ISBN 978-1-61377-524-0 First printing: November 2012. Printed in Korea.

COVER COLLAGE: an original illustration by Steven Chorney celebrates the top six fantasy
movies as ranked by this book. 1st PAGE: The memorable *Wizard of Oz* cast in a larger-than-life
publicity image (Metro-Goldwyn-Mayer, 1939). ABOVE: Middle Earth mutation Gollum
(Andy Serkis) from *The Lord of the Rings: The Two Towers* (New Line Cinema, 2002).

FANTASTIC PRESS

presents

TOP 100 Fantasy MOVIES

Written, Edited and Designed by
GARY GERANI

KEN RUBIN
Production Coordinator

POSTER/PHOTO CREDITS: Polygram Filmed Entertainment (10), New Line Cinema (69, 70, 71, 132, 133, 190, 191, 192, 193, 194, 196), Metro-Goldwyn-Mayer (32, 40, 41, 42, 43, 48, 49, 50, 51, 56, 57, 62, 68, 76, 77, 84, 85, 184, 185, 186, 187, 194, 195), Lopert Pictures (182, 183), Janus Films (146, 152, 182, 183), Paramount Pictures (22, 23, 29, 72, 74, 75, 81, 134, 135, 147, 180, 181, 194), Columbia Pictures Corporation (31, 54, 86, 87, 116, 117, 128, 137, 150, 151, 164, 165, 166, 167, 195), Liberty Films (178, 179), RKO Radio Pictures (11, 122, 123, 124, 125, 139, 195), Rizzoli Film (172, 173), J. Arthur Rank (170, 171), Universal Studios: (8, 9, 16, 17, 22, 23, 24, 60, 61, 63, 64, 65, 72, 81, 102, 103, 136, 138, 154, 155, 156, 194), 20th Century Fox Film Corporation (18, 19, 30, 106, 107, 108, 129, 140, 141, 148, 149, 157, 168, 194), United Artists (28, 53, 66, 67, 80, 99, 104, 158, 159, 160, 161, 194), Renown Pictures (158, 159), Chamartín Productions (153), UMPO (153), Svensk Film Industry (152), Warner Bros. Pictures (26, 27, 32, 40, 41, 42, 43, 50, 51, 52, 58, 59, 62, 76, 77, 82, 83, 84, 98, 112, 113, 118, 119, 120, 121, 122, 123, 124, 127, 130, 131, 139, 142, 143, 144, 145, 147, 194), Marianne Productions (146), Picturehouse Entertainment (142, 143, 144, 145), Kennedy Miller Productions (138), Selznick Productions (126, 127), Romulus Films (11, 110), Orion Pictures Corporation (105, 195), London Films (104), Republic Pictures (63, 64, 65, 102, 103), Mosfilm (100, 101), Valiant Films (100, 101), Walt Disney Productions (12, 13, 44, 45, 46, 47, 78, 79, 88, 89, 94, 95, 96, 97, 194), Miramax Films (73), USA Films (55), General Film Distributors (33, 53), Handemade Films (38, 39), Avo Embassy Pictures (20, 21, 38, 39), TriStar Pictures (36, 37, 195), Eagle-Lion Films (33, 195), Galatea Films (20, 21), Lou Bunin Productions (14, 15).

PHOTO SOURCES: The Gary Gerani Photo and Poster Collection, Photofest (special thanks to Buddy Weiss); Jerry Ohlinger's Movie Material Store, Hollywood Movie Posters (Ronald V. Borst), Hollywood Book and Poster (Eric Caiden), Porkepyn, Stephen Sally, other sources.

Table of Contents

LEFT: an enchanted vista from *Bridge to Terabithia* (Walt Disney Productions, 2004). ABOVE, TOP: Jennifer Connelly and David Bowie trip the light fantastic in *Labyrinth* (TriStar, 1986). ABOVE, BOTTOM: Rex Harrison bids farewell to Gene Tierney in *The Ghost and Mrs. Muir* (20th Century Fox, 1947).

INTRODUCTION
FRANK DARABONT

Movies, the best ones, offer us indelible images that become iconic. These images get stamped into our brains forever as treasured sense-memories. Some are so potent that they achieve the amazing trick of being instantly recognized even by people who've never *seen* those movies:

Humphrey Bogart and Ingrid Bergman say farewell on a fog-shrouded tarmac while a Lockheed Electra runs up its engines for its flight to Lisbon...

Vivien Leigh makes her way through a vast sprawl of wounded and dying soldiers in an Atlanta railroad yard...

Peter O'Toole, resplendent in spotless white Arabian robes and headdress, leads a charge of troops into battle astride a galloping camel...

These examples transcend being just "great movie moments" and become shared cultural legacies. We know instantly what those images are, what films they represent. Once we've experienced those moments through the skillful manipulation of light captured through a lens and committed to celluloid at 24 frames per second (my jury's still out on that digital stuff everybody's switching to nowadays), it's as if we ourselves had lived those moments. They wind up feeling like dreams we've all had. That's how powerful the motion-picture image can be.

This dynamic deepens the more we shift our focus into the realm of *fantasy* films, which by their nature take us closer to the pure dreamlike state that is the special province of films. Because fantasy films are our gateway to creatures and worlds that dwell beyond the borders of reality and depict events and realms that are wondrous and impossible, I think they strike the deeper nerve:

A cyclops battles a horned dragon to the death on a remote, rocky island while Kerwin Matthews and Kathryn Grant look on in breathless anticipation...

An invisible monster from the Id is revealed in all its pissed-off glory in the surging force-field perimeter "fence" of United Planets Cruiser C-57D (my vote for the coolest flying saucer and the best creature reveal in movie history)...

A young Judy Garland dances arm-in-arm with a Scarecrow, a Tin Man, and a Cowardly Lion down a yellow brick road on a quest to find a wizard...

Indelible images. Unforgettable moments. The purest of gifts from our best storytellers and most outré dreamers. These and countless more crowd my brain and are my favorite sense-memories. They lit up my imagination like a pinball machine as a youngster, and from my earliest recollection made me yearn to do what I now do for a living.

I've been surprised and delighted many times through the years to find that I was far from alone in this.

In 2003, I was honored to present Ray Harryhausen his richly deserved (and long overdue!) star on Hollywood Boulevard's Walk of Fame. For me, having grown up steeped in the cinema of the fantastic and having feasted throughout childhood on a steady diet of Mr. Harryhausen's stop-motion wonders, being a presenter that day was a privilege beyond measure.

The crowd that showed up for the occasion included a huge array of film industry professionals: writers, directors, actors, producers, animators, visual and makeup effects artists—you name it, they were there, representing every facet of film production. A few were famous, some legends in their fields.

As varied as their specialties were, I knew that their presence at this event meant we all shared one thing in common: We'd all been smitten by the same flights of filmic fantasy as kids, had all shared the same wallops of pleasure and inspiration. All of us had been spurred to professional adulthood by the same influences, the same "manufactured dreams." It had been master film fantasists like Harryhausen, and many more like him, who had spun us those dreams and given us the push.

In honor of that fact, I told the following anecdote during my speech:

One day during the filming of *The Green Mile*, I turned to Tom Hanks and asked him this question: "What sparked your passion for acting? Was there a specific thing that set you on your path in life?"

Hanks replied without hesitation: "Seeing *Jason and the Argonauts* when I was a kid. Jason sword-fighting the skeletons melted my brain. I knew right then and there what I had to be when I grew up! I had to be Jason! I wanted to fight skeletons!"

In answering so succinctly, Tom Hanks had eloquently summed up for all of us who love them why fantasy films matter: Inside every grownup is a kid who wants to kick some skeleton ass. It's as simple and profound as that.

I leave you now to turn the page and be swept away by creatures and worlds that dwell beyond the borders of reality, that depict events and realms both wondrous and impossible...

Frank Darabont, 2012

OVERVIEW

GARY GERANI

Does a good fantasy story provide an escape from reality, or an incisive, imaginative reflection of it? Both, if the tale's working the way it should. Fantasy at its best returns the reader or viewer to a childlike state of open possibilities, enabling him to dream with his eyes wide open. Through the patently absurd we learn about humanity's perplexing contradictions, and by laughing at these colorful Catch 22s we come to peace with our inherent pros and cons. If horror sheds a light on the darker side of human behavior, and sci-fi opens our minds to technological and social advancement, then fantasy points the way to a better understanding of the deepest, most fundamental concerns, those impossible questions we all ask from childhood to grave. Through the balm of pure imagination, we humans theorize about God, eternity, the afterlife, our moral place in the cosmos. Fantasy enables us to explore these issues with cleverness and, more often than not, uninhibited fun. Phrased a little differently, it's that spoonful of sugar that helps the medicine go down in the most delightful way.

So, like little Alice resurfacing in Wonderland, join us now as we take in all the outlandish sights and sounds of fantasy cinema, an irresistible parallel universe where dreams come true and just about anything is possible. Just ask John Malkovitch!

Gary Gerani, 2012

ABOUT THE BOOK

The 100 movies you're about to read about represent my choices for the cinema's most significant fantasy endeavors. Sorry, no comic book superhero or animated features in this line-up, as they belong to very active subgenres (and future studies) of their own. Ranking is a subjective party game, of course. But all of the movies showcased here are worth experiencing, from the celebrated classics to way-below-the-radar obscurities and foreign efforts.

ABOUT THE AUTHOR

Gary Gerani is a screenwriter (Stan Winston's *Pumpkinhead*, an upcoming John Travolta comedy), graphic novelist (*Dinosaurs Attack!*, *Bram Stoker's Death Ship*), children's product developer (hundreds of products for Topps), film and TV historian (1977's *Fantastic Television*), award-winning art director (for renderings by Drew Struzan, Jack Davis, Joe Smith, etc.), photo editor, designer and publisher (the Fantastic Press trade paperback book series).

KEY TO UNDERSTANDING

(100) 1.85 🎧🎧

Clock: Running time
Monitor: Aspect ratio

Full headphone: Stereo soundtrack
Half headphone: Mono soundtrack

100

LEGEND 1985

94   2.35

WHO MADE IT:

20th Century-Fox/Embassy International Pictures (U.S./U.K.). Director: Ridley Scott. Producers: Joseph P. Grace, Tim Hampton, Arnon Michan. Writer: William Hjortsberg. Cinematography (Technicolor): Alex Thompson. Music: Tangerine Dream; Jerry Goldsmith (European version). Starring Tom Cruise (Jack), Mia Sara (Lili), Tim Curry (Darkness), David Bennent (Gump), Alice Playten (Blix), Billy Barty (Screwball), Robert Picardo (Meg Mucklebones).

WHAT IT'S ABOUT:

Sweet Princess Lili would rather spend her time in the woods with feral companion Jack than deal with royal duties. But Lili's impulsive nature soon causes trouble, and the unexpected shooting of a unicorn before her horrified eyes triggers a series of deadly-dangerous events. Threatening all is a monstrous, hulking demon known as the Darkness, who seeks to create eternal night by destroying daylight and marrying an apparently corrupted Lili. Only resourceful Jack and his forest creature friends stand between this monster and the end of their world.

WHY IT'S IMPORTANT:

After the groundbreaking experiences of *Alien* and *Blade Runner*, much was expected from Ridley Scott's take on all things magical and fable-like. But *Legend*, while awash with expected visual delights, disappointed audiences of the day, which were still wary of pixies, goblins and the inherently bizarre attendant elements of free-flowing fantasy. Like Ron Howard's *Willow*, the film was dismissed as an ambitious misfire with cool visual effects and that was pretty much that. Meanwhile, the European cut of *Legend*, blessed with a symphonic Jerry Goldsmith score, suggested that something far better had been prepared by Scott and his team, before a disastrous screening in Berlin forced the director to make significant alterations. Apart from the inclusion of a blissful, youth-friendly score by Tangerine Dream, the movie was re-edited, shaving down characterizations (Gump) and minimizing Lili's status as a spoiled princess with a sense of royal entitlement – rescuer Jack is her stated "knight" in the Euro cut. Most importantly, Scott holds back on his key reveal of Tim Curry's Darkness until after Lili is transformed, making this demonoid's claw-and-hoofed emergence from an enchanted mirror all the more terrifying. In the commercially-driven U.S. incarnation, mega-horned Darkness is showcased at every opportunity, initially presented with garishly glowing eyes and fingernails.

Hasty changes aside, both versions allow director Scott to whip up a wondrous nether-world of ethereal events, mixing and matching plot/thematic elements that suggest Adam and Eve's expulsion from Heaven, ancient Finnish folk tales of a snow-besieged planet, beauty and the beast, the last unicorn, etc. What emerges from this pastiche is a simple – perhaps too simple – rendering of Good against Evil (or Light vs. Dark) in relatively straightforward adult terms. Young Cruise is fine as the feral hero and Sara letter-perfect as the innocent but headstrong virgin princess he loves. Although rubber-costumed Curry is saddled with mostly fortune-cookie dialogue ("The dreams of youth are the regrets of maturity," he informs unimpressed Lili), his monstrous, austere countenance is never anything less than iconic.

In its final twin incarnations, *Legend* may not be the last word on magical adventure, but it paved the way for a new generation of filmmakers intrigued by the fanciful genre and the challenge of making it palatable for a mainstream audience.

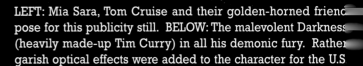

LEFT: Mia Sara, Tom Cruise and their golden-horned friend pose for this publicity still. BELOW: The malevolent Darkness (heavily made-up Tim Curry) in all his demonic fury. Rather garish optical effects were added to the character for the U.S.

BELOW: *Legend* offers a plethora of fairy tale-like entities including a sadistic goblin (Robert Picardo as Meg Mucklebones) and a buzzing fairy with pre-CGI wings. It would be a full decade later before fx technology could easily accommodate such creations.

Legendary film composer Jerry Goldsmith's classical-style background music was replaced in the U.S. by Tangerine Dream's breezier, though no less effective pop score.

Innocent heroine Lily succumbs to dark temptation, much to Jack's deep regret.

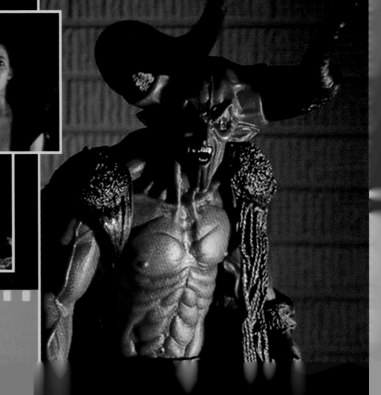

The Darkness required a full body-suit (by Rob Bottin and Nick Dudman), similar to the one developed for *Hellboy* years later.

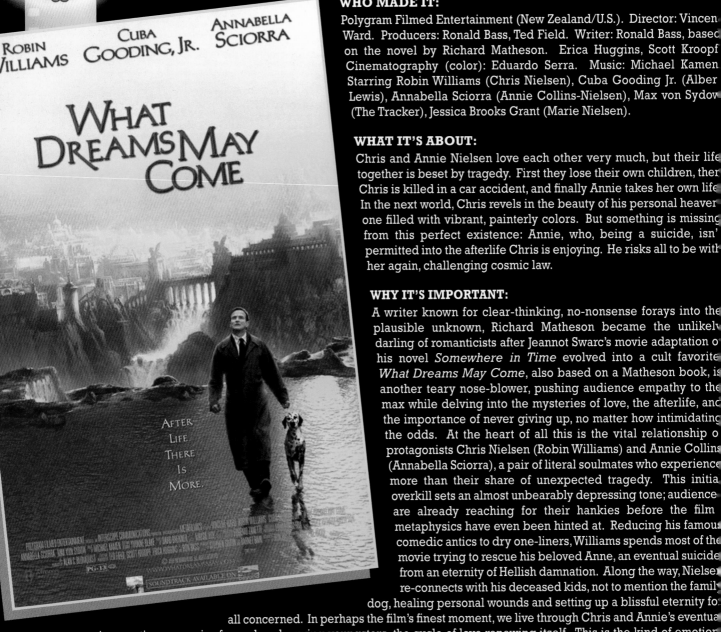

WHO MADE IT:

Polygram Filmed Entertainment (New Zealand/U.S.). Director: Vincen
Ward. Producers: Ronald Bass, Ted Field. Writer: Ronald Bass, based
on the novel by Richard Matheson. Erica Huggins, Scott Kroopf
Cinematography (color): Eduardo Serra. Music: Michael Kamen
Starring Robin Williams (Chris Nielsen), Cuba Gooding Jr. (Alber
Lewis), Annabella Sciorra (Annie Collins-Nielsen), Max von Sydow
(The Tracker), Jessica Brooks Grant (Marie Nielsen).

WHAT IT'S ABOUT:

Chris and Annie Nielsen love each other very much, but their life
together is beset by tragedy. First they lose their own children, ther
Chris is killed in a car accident, and finally Annie takes her own life
In the next world, Chris revels in the beauty of his personal heaven
one filled with vibrant, painterly colors. But something is missing
from this perfect existence: Annie, who, being a suicide, isn'
permitted into the afterlife Chris is enjoying. He risks all to be with
her again, challenging cosmic law.

WHY IT'S IMPORTANT:

A writer known for clear-thinking, no-nonsense forays into the
plausible unknown, Richard Matheson became the unlikely
darling of romanticists after Jeannot Swarc's movie adaptation of
his novel *Somewhere in Time* evolved into a cult favorite
What Dreams May Come, also based on a Matheson book, is
another teary nose-blower, pushing audience empathy to the
max while delving into the mysteries of love, the afterlife, and
the importance of never giving up, no matter how intimidating
the odds. At the heart of all this is the vital relationship o
protagonists Chris Nielsen (Robin Williams) and Annie Collins
(Annabella Sciorra), a pair of literal soulmates who experience
more than their share of unexpected tragedy. This initia
overkill sets an almost unbearably depressing tone; audience
are already reaching for their hankies before the film
metaphysics have even been hinted at. Reducing his famous
comedic antics to dry one-liners, Williams spends most of the
movie trying to rescue his beloved Anne, an eventual suicide
from an eternity of Hellish damnation. Along the way, Nielser
re-connects with his deceased kids, not to mention the family
dog, healing personal wounds and setting up a blissful eternity fo
all concerned. In perhaps the film's finest moment, we live through Chris and Annie's eventua
reincarnation as a pair of somehow knowing youngsters, the cycle of love renewing itself. This is the kind of emotior
churning parable critics either go with, or blast as morbidly sentimental. By the time we're suffering through Nielsen's final sacrifice
so many afterlife rules have been stuffed into our woozy brains that sympathy for the Nielsens threatens to turn into impatience
Fortunately, Williams holds it all together, ably supported by leading lady Sciorra and a pair of heavyweight spiritual helpers (breezy
Gooding Jr. and intimidating, mysterious von Sydow). Still, the real "stars" of this movie are the special effects landscapes, dazzling
dreamlands that required rarely-used camera technology to realize. From the first visit to a painted universe (reflecting Annie's wor
and Chris' own love for art) to Hell as a monstrous Sargasso sea of burning ships and wretched souls, these amazing Dreams comman
our interest even as they forward the plot.

Moist, frequently downbeat, ultimately alive with the joy of emotional continuit
What Dreams May Come is a soothing balm for those who have loved and los
something even its hard-to-please author considers a "good thing." Amen to tha

WHO MADE IT:

RKO Radio Pictures (U.S.). Directors: Lansing C. Holden, Irving Pichel. Producers: Merian C. Cooper, Shirley Burden. Writers: Ruth Rose, Dudley Nichols, from the novel by H. Rider Haggard. Cinematography (b/w): J. Roy Hunt. Music: Max Steiner. Starring Helen Gahagan (She), Randolph Scott (Leo Vincey), Helen Mack (Tanya Dugmore), Nigel Bruce (Horace Holly), Samuel S. Hinds (John Vincey), Jim Thorpe (Captain of the Guard).

WHAT IT'S ABOUT:

The dying uncle of adventurer Leo Vincey tells about a lost kingdom visited by Vincey's ancestor 500 years ago. Inspired, Leo and family friend Horace Holly set out for this fabled empire in the frozen Russian arctic, hoping to discover if it truly contains the secret of immortality within a mystic fire, as ancient legends insist. Together with Tanya, a guide's daughter, they survive a monstrous avalanche and find their way into Kor, ruled by the mysterious, merciless She. This beautiful leader believes Leo Vincey to be his own ancestor, whom she once loved, and invites him to share immortality with her.

WHY IT'S IMPORTANT:

Like Edgar Rice Burroughs (and Alex "Flash Gordon" Raymond, for that matter), H. Rider Haggard achieved pop culture immortality with fanciful, decidedly outlandish adventure tales. *She* offers up the prerequisite stalwart explorers, a lost kingdom in the middle of nowhere, the secret of eternal youth, and a spiteful, beautiful empress smitten with the macho leading man. This prototypical pulp romance has its origins in ancient legends of Atlantis, but golden age Hollywood was extremely wary of far-out extravaganzas once the sound era began. Only RKO producers Merian C. Cooper and Ernest Schoedsack were willing to push the outdoor adventure envelope to absurd, logic-challenging extremes. After an enigmatic encounter with a frozen sabertooth tiger, the closest this film gets to a 'monster,' our intrepid explorers narrowly avoid being buried alive in a spectacular avalanche. Soon they're the nervous guests of an ancient, hybrid civilization that somehow embraces eye-popping art deco sensibilities (anticipating Capra's Shangri-la one year later). Young Randolph Scott puts his spin on a heroic role usually reserved for Bruce Cabot, a pre-Dr. Watson Nigel Bruce is all reckless enthusiasm as expedition scientist Holly, and waifish Helen Mack, last seen bandaging *The Son of Kong*, is the down-to-earth rival for Scott's affection. And She herself? Helen Gahagan, Mrs. Melvyn Douglas and future political nemesis of Richard Nixon, was certainly a curious casting choice; she's more disillusioned spinster schoolteacher than primitive despot. Imagine Shangri-la's High Lama losing faith in mankind's potential and bitterly turning inward, all plans for a progressive tomorrow abandoned. When a seemingly civilized person like this is compelled to bark murder orders, the effect is unexpectedly chilling. Gahagan's spectacular demise, accomplished with a series of progressively more grotesque old-age makeups, is a high point of the film.

Along with *Kong* and 1935's *The Last Days of Pompeii*, *She* comprises Cooper's "ancient civilization" trilogy. Blessed with imaginative production design, agreeable players and Max Steiner's inventive music score, it's a grandly conceived fantasy-adventure, nothing less than a feature-length cliffhanger with all the trimmings.

Subtitle: The Curse of the Black Pearl   Poster/photos: © 2003 Walt Disney Pictures

WHO MADE IT:

Walt Disney/Jerry Bruckheimer Films (U.S.). Director: Gore Verbinski. Producers: Jerry Bruckheimer, Paul Deason, Bruce Henricks, Chad Oman, Mike Stenson. Writers: Ted Elliott & Terry Rossio, Stuart Beattie, Jay Wolpert. Cinematography (color): Dariusz Wolski. Music: Klaus Badelt. Starring Johnny Depp (Jack Sparrow), Geoffrey Rush (Barbossa), Orlando Bloom (Will Turner), Keira Knightley (Elizabeth Swann), Jack Davenport (Norrington), Jonathan Pryce (Governor Weatherby Swann), Lee Arenberg (Pintel), Mackenzie Crook (Ragetti), Damian O'Hare (Lt. Gillette), Giles New (Murtogg), Angus Barnet (Mullroy), David Bailie (Cotton), Michael Berry Jr. (Twigg), Zoe Saldana (Anamaria), Kevin McNally (Gibbs).

WHAT IT'S ABOUT:

Sly and savvy pirate Captain Jack Sparrow teams with Will Turner, a blacksmith who can handle himself in a fight, to find Will's lost sweetheart Elizabeth Swann (who is also the governor's daughter). She's been kidnapped by dreaded Captain Barbossa, Sparrow's former skipper and a man with a most curious problem: he and his crew have been damned to an existence that is neither life or death. Only a blood sacrifice can end this terrible curse, prompting Captain Sparrow into some resourceful counter-planning.

WHY IT'S IMPORTANT:

This uneven but mostly spirited romp, inspired by the much-beloved Disneyland theme park attraction, wound up launching an unlikely new powerhouse franchise, one that, for better or worse, shows no signs of drifting away. Twisty plotting and imaginative CG effects aside, it's the casting of indispensible Johnny Depp as possibly mad, wildly theatrical Captain Jack Sparrow that dominates *Pirates of the Caribbean*. Like Robert Downey Jr. in the *Iron Man* or *Sherlock Holmes* films, he's more than just the right actor for the part; for many audience members, he's the main reason they bought their tickets in the first place.

It would be tempting to say that this film and its sequels resurrected the moribund 'pirate' film genre, but that never actually happened; alas, swashbuckling sea stories remain decidedly unpopular with modern viewers. Somewhere between the failed excesses of *Hook* and *Cutthroat Island* lies *Pirates*, transformed into a crowd-pleaser mostly because of Depp's oddball turn, but also due to the high quotient of scarifying fantasy set pieces and other over-the-top elements. The result is an entertaining family movie from Disney with enough spins-on-spins to bemuse all but the snobbiest critic. Granted, somewhere within this rollercoaster of a confection is an enchanting premise about a young girl from a regressive era who dreams about living as a free-spirited pirate, only to get her chance in real life. But mostly, this initial POTC extravaganza is agreeable flapdoodle, fun and frivolous like the ride it celebrates. The "damned crew" angle certainly allows for some breathtaking ILM special effects, with Barbossa's yo-ho-ho-horrors doggedly walking across the ocean floor to surprise a ship full of soldiers being a standout sequence.

Appearing very much at home in their roles are Orlando Bloom (the *Rings* trilogy) and Keira Knightley (*Princess of Thieves*) as angst-ridden young lovers who share a precious, significant moment from the past. Equally convincing is resident villain Geoffrey Rush, and pompous romantic rival Jack Davenport. But it's pretty much Depp's movie, whether he's preening like a diva or diving to Knightley's rescue with Tarzan-like machismo. For this bit of casting, and providing a fresh, colorful take on seafaring ghost stories in general, *Pirate*

ABOVE: Intrepid if eccentric Captain Jack Sparrow (Johnny Depp) and unlikely partner Will Turner (Orlando Bloom) keep an eye out for trouble, which is not long in coming…

ABOVE: Elizabeth Swann (Keira Knightley) is temporarily menaced by future ally and potential lover Jack Sparrow (Depp).

ABOVE: Swashbuckling Sparrow tests the mettle of Will Turner (Orlando Bloom, channeling his Legolas character from *The Lord of the Rings*). Bloom would return for the next two *Pirates* installments.

LEFT: Vile Captain Barbossa (Geoffrey Rush) is even fouler in ghost-form, the result of a potent curse. Errol Flynn never faced villains like this!

LEFT: Johnny Depp on set. RIGHT: Concept painting of the ghost pirates' underwater walk.

WHO MADE IT:

Lou Bunin Productions (U.S./U.K./France). Director: Dallas Bower. Producer: Lou Bunin. Writers: Henry Myers, Albert Lewin, Edward Eliscu, based on the novel by Lewis Carroll. Cinematography (Anscocolor): Gerald Gibbs, Claude Renoir. Music: Sol Kaplan. Starring Carol Marsh (Alice), Stephen Murray (Lewis Carroll/Knave of Hearts), Ernest Milton (Vice Chancellor/White Rabbit), Pamela Brown (Queen/Queen of Hearts), Felix Aylmer (Dr. Liddel/Cheshire Cat), David Reed (Prince Consort/King of Hearts), Joyce Grenfell (Ugly Duchess/Dormouse), Raymond Bussieres (Tailor/White Rabbit), Peter Bull (Puppet Character – voice).

WHAT IT'S ABOUT:

Instructor/author Lewis Carroll is inspired by various individuals in his midst, especially a remarkable young lady named Alice. One day, enjoying a boat ride with the girl and her sisters, he concocts an outlandish yarn and populates it with fantasy variations of people he knows. Young Alice is cast as the protagonist, lost in a mad universe of literal ups and downs, which she actually sings about. After encountering a plethora of unique personalities, the Cheshire Cat and Ugly Duchess among them, Alice survives the Queen's wrath and eventually finds her way back to the real world.

WHY IT'S IMPORTANT:

Transposing Lewis Carroll's famous novel into a movie or play has always been problematic: it's sweet and sour, innocent and knowing, cynical yet hopeful. Too often this results in family-friendly adaptations that embrace cloying set-pieces, reducing Carroll's social satire to a disconnected series of campy vignettes. Facing the challenge admirably is this fascinating combo of live-action material and stop-motion photography, all in jarring Anscocolor. Director Dallas Bower nails the correct tone instantly, and he's helped by two significant factors: first, a real-world prologue that provides some welcome context for the outrageous adventure ahead, a la *Wizard of Oz*. Depicting Alice, the Queen, and other real-life individuals who inspired *Wonderland*'s famous characters is certainly a gimmick, but it yields enormous creative rewards. The bittersweet aspects of this oft-told tale take on deeper resonance once we understand precisely who the author is referencing, and why. By allowing the self-contained fantasy narrative (Alice's "dream") to play out as a film-within-a-film, Dallas winds up achieving the best of both worlds.

Secondly, there is a sophisticated edge to this film's animation that distinguishes it from straightforward children's entertainment in the vein of George Pal. These twisted entities have an almost pre-Jay Ward/Matt Groening anti-Disney sensibility, a grandly irreverent streak Carroll himself would have appreciated. It's actually rather startling to watch live-action Alice sharing the same universe with Louis Bunin's puppets, and not because the fx are crude: this film's production design is so inventive (Bernice Polifka), obvious split-screen composites provide surreal new perspectives, casually transferring the young protagonist's disorientation to awed viewers.

And then there's Alice herself. 20 year-old Carol Marsh was something of a British Deanna Durbin, the wholesome girl-next-door whose budding sexuality proved irresistibly charming to English moviegoers. Not surprisingly, this on-the-cusp quality made Marsh ideal for Carroll's inquisitive heroine, and it's hard to imagine another U.K. ingénue playing the role so skillfully. *Alice* '49 also offers some tolerable musical numbers, boasting Marsh, a trained performer, miming her signature ditty with fresh-faced bravado (an uncredited Adele Leigh does the actual singing).

Sadly, *Alice in Wonderland* has been out of circulation for several decades, and for a very specific reason: Disney wanted to clear the decks for his '51 adaptation, which made all the mistakes Bower's take skillfully avoided. As a result, there is no pristine "special edition" of this pseudo-classic to revel in nowadays, just inferior, mostly elusive video-taped transfers. Still, this is the *Alice* for discerning viewers

A "real world" prologue featuring Lewis Carroll (Stephen Murray) and Alice (Carol Marsh) sets up the fable.

ABOVE: Live-action Alice shares the frame with a flustered White Rabbit, brought to life via stop-motion animation.

...interacts with an optically-composited Alice in this famous scene.

The Caterpillar as articulated puppet...

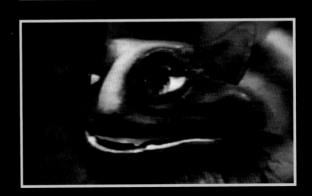

Louis Bunin's funky, beautifully-sculpted animation puppets have personality to spare. Bunin also produced this mostly-forgotten British adaptation.

LEFT: W.C. Fields as Humpty Dumpty from 1933's *Alice*. RIGHT: Helena Bonham Carter in Tim Burton's ambitious 2010 take.

Poster/photos: © 1980 Universal Studios

Someday in the past he will find her....

Somewhere in Time

CHRISTOPHER REEVE IN A RASTAR/STEPHEN DEUTSCH PRODUCTION A JEANNOT SZWARC FILM "SOMEWHERE IN TIME" STARRING JANE SEYMOUR · CHRISTOPHER PLUMMER AS W. F. ROBINSON CO-STARRING TERESA WRIGHT SCREENPLAY BY RICHARD MATHESON BASED ON HIS NOVEL "BID TIME RETURN" PRODUCED BY STEPHEN DEUTSCH MUSIC BY JOHN BARRY DIRECTED BY JEANNOT SZWARC A UNIVERSAL PICTURE

WHO MADE IT:

Universal Pictures (U.S.). Director: Jeannot Swarc. Producers: Stephen Deutsch, Steve Bickel, Ray Stark. Writer: Richard Matheson, based on his novel "Bid Time Return." Cinematography (Technicolor): Isidore Mankofsky. Music: John Barry. Starring Christopher Reeve (Richard Collier), Jane Seymour (Elise McKenna), Christopher Plummer (William Fawcett Robinson), Teresa Wright (Laura Roberts), Bill Erwin (Arthur Biehl), George Voskovec (Dr. Finney), Susan French (Older Elise), Eddra Gale (Genevieve), William H. Macy (Critic).

WHAT IT'S ABOUT:

Writer Richard Collier receives an artifact from the past and a curious request during a reception for his first play. Intrigued, he becomes fascinated with the old woman who approached him, a famous stage actress named Elise McKenna from the early 1900s. Determined to see her in her prime, he uses a curious mental process to travel back through the years, and they fall deeply in love. This union is resented by Elise's manager, and before long an unexpected accident yanks Richard back to the present. He desperately tries to return, but fails, until the afterlife reunites both time-torn lovers.

WHY IT'S IMPORTANT:

An earnest but uneven adaptation of Richard Matheson's romantic novel, *Somewhere in Time* is a lilting, fragile tearjerker in the tradition of William Dieterle's *Portrait of Jennie*. Driven by mysterious passions, time-crossed lovers Richard Collier (Christopher Reeve) and Elise McKenna (Jane Seymour) find themselves in a heartbreaking paradox; they are ultimately ripped from each other by fate, with only death enabling them to reunite. Matheson has explored the afterlife in many of his works, most significantly *What Dreams May Come*, but the focus here is on a romance that begins only after Collier has completed his inexplicable time trip, drawing comparisons with the venerable *Berkeley Square/I'll Never Forget You*. Lock yourself away from reality, fill the room with artifacts of the past, and a person can somehow propel himself into another age. That's one method of time travel H.G. Wells never considered, although determined John Carter mind-projecting himself to Mars is a vaguely similar wish-fulfillment notion.

Big and hunky, star Christopher Reeve is game but slightly miscast as the obsessed playwright protagonist, his Clark Kent-style 'awkward comedy' routine often at odds with the tale's elegant tone. More effective is Seymour, her spontaneous changing of dialogue during a stage performance to convey her preternatural love for Richard providing the film's most memorable scene. Also around for some minor personal conflict is 2011 Oscar winner Christopher Plummer, appropriately dour as Seymour's jealous guardian/Svengali-like mentor.

Hampered by a story perhaps better suited to an hour treatment (it would have been perfect as one of those 60-minute *Zones* or an extended *Night Gallery* episode), *Somewhere in Time* failed at the boxoffice but became an instant cult favorite on VHS, recommended enthusiastically by gushing video store clerks. It also inspired a Broadway incarnation that never materialized, penned by Matheson with original music by Billy Goldenberg. It was the "lack of a third act" that torpedoed this project, reflecting a basic weakness in the movie version as well. But from its bittersweet plot to John

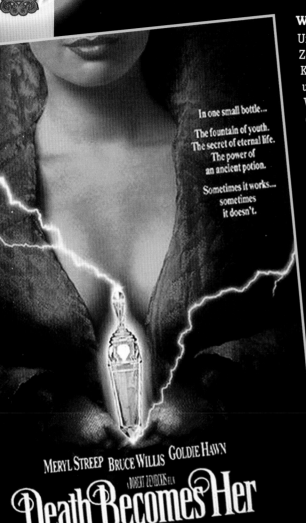

In one small bottle...

The fountain of youth.
The secret of eternal life.
The power of
an ancient potion.

Sometimes it works...
sometimes
it doesn't.

MERYL STREEP   BRUCE WILLIS   GOLDIE HAWN

A ROBERT ZEMECKIS FILM

Death Becomes Her

COMING SOON

WHO MADE IT:

Universal Pictures (U.S.). Director: Robert Zemeckis. Producers: Robert Zemekis, Steve Starkey, Joan Bradshaw. Writers: Martin Donovan & David Koepp. Cinematography (color): Dean Cundey. Music: Alan Silvestri. Make-up Designer: Dick Smith. Starring Meryl Streep (Madeline Ashton), Bruce Willis (Ernest Menville), Goldie Hawn (Helen Sharp), Isabella Rossellini (Lisle Von Rhuman), Ian Ogilvy (Chagall), Adam Storke (Dakota), Nancy Fish (Rose) Alaina Reed Hall (Psychologist), Michelle Johnson (Anna), Mary Ellen Trainor (Vivian Adams).

WHAT IT'S ABOUT:

Close friends Madeline Ashton and Helen Sharp are, in truth, insanely jealous of one another. When actress Madeline steals writer Helen's fiancé Ernest for herself, war is declared. Helen plots a monstrous revenge over the course of years, but Madeline has some bizarre ideas of her own. A mysterious woman named Lisle Von Rhuman provides a magical potion that gives these vindictive harpies

neverending life… they just need to protect their bodies from physical harm. Some twisted limbs and a shotgun blast in the chest later, both are still sniping at each other, and will continue to do so for all eternity.

WHY IT'S IMPORTANT:

Sort of a dark cousin to *Who Framed Roger Rabbit*, *Death Becomes Her* enables director Bob Zemeckis to revel in madcap humor and macabre make-up effects, the last of their elaborate kind before CG pretty much replaced most on-set fabrications. Fortunately, Dick Smith's contorted appendages and fat suits work hand-in-hand with this twisted yarn about jealousy, vanity, and a pair of slick chicks (Streep and Hawn, both brilliant) who spend their entire lives – and deaths – trying to outdo one another. Caught in this absurd crossfire is equally pathetic Ernest Menville (nerdier-than-usual Bruce Willis), who at least has enough sense to reject a Faustian bargain when it's shoved in his face. This puts him ahead of our leading ladies, who are so relentlessly superficial that they don't even notice the horrific consequences of their soul-damning deal… May they both rest in pieces.

Although the showcased make-ups made a bigger impact in 1992, before viewers became accustomed to (even resentful of) "we can do anything" special effects, *Death Becomes Her* still elicits a crooked smile, due mostly to the unrestrained fun all three stars seem to be having with their campy material. If Donovan & Koepp's screenplay had been a tad less broad, the movie might have played like an American variation of Shaw's *Blithe Spirit*. As it is, Zemeckis and company provide a perceptive, gleefully bitchy farce, with influences as diverse as Lillian Hellman, Harold Lloyd, and William Castle.

Tidbit: A role played by Tracey Ullmann was entirely cut from the film after a disasterous preview screening prompted some drastic re-editing and a new ending (Ullmann still turns up in the trailer, however).

NIGHT AT THE MUSEUM 2006

108   1.85

EVERYTHING COMES TO LIFE

BEN STILLER
NIGHT AT THE MUSEUM

WHO MADE IT:

20th Century Fox/Ingenious Film Partners/1492 Productions (U.S./U.K.)
Director: Shawn Levy. Producers: Thomas M. Hammel, Mark Radcliffe,
Ira Shuman, Michael Barnathan, Chris Columbus, Shawn Levy. Writers:
Robert Ben Garant & Thomas Lennon, based on the book by Milan
Trenc. Cinematography (color): Guillermo Navarro. Music: Alan
Silvestri. Starring Ben Stiller (Larry Daley), Carla Gugino (Rebecca),
Dick Van Dyke (Cecil), Mickey Rooney (Gus), Bill Cobbs (Reginald),
Jake Cherry (Nick Daley), Ricky Gervais (Dr. McPhee), Robin Williams
(Teddy Roosevelt), Kim Raver (Erica Daley), Patrick Gallagher (Attila
the Hun), Anna Meara (Debbie).

WHAT IT'S ABOUT:

Down on his luck, unemployed and divorced Larry Daley takes a job
as night watchman at the Museum of Natural History. But a shocked
Larry discovers that, after the sun sets, various exhibits miraculously
come to life, including a most playful T-rex skeleton. It's all because
of a curse placed on an ancient Egyptian stone displayed in the
museum, an all-powerful object sought after by three former
security guards. Summoning his fortitude, Larry organizes all the
historical characters into a makeshift army. He winds up saving
the museum along with his own self-esteem – earning his son
Nick's respect in the process.

WHY IT'S IMPORTANT:

The notion of what might "come alive" at a museum after dark is
a powerful and evocative one. With *The Relic* squandering
inherently spooky possibilities a decade earlier, it fell to Chris
Columbus' 1492 Productions to find whimsy and family-style
warmth in this fanciful notion. The resulting film serves as both
a special effects extravaganza and a more than serviceable
vehicle for dour-faced Ben Stiller.

Screenwriters Garant and Lennon wisely set up his character
Larry Daley as a decent enough loser kept alive by offbeat
hopes and dreams; he's also a divorced dad with serious self-
respect issues and, as this parable gets underway, no means
of financial support. When his disillusioned son Nick cuts to
the chase and suggests that maybe dad's just "an ordinary guy who
should get a job," it pretty much bursts Larry's bubble and opens his eyes to responsibility. A regular
position as night guard at the Museum of Natural History seems to take the pressure off... at first.

With a plethora of living exhibits to contend with, besieged Larry finds his mettle tested in ways he never imagined. But there's no way
this guy's quitting now, not with so much riding on his job success. To deal with the various personal conflicts depicted in museum
dioramas, he must bone up on ancient history in a hurry, using this knowledge to promote understanding among the building's unruly
inhabitants. There is a smart suggestion here that Daley is bettering himself through self-education. Our everyman hero literally gets
his house in order, foils the lovable baddies (former night guards with an agenda, led by none other than Dick Van Dyke), and earns the
admiration of his wide-eyed son in the process.

Offering a fanciful high concept supported by a logical explanation (it's an ancient Egyptian artifact on display that inadvertently bestows
"life" to all exhibits), *Night at the Museum* succeeds in balancing zestful imagination with everyday reality, comedy with gentle pathos.
It may even inspire some youngsters to develop a legitimate interest in natural history... with or without a pet dinosaur to play with.

ABOVE: New guard Larry is pursued by a T-Rex exhibit! RIGHT: It's party time in the museum's atrium.

Larry Daley (Ben Stiller) has his hands full with various museum personalities, living incarnations of mini-cowboys (Owen Wilson) and ex-Presidents (Robin Williams) among them.

Suddenly-alive Neanderthals hold scheming museum guards Reginald (Bill Cobbs) and Gus (Mickey Rooney) captive in the outlandish climax.

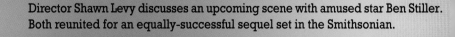

Director Shawn Levy discusses an upcoming scene with amused star Ben Stiller. Both reunited for an equally-successful sequel set in the Smithsonian.

IGHTY SAGA OF THE WORLD'S MIGHTIEST MAN !

JOSEPH E. LEVINE
PRESENTS

HERCULES

STEVE REEVES

SYLVA KOSCINA · GIANNA MARIA CANALE

FABRIZIO MIONI · IVO GARRANI · ARTURO DOMINICI · MIMMO PALMARA · LIDIA ALFONSI · GINA ROVERE
DIRECTED BY PIETRO FRANCISCI · EASTMAN COLOR by Pathé · DYALISCOPE · O.S.C.A.R. FILM · GALATEA · DISTRIBUTED BY WARNER BROS

WHO MADE IT:

Galatea Film(Italy)/Embassy Pictures (U.S.). Director: Pietro Francisc
Producer: Federico Teti. Presenter: Joseph E. Levine. Writers: Ennio De
Concini, Pietro Francisci, Gaio Frattini. Cinematography
(Eastmancolor): Mario Bava. Music: Enzo Masetti. Starring Steve
Reeves (Hercules), Sylva Koscina (Iole), Fabrizio Mioni (Jason), Ivo
Garrani (Pelias), Gianna Maria Canale (Antea), Arturo Dominic
(Eurysteus), Lifdia Alfonsi (The Sybil), Gabriele Antonini (Ulysses).

WHAT IT'S ABOUT:

While in the service of King Pelias, Hercules cannot save the life of the
ruler's arrogant son, but falls in love with his comely daughter Iole
He renounces his immortality for the joys of a normal life, but soon
finds himself accompanying Jason in his fabled quest for the Golden
Fleece. The brave Argonauts endure various life-threatening
adventures and are nearly defeated by the beautiful but treacherous
Amazons. Jason ultimately finds the Fleece, and Hercules helps him
to reclaim his stolen kingdom from Pelias. The demi-god ultimately
claims Iole as his bride and they face new adventures together.

WHY IT'S IMPORTANT:

After hitting paydirt with his U.S. release of Japan's *Godzilla* in
1956, producer Joseph E. Levine smelled similar box-office
potential in *The Labors of Hercules*, a widescreen Italian effort
showcasing American body builder Steve Reeves. The film
became an even bigger success stateside, buoyed by an
aggressive advertising/exploitation campaign. It also launched
the colorful sub-genre known as sword-and-sandal (or
"peplum"), which sold a lot of popcorn to international movie
audiences in the late '50s/early '60s. Biblical superheroes had
been the subject of mainstream movies before, most notably
Cecil B. DeMille's high-profile *Samson and Delilah* in 1949
More of a direct influence on *Labors* was Italy's highly
successful *Ulysses* from just a few years earlier ('54), boasting
an unforgettable Cyclops encounter and the megawatt star
presence of Kirk Douglas and Anthony Quinn. But Galatea's
Hercules was something else again. Part mythological
history lesson, part comic book (and, with gothic-minded
Mario Bavo lighting the shots, horror movie), this energetic
confection pushed its pepla pleasures to the max. Zeus' muscular
offspring is redefined for postwar audiences as a surly pre-Bond, the ultimate man's man; but
he's also suave and charming, a toga-adorned lady killer. This canny characterization was complete once an appropriate
God-like voice was found to match Reeves' imposing physical presence (enter Norman Rose). Unfortunately, current widescreen editions
of the film are mastered from an earlier cut, before this significant audio improvement was made.

Wrapped about the legend of Jason's quest for the Golden Fleece, *Hercules* concerns itself with two key issues: the title character's
desire to renounce immortality for a normal life, and outcast Jason regaining his stolen throne. Some of Galatea's most recognizable
performers show up for this pseudo-Biblical morality play/serial adventure, *Black Sunday*'s Ivo Garrani and Arturo Dominici among
them. Sylva Koscina is quite irresistible as star-crossed heroine Iole, and it's easy to understand why Hercules would forfeit his Olympian
heritage for marital bliss with such a lovely creature.

Although hindered slightly by uneven special effects (that "Hydra" guarding the Golden Fleece turns out to be a rubbery, dragon-like
dinosaur with Godzilla's distinctive roar), *Hercules* is nevertheless a great-looking film in anamorphic widescreen, offering a fantastica
color palette and a self-assured sense of dramatic spectacle that matches the Herculean countenance of Mr. Reeves himself. Followed
almost instantly by the equally enjoyable and even spookier *Hercules Unchained*, Levine's 1959 import remains the definitive scree

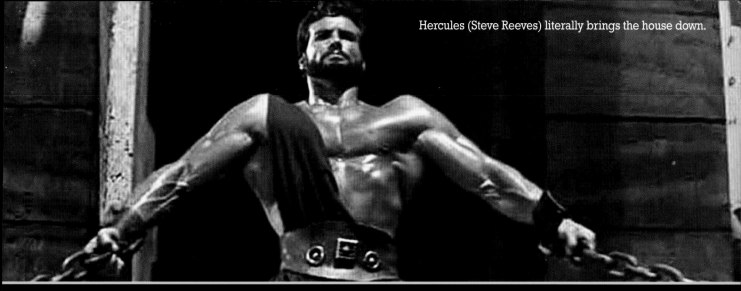

Hercules (Steve Reeves) literally brings the house down.

BELOW: Monsters reared their ugly heads in two key scenes, with a dinosaur-like dragon standing in for the seven-headed hydra.

ABOVE: Galetea stock players Arturo Dominichi (Eurysteus) and Ivo Garrani (King Pelias); both would later appear in Mario Bava's *The Mask of Satan*. LEFT: Reeves with lovely co-star Sylva Koscina. Both would return for the following year's sequel, *Hercules Unchained*.

Although Steve Reeves embodied the role of Hercules, his ordinary speaking voice was replaced by voice artist Norman Rose's more commanding tones.

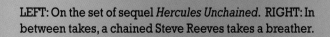

LEFT: On the set of sequel *Hercules Unchained*. RIGHT: In between takes, a chained Steve Reeves takes a breather.

WHO MADE IT:

Paramount Pictures (U.S.). Director: Tay Garnett. Producer: Robert Fellows. Writers: Edmund Beloin, based on the novel by Mark Twain. Cinematography (Technicolor): Ray Rennahan. Music: Victor Young. Starring Bing Crosby (Hank Martin), Rhonda Fleming (Alisande La Carteloise), Cedric Hardwicke (Lord Pendragon/King Arthur), William Bendix (Sir Sagramore), Murvyn Vye (Merlin), Virginia Field (Morgan Le Fay), Joseph Vitale (Sir Logris), Henry Wilcoxon (Sir Lancelot).

WHAT IT'S ABOUT:

An amiable mechanic from Connecticut suddenly finds himself catapulted back to the days of King Arthur. As first mistaken for a demon, Hank Martin wins over Arthur's no-nonsense crowd with his charm and good humor. He falls in love with beautiful "Sandy," becomes pals with his initial 'captor,' Sir Sagramore, and runs afoul of Arthur's enemies, most importantly Merlin the Magician. An attempt to open Arthur's eyes to injustice in his realm backfires, with Hank and friends taken prisoner. But his resourcefulness – and a handy almanac – saves the day. Eventually returned to his own time, Martin discovers that romance wasn't so very far away after all.

WHY IT'S IMPORTANT:

Mark Twain's fanciful story has inspired a number of movie incarnations, including an early sound effort boasting Will Rogers. But Paramount's 1949 Technicolor opus, ostensibly a vehicle for mega-star Bing Crosby, is the only adaptation that comes close to achieving a *Wizard of Oz*-like sense of endearing immortality. Combining a pleasing Victor Young score with eye-popping photography and a playfulness that keeps Twain's social satire in check, this very Hollywood *Yankee* was made for the masses. Even by 1949 the wraparound structure was something of a cliché, although studio bosses wisely resisted the temptation to present these bookends in black-and-white. A convenient blast of lightning hurls car mechanic Hank Martin into period England (wonder if he bumped into fellow time-traveler Peter Standish along the way?). While a total enigma to King Arthur and his cronies, he is soon back in business, horseshoeing local nags for visiting royalty… and making some humane 20th Century suggestions that inevitably rock the boat. With no one less than Merlin the Magician to contend with, resourceful Hank has his work cut out for him. Of course, he also has Rhonda Fleming's "Sandy" for ongoing inspiration, and the King himself (Cedric Hardwicke) as an eventual ally. Meanwhile, William Bendix is busy scoring major laughs as boastful-but-lovable Sir Sagramore ("Clarence" to Hank), especially in a showcase moment where he innocently fiddles with a loaded pistol his buddy from tomorrow has just fashioned.

The whole show, of course, rests on crooner Crosby's genial shoulders. America's most successful entertainer in '49, he's blessed with an easy, charming, nice guy persona that transcends any plot development. Bing's a more than perfect fit for take-it-all-in-stride Hank Martin, whether romancing local royalty, acing an unexpected joust, or saving his own life during a public execution, rescued by an almanac in his pocket and a convenient solar eclipse.

Self-assured and buoyant like its hero, *A Connecticut Yankee in King Arthur's Court* has stood the test of time quite well. Twain's satiric edge may be blunted a bit by Hollywood requirements, but it's not totally invisible (poverty and injustice during Arthur's reign are addressed). As for Crosby, he never made another fantasy film, and that's a shame. His one foray into the gleefully outlandish yielded impressive box-office returns in 1949, and continues to entertain viewers more than a half-century later t

LEFT: Amiable smitty and car doctor Hank Martin (Bing Crosby) amuses some local kiddies with a cheerful can-do song before being catapulted into the past.

RIGHT: Boastful Sir Sagramore (William Bendix) tells an extremely tall tale about the capture of stranger-in-a-strange land Martin. Adept at both comedy and drama, the versatile Bendix, famed for his *Life of Riley* TV series, is hilarious in this movie. His foolish fiddling with Hank's loaded pistol is a memorable bit-of-business.

ABOVE: One of several breathtaking matte paintings featured in *Yankee*, optically printed into the color frame.

ABOVE: King Arthur (Cedric Hardwicke) holds court, with treacherous Merlin (Murvyn Vye) by his side. LEFT: The disguised boys are "busy doin' nothing' in a charming musical number. RIGHT: Hank finds the girl of his dreams in Alisande ("Sandy," played by Rhonda Fleming). Bing Crosby first appeared in period garb one year earlier for Billy Wilder's *The Emperor Waltz*, a pleasing but less entertaining romp.

LEFT: the silent version (yikes!). RIGHT: On set with star Crosby, producer Robert Fellows and director Tay Garnett.

Rhonda Fleming as Bing Crosby's medieval sweetheart Sandy dazzled 1949 audiences in *A Connecticut Yankee in King Arthur's Cou* mostly bedecked in regal attire (ABOVE), but just as sexy disguised as a page boy (BELOW, with fellow prisoner Crosby). Meanwhi former Sopranos star James Gandolfini provides the voice and persona of Carol (RIGHT), who dwells *Where the Wild Things Are*.

ANOTHER TIME,
ANOTHER PLACE

WHO MADE IT:

Warner Bros. (U.S./Australia/Germany). Director: Spike Jonze. Producers: Bruce Berman, Scott Mednick, Thomas Tull, Tom Hanks, Gary Goetzman, Maurice Sendak. Writers: David Eggers, Spike Jonze, based on the book by Maurice Sendak. Cinematography (color): Lance Acord. Music: Carter Burwell, Karen Orzolek. Starring Max Records (Max), James Gandolfini (Carol - voice), Catherine O'Hara (Judith - voice), Lauren Ambrose (KW – voice), Forest Whitaker (Ira - voice), Catherine Keener (Mom), Alexander (Paul Dano), Pepita Emmerichs (Claire), Mark Ruffalo (The Boyfriend).

WHAT IT'S ABOUT:

Ignored and under-appreciated by his family (or so he thinks), young, tantrum-prone Max runs away and becomes "king" on an island inhabited by wondrous, but somewhat mixed-up monsters. Max soon realizes that he can't solve their various emotional problems, and begins to see the error of his own out-of-control ways and behavior.

WHY IT'S IMPORTANT:

Filled with hate and rage, kids? Uncle Maurice has the answer... Just spend a little time *Where the Wild Things Are* and work out those frustrations, lickety-split. Like the offbeat Sendak book that inspired it, Spike Jonze's movie fearlessly eschews light-heartedness in favor of sustained melancholy. This is no fanciful trip to a gaily-colored wonderland, but a depressing journey of self-discovery undertaken by a lonely little boy with some real anger management issues. In short, it's one of the most realistic depictions of childhood angst ever put on film. Not exactly abandoned by his sister (she's just a normal self-absorbed teen) and his divorced mom (under job pressure, a new boyfriend, but still there for him), frustrated youngster Max (Max Records) finds solace with the weird wild creatures he bonds with after "sailing off" to a mysterious isle. We're not really sure how much of this journey takes place in his mind – he is gone for a stretch – but the life lessons he absorbs are nonetheless real. Enormous troll Carol (James Gandolfini) is something of a Max doppelganger, giving into rage and jealousy whenever things don't go exactly as planned, while nurturing KW is a surrogate sister/mom combo, even "giving birth" to the concealed boy (hiding from enraged Carol) when he's pulled from her innards. Proclaimed "King" of these lovable but messed-up monsters, Max soon realizes that bringing harmony to his adopted realm is a lot harder than he thought. Indeed, "You're out of control!" is as much a signature line for this movie as "Let the wild rumpus begin!" (signaling unrestrained mayhem and, usually, playful violence). Max even comes to grips with the physical harm he can cause others during his tantrums, which is where this unique adventure began (he bites mom in a fit of rage). When the boy finally returns home and his relived mother can finally close her eyes and rest easy, the youthful Monster King smiles contentedly. Like sleeping in a massive pile with his loved ones, he now feels safe and secure.

Director Spike Jonze (*Being John Malkovitch*, *Adaptation*) deftly adapts Maurice Sendak's mostly-illustrated book and embraces semi-disturbing material, running the risk of alienating mainstream viewers who might turn off to loud, abrasive Max. The monster friends are essentially giant shaggy suits with CGI faces, an ideal fx combination that enables actor Max Records to convincingly interact with them. Also carefully thought out is the choice of background music, with Karen O's jaunty "Building All is Love" (played during the building of Max's fort) being especially memorable. Not for all tastes (most Spike Jonze movies aren't), *Where the Wild Things Are* redefines its generally upbeat genre for a more sophisticated audience. In many ways, it's *The Wizard of Oz* for a dysfunctional generation: there is no place like home, and this is especially true in the frustrating, super-difficult 21st Century.

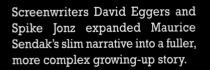
Unhappy youngster Max (Max Records) works out his frustrations with lovable monster friends, who make him King of their island.

Screenwriters David Eggers and Spike Jonz expanded Maurice Sendak's slim narrative into a fuller, more complex growing-up story.

ormer *Sopranos* star James Gandolfini provides the oice for an intimidating but good-hearted ogre.

"Let the wild rumpus begin!" cries Max, which is a fine idea if you can avoid being trampled by your oversized monster buddies.

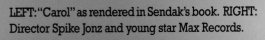

LEFT: "Carol" as rendered in Sendak's book. RIGHT: Director Spike Jonz and young star Max Records.

89 ANGEL ON MY SHOULDER 1946 ⊙100 1.37

WHO MADE IT:

United Artists (U.S.). Director: Archie Mayo. Producers: Charles R. Rogers, David W. Siegel. Writers: Harry Segall, Roland Kibbe. Cinematography (b/w): James Van Trees. Music: Dimitri Tiompkin. Starring Paul Muni (Eddie Kagle/Judge Frederick Parker), Anne Baxter (Barbara Foster), Claude Rains (Nick), Onslow Stevens (Dr. Matt Higgins), George Cleveland (Albert), Erskine Sanford (Minister), Hardie Albright (Smiley Williams), James Flavin (Bellamy).

WHAT IT'S ABOUT:

High-class hoodlum Eddie Kagle is blasted by one of his own criminal cohorts, Smiley Williams. In Hell, fast-thinking Eddie makes an arrangement with Nick, the Prince of Darkness himself. The underworld kingpin returns to Earth in the form of respected Judge Parker, part of the Devil's plan for wider corruption. But Eddie is more interested in getting even with his own murderer. As he deals with hate, love and hope with friends and foes alike, Kagle begins to see the world and his responsibility to it in a different light.

WHY IT'S IMPORTANT:

How about *Mr. Jordan* in reverse? There's no question the popularity of Columbia's 1942 fantasy inspired this two-character study of corruption and redemption, with the inevitable casting of Claude Rains cementing the parallel. Once again a deceased soul is returned to Earth in order to inhabit a living body, only this time the "hero" is vengeful gangster Eddie Kagle (Paul Muni), obsessed with slaying a former friend and cohort (Hardie Albright) who guns him down without mercy eight minutes into the film. "My children, my children, what would you do without me?" sighs philosophical Nick as only honey-and-gravel-voiced Rains can. Sure of his infernal powers and uncanny ability to darkly influence, he's hoping to use the seemingly single-minded Kagan to replace a do-gooder lookalike and further the cause of Evil on Earth. As with *Jordan*, the reborn hero falls in love (a more sedate than usual Anne Baxter), but in *Angel* it's part of an overall second chance Fate has provided. Significantly, Kagan resists the Devil's chummy friendship, pegging Pal Nick as a sophisticated con man and never missing an opportunity to remind this amiable escort of his loathsome nature. This is a literal "beat the devil" parable, matching Lucifer with a worthy adversary from a very different kind of Underworld. Although the political material isn't as front-and-center as it is in comparable movie fables like *The Devil and Daniel Webster* and *Gabriel Over the White House*, it provides the required moral challenges and opportunities for Kagel, which he aces.

Frequently criticized by modern viewers for overacting, Muni tones it down as the tough guy protagonist, keeping a welcome lid on his character's potentially volatile personality. It's important that Kagel be just as smooth and self-assured as Nick during the course of their uneasy alliance, anticipating soul-threatening tricks and, whenever possible, reversing them. While it's true that this crime boss needs to account for considerable sins, his brief, inspiring return to Earth assures him of the moral high ground. Both he and the Prince of Darkness head back to infernal regions as the final shot fades, but the story really doesn't end here: it's clear that Nick, foiled and literally blackmailed by this wily gangster, will be given "Hell" by his ex-partner at every turn.

GHOST 1990

WHO MADE IT:

Paramount Pictures (U.S.). Director: Jerry Zucker. Producers: Steven-Charles Jaffe, Bruce Joel Rubin, Lisa Weinstein. Writer: Bruce Joel Rubin. Cinematography (Technicolor): Adam Greenberg. Music: Maurice Jarre, Alex North. Starring Patrick Swayze (Sam Wheat), Demi Moore (Molly Jensen), Whoopi Goldberg, Tony Goldwyn (Carl Bruner), John Hugh (Surgeon), Rick Aviles (Willie Lopez), Vincent Schiavelli (Subway Ghost).

WHAT IT'S ABOUT:

Young businessman Sam Wheat is killed in what appears to be an act of senseless violence, leaving his grieving young widow Molly behind. But Sam remains on Earth as a ghost, much to his own astonishment. After initial disorientation, he learns how to operate in the world of the living, and eventually enlists the aid of a fortune-telling bunko artist – who happens to have genuine psychic powers – to bring his own murderer to justice. This turns out to be his best friend Carl, who is claimed by hellish demons following his own unexpected demise. Sam bids his great love Molly a last farewell before ascending into the higher regions, his purpose on Earth fulfilled.

WHY IT'S IMPORTANT:

Ghost won an Oscar for it's screenplay, and it's easy to understand why: Bruce Joel Rubin hatches a simple fantasy premise and runs with it, making clever use of all logical plot extensions, setting up and paying off gags, always moving Jerry Zucker's supernatural murder-romance into slightly different, mostly interesting conceptual territory. If best friend Carl's yuppie untrustworthiness seems apparent from the start, the eventual twisty turns, especially those involving his stolen check, provide enough 'gotcha!' moments to keep viewers happy. And Whoppi Goldberg's endearing bunko psychic (she earns the film's second Oscar) doesn't show up until relatively late in the day, only to be used exceptionally well – even enabling the life-separated lovers to enjoy one last dance through the (mostly implied) use of her spirit-inhabited body. Minor characters like the Subway Ghost (Vincent Schiavelli), necessary to the plot so that Sam can learn how to move objects with his mind, add their own surprisingly fresh pleasures (this haunted wretch was apparently a jumper; now we've learned what happens to suicides, or at least one of them). But it's that kind of a movie, hooked on its own free-flowing imagination and sense of manipulative vitality. At the heart of *Ghost*, of course, is the preternatural loving relationship of Sam and Molly (Patrick Swayze, Demi Moore). Their mutual physicality is nicely conveyed in the film's famous pottery molding scene, as hands and clay take a one-of-a-kind sensual journey. This is promptly referenced in the actual bedroom scene, with Sam's body seeming to change form in Molly's eager hands – another self-aware reference, as his body will soon transform literally. Given *Ghost*'s zingy "every scene a new angle!" structure, it's refreshing that both Moore and Swayze are allowed some personal moments that aren't specifically plot-related... for Moore, it's her beautiful scene with the disbelieving but sympathetic cop, as she deals with loss and denial in very realistic, relatable terms; for Swayze, it's his primal outburst at newly-discovered best friend betrayer Carl (Tony Goldwyn): "I had a life!"

Finally, as if the winning romance, Whoppi Goldberg, savvy personalization of ghosthood and oh-so-clever story twists weren't enough, Rubin throws a bone to the horror crowd by rolling out a swarm of hellish black wraiths to claim bad characters (another set-up, of course, and it's fun to watch deserving Carl go

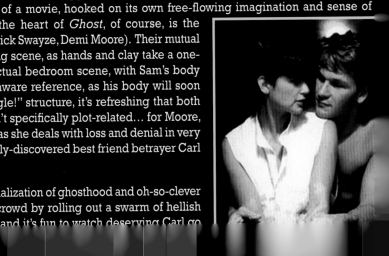

WHO MADE IT:

20th Century-Fox (U.S./U.K.). Director: Roy Ward Baker. Producer: So
C. Siegel. Writers: Ronald MacDougall, based on the play "Berkele
Square" by John L. Balderston. Cinematography (b/w, Technicolor)
Georges Perinal. Music: William Alwyn. Starring Tyrone Power (Pete
Standish), Ann Blyth (Helen Pettigrew/Martha Forsyth), Michael Rennie
(Roger Forsyth), Beatrice Campbell (Kate Pettigrew), Kathleen Byror
(Duchess of Devonshire), Raymond Huntley (Mr. Throstle).

WHAT IT'S ABOUT:

Dissatisfied with the atomic-era world he lives in, nuclear physicis
Peter Standish is struck by lightning and hurled back to Victorian

London. He takes the place of
his ancestor of the same name,
and begins a new life. But
Standish is out of place in this
era; moreover, he realizes that
he has viewed period times
through the eyes of a hopeless
romantic, and is repulsed by
the degree of ignorance and
arrogance in his midst. Only love for a beautiful cousin makes the
experience bearable. When Peter finally returns to his own time
he realizes that paradise wasn't so very far away after all.

WHY IT'S IMPORTANT:

The notion of escaping into another, seemingly more satisfying
period of history has inspired many a science fiction writer
Usually there is a tangible method of transport involved, a time-
traveling machine of some kind. But in fantasy, trips to the pas
tend to be much cleaner and far more mysterious, often
accomplished by sheer force of will. *I'll Never Forget You*
gamely updates John L. Balderston's seminal play *Berkele*
Square to the no-nonsense atomic age, partially to ground
hero Peter Standish as a level-headed rational thinker
Earnestly explaining his expected departure to skeptica
colleague Roger Forsyth (Michael Rennie, prior to being
cast in *The Day the Earth Stood Still*), Standish is much like
H.G. Wells' discontented George, a man of great passion stuck in a society tha
appreciates only the practical benefits of his considerable skills. A blast of heavenly lightning hurls Peter
back to Victorian era London, nicely etched in darker-than-usual Technicolor, even as his anachronistic counterpart assumes the
scientist's identity in 1951. Unlike Frank Lloyd's 1933 film adaptation, which followed the
century-spanning misadventures of both Standishes, *I'll Never Forget You* is content to
remain with the modern hero throughout, tracking both his initial elation and ultimate
disillusionment with unfair, uncivilized, unclean period London.

Clearly the inspiration for writer Richard Matheson's substantial work in this sub-genre
(his much beloved *Somewhere in Time* is practically a remake), Balderston's tale
established the template for all romantic time-tripping fantasies to come, first on stage
then in the cinema. More accessible than Fox's 1933 film incarnation, *I'll Never Forge*
You is a reasonably effective rendering, enhanced by attractive Hollywood leads and

WHO MADE IT:

Columbia Pictures Corporation (U.S.). Director: Terry Gilliam. Producers: Debra Hill, Lynda Obst, Tony Mark, Stacey Sher. Writer: Richard LaGravenese. Cinematography (Technicolor): Roger Pratt. Music: George Fenton. Starring Jeff Bridges (Jack Lucas), Robin Williams (Parry), Mercedes Ruehl (Anne), Amanda Plummer (Lydia), Michael Jeter (Homeless Cabaret Singer), Kathy Najimy (Crazed Video Customer), David Hyde Pierce (Lou Rosen), Ted Ross (Limo Bum), Lara Harris (Sondra), Warren Olney (TV Anchorman), Frazer Smith (News Reporter), Harry Shearer (Sitcom Actor).

WHAT IT'S ABOUT:

An arrogant and cynical disc jockey named Jack Lucas makes a statement on the air that leads to an act of bloody violence. Consumed by guilt, Lucas eventually runs into a survivor of this tragedy, delusional but delightful former teacher Parry, and befriends him. Parry, who sees a monstrous Red Knight whenever his confidence or sense of reality threatens to return, begs his new ally to join him on a questionable quest to steal the Holy Grail from a local millionaire. By helping this poor soul with his various problems, Lucas hopes to get his own ruined life in order.

WHY IT'S IMPORTANT:

Terry Gilliam is an artist fascinated by insanity, both as a clinical condition and as a springboard for creative expression. Madness is the only method of escape from a totalitarian state in *Brazil*, and here, both Robin Williams and Jeff Bridges play wounded characters who take turns facing dragon-monsters and ghostly assassins to keep themselves alive, and at least semi-hopeful. Using the quest for the Holy Grail for inspiration, along with New York City as a colorful backdrop, Gilliam spins an emotionally-ripe tale of vanity, tragedy, and eventual redemption. "I just want to pay the fine and go home," chokes out guilt-ridden shock jock Jack Lucas to earthy, sympathetic girlfriend Anne (Mercedes Ruel) after his reckless on-air remarks lead to a mass killing. Coming to the aide of an endearingly deranged survivor named Parry (Williams), Jack endures a plethora of weirdly embarrassing episodes, a few of them challenging his own tenuous hold on sanity. A matchmaking subplot that introduces Amanda Plummer's character Lydia into the narrative dominates Act III, providing the movie's most amusing visual set-piece. It's a dinner for four at a Chinese restaurant, complete with optical wipes signaling the passage of time, as oddest of couples Parry and Lydia defy common sense and hit it off, much to the happy astonishment of their sponsors.

But laughs and graphic displays of magical entities aside (the fiery Red Knight works in just about every dramatic context, and is especially interesting charging through Central Park), it's human relationships and finding a reason for being that this movie is mainly concerned about. Self-destructive Jack keeps screwing up right until the end, and only the legitimate miracle of the retrieved Grail manages to turn him around. In a lovely bit of irony, Jack unexpectedly prevents the Grail owner's suicide by stealing the object and tripping sensory alarms, bringing police and life-saving first aid promptly to the spot.

Like all of Gilliam's films, a certain playful maturity and patience with the abstract are required for maximum satisfaction. Those who can tune into this eclectic filmmaker's skewed wavelength will find their brain cells tickled and their hearts enriched.

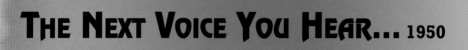

THE STORY OF WHAT HAPPENED AT **8:30** P.M. TO THE JOE SMITHS AND FAMILIES LIKE THEM ALL OVER THE WORLD!...

an M·G·M picture

The Next Voice You Hear...

JAMES WHITMORE · NANCY DAVIS   CHARLES SCHNEE   GEORGE SUMNER ALBEE
WILLIAM A. WELLMAN   DORE SCHARY   A METRO-GOLDWYN-MAYER PICTURE

WHO MADE IT:

Metro-Goldwyn-Mayer (U.S.). Director: William A. Wellman. Producer: Dore Schary. Writers: Charles Schnee, from a story by George Sumner Albee. Cinematography (b/w): William Mellor. Music: David Raksin. Starring James Whitmore (Joe Smith), Nancy Davis (Mrs. Mary Smith), Gary Gray (Johnny Smith), Lillian Bronson (Aunt Ethel), Art Smith (Fred Brannan), Tom D'Andrea (Harry 'Hap' McGee), Jeff Corey (Freddie).

WHAT IT'S ABOUT:

The voice of God coming over the radio for a week causes wonder, consternation and fear. Among those in awe of the event are American factory worker Joe Smith and his family. People everywhere begin to discover that the secret to living a happy life is to relax and appreciate the many wonders about them – love first of all. As new life comes into the world, the miracle of the Voice, which

could not be recorded, will be remembered and spoken about by those who were fortunate enough to hear it first hand.

WHY IT'S IMPORTANT:

After giving MGM a sizable hit in *Battleground*, director William Wellman was allowed this offbeat experiment in low-budget efficiency, a quietly meaningful B+ quasi-religious think piece supported wholeheartedly by message-friendly studio boss Dore Shary. *The Next Voice You Hear...* has a lot to say about 1950s social attitudes and the nobility of common folk, some of it wise, some of it reeking of Hollywood condescension. "God" in this scenario is clearly the Big He as presented in Sunday School and Christmas cards; among other things, He's apparently camera shy, and since His radio messages always come through with "static free reception," one can only wonder what was on TV screens during these intervals (a black void? Too ominous!). Since most of the film's audience was still radio-centric in 1950, this question was easily overlooked. It's also interesting that God chooses 8:30 pm Pacific Time to speak, meaning that the broadcast is heard in Manhattan at 11:30 – just in time for all elitist East Coast night-lifers to get home.

Wellman is clearly having fun on a number of levels. As with *Ben-Hur*, the picture begins without Leo the Lion roaring (this movie's about PEACE, get it?), serving up a freeze-frame logo and some church bells instead. The film's structure is dictated by the week in which this miracle occurs, each day labeled reverently in screen titles. Repeating a smart move he first employed in *Battleground*, Wellman limits background musical scoring to the opening and ending of his movie, subtly increasing a sense of reality. That said, there is a considerable amount of music featured in *Next Voice*, almost all of it emanating from radios. This clever use of aural counterpointing (we call it 'needle-drop' today) captures our protagonist's mood perfectly. It's no accident that Jerome Kerns' "All the Things You Are," generally regarded as one of the most beautiful love songs ever written, accompanies Whitmore's first wistful musings about the mysterious Voice.

Despite good intentions, Wellman and writer Charles Schnee manage to screw up some major supporting characters, probably because time constraints wouldn't allow for re-writes. *Next Voice* can't decide whether Aunt Ethel (Lillian Bronsan) is a howling fanatic or laughable case of self-parody, while Whitmore's noxious boss Art Smith "arcs" into a lovable neighborhood sage – one of God's miracles, or just rushed screenwriting? Still, the film gets points for being... well, just being. And when all else fails, there's always the "new Spencer Tracy," James Whitmore, Wellman's Oscar-nominated discovery from *Battleground*, he's a pleasure to watch in just about anything.

THAT
WONDERFULLY FUNNY
MOTION PICTURE...

Miranda

Starring

GLYNIS JOHNS · GOOGIE WITHERS
GRIFFITH JONES · JOHN McCALLUM

David Tomlinson · Yvonne Owen
Sonia Holm · Margaret Rutherford

Produced by Betty E. Box · Directed by Ken Annakin
Screenplay by Peter Blackmore
A Sydney Box Production for Gainsborough

A J. ARTHUR RANK Presentation
An EAGLE LION FILMS Release

Miranda HAS Everything !

WHO MADE IT:

General Film Distributors (U.K.)/Eagle-Lion Films (U.S.). Director: Ken Annakin. Producers: Betty E. Box, Roy Rich. Writers: Peter Blackmore, based on his play. Additional dialogue by Dennis Waldock. Cinematography (b/w): Ray Elton. Music: Temple Abady. Starring Glynis Johns (Miranda Trewella), Googie Withers (Clare Martin), Griffith Jones (Dr. Paul Martin), John McCallum (Nigel), Margaret Rutherford (Nurse Carey), David Tomlinson (Charles), Yvonne Owen (Betty), Sonia Holm (Isobel), Zena Marshall (Secretary), Brian Oulton (Manell).

WHAT IT'S ABOUT:

On a fishing holiday, young Dr. Paul Martin hooks an alluring, comically talkative mermaid named Miranda. Against his better judgment, he gives in to her request to see London, effectively passing her off as a wheelchair-bound invalid. Adorable but unable to control her amorous instincts, Miranda begins flirting with every eligible male in sight, throwing the doctor's world into a tizzy.

WHY IT'S IMPORTANT:

Ken Annakin's *Miranda* is a very different kettle of fish than its American counterpart, *Mr. Peabody and the Mermaid.* Both films were released the same year, obviously a trick of wily King Neptune, and both possess charms that hold up rather nicely today. But unlike Ann Blyth's mute, childlike siren who only has doe eyes for William Powell, Miranda is coquettish irony personified, mad about men in general and addicted to capturing their hearts. Plunking this amorous creature in the middle of upper-class England leads to all sorts of over-the-top situations, made all the more entertaining by star Glynis Johns' irresistibly disarming voice. It's hard to imagine anyone other than Johns in this part, so thoroughly does she infuse her infectious "playful flirt" on-screen persona into it. Miranda is delightfully amoral, and the nonchalant way she discusses life-or-death issues is hilarious and distantly chilling at the same time. This wide-eyed babe is a siren, after all, who preys on attentive human men and shrugs her tail at the consequences (the last image in the movie is a shocker). A befuddled Griffith Jones plays the

vacationing doctor who stumbles upon Miranda and rather foolishly brings her to civilization, passing her off as a wheelchair-bound patient whose legs are forever covered. This last gag is borderline offense, and briefly suggests a deeper resonance: is Miranda Trewella "different" because she's a mermaid, or because she's handicapped? If this plot gimmick were to be retained in a contemporary remake, savvy screenwriters would seize the subtext possibilities and run with them.

But as is, *Miranda* thoroughly entertains and provides enough mild social satire to justify its fanciful premise. The effervescent Johns would repeat her signature role in a full-color sequel, *Mad About Men* (1954), and also play Miranda uncredited in the nutsy British satire, *Helter Skelter*, featuring frequent co-star David Tomlinson (Charles in *Miranda*, Johns' fussy husband years later in *Mary Poppins*). As for 1948's mermaid wars, *Mr. Peabody* easily conquered North America, while *Miranda* became Europe's sea cow of choice (sorry about the unthinking words

CHILD CARE WITH A TWIST

Miranda the mermaid (Glynis Johns) and her gurgling newborn left bemused 1948 audiences with something
to ponder about. Meanwhile, nefarious Witch King David Bowie entertains the kidnapped little brother of
teenage nemesis Jennifer Connelly in *Labyrinth*. Imperiled children have been a mainstay of fantasy fiction
since the earliest folk tales. Significantly, characters like Lewis Carroll's Alice or Frank Baum's Dorothy Gale
are far younger on the page than they have been in mainstream movie adaptations, which frequently play as

83

LABYRINTH 1986

-101- 2.20

WHO MADE IT:

Tri-Star Pictures/Henson Associates/Lucasfilm (U.K./U.S.). Director: Jim Henson. Producers: David Lazer, George Lucas, Eric Rattray. Writers: Terry Jones, based on a story by Dennis Lee and Jim Henson. Cinematography (color): Alex Thomson. Music: Trevor Jones. Starring: David Bowie (Jareth the Goblin King), Jennifer Connelly (Sarah), Toby Froud (Toby), Shelley Thompson (Stepmother), Christopher Malcolm (Father), Natalie Finland (Fairy), Shari Weiser (Hoggle), Frank Oz (The Wiseman), Brian Henson (Hoggle/Goblin – voice).

WHAT IT'S ABOUT:

Annoyed 15 year-old Sarah, left to baby sit her little brother Toby, accidentally wishes him into a deadly-dangerous fantasy world dominated by the enigmatic Goblin King, Jareth. Now Sarah must enter Jareth's oddly challenging labyrinth in order to find her imperiled sibling and beat the mysterious King at his own nefarious game. For if she does not rescue Toby by midnight, the boy will be transformed into a goblin himself!

WHY IT'S IMPORTANT:

Once Yoda bridged the gap between puppetry and live-action performance in *The Empire Strikes Back*, a creative collaboration between '80s fantasy masters Jim Henson (The Muppets) and George Lucas seemed inevitable. Produced on a healthy budget with all the widescreen trimmings, their semi-musical *Labyrinth* is an *Alice in Wonderland/Wizard of Oz*-like scenario dominated by the austere figure of David Bowie, perfectly cast as resident villain Goblin King. But he is more of a challenging figure than a purely malevolent one, inspiring adolescent rescuer Sara (Jennifer Connelly) even as he threatens to transform her kidnapped little brother into one of his own. Facing a plethora of obstacles in the perplexing Labyrinth while befriending various oddball entities, young Sarah survives the tale's inevitable growing-up trajectory and learns that dire consequences can result from reckless behavior and self-centered thinking. That said, there's a curious paradox to the film's message: escaping headlong into fantasy warps Sarah's perception of true values, while at the same time it provides her with the inspiration and confidence she requires to get through life in general. Lucas once said something similar about his own personal therapy, admitting that, whenever the pressure-filled real world gets too much for him, he visits his made-up universe and spends quality time with the various "friends" of his imagination. At the end of *Labyrinth*, following her complicated maze-quest and tentative dance with the seductive Goblin King – what fifteen year-old girl isn't mesmerized by a sexy rock star? – wiser, more responsible Sarah finally gets her priorities straight. People should really live in both worlds, this movie's telling us, the tangible one and an always-comforting, frequently absurd parallel universe where anything is possible.

Technically, *Labyrinth* is a breath-taker, Brian Froud's brilliantly conceived on-set characters and landscapes providing a unique wonderland that never fails to amaze. Walking sticks have irksome personalities, rocks roll about with dogged purpose and quaint communities literally spring to life as director Jim Henson's genius for giddy make-believe is extravagantly showcased. Yes, many of these fanciful entities are flop-flimsy wailers that remind us of their Muppet heritage, but as an alternative to the 21st Century's super-smooth, digitally synthetic CG creations, they are most welcome indeed.

Although rarely breaking new ground, *Labyrinth* successfully charts its coming-of-age fairy tale requirements with style, good will and flamboyantly imaginative production design worthy of its seasoned co-creators. Still, visitors to this monster maze take heed: Never say "piece of cake" after solving a problem, or you may wind up in that foulest, most flatulent of destinations: the Bog of Eternal Stench!

Pretty teenager Sarah (Jennifer Connelly) learns about responsibility the hard way after Witch King Jared (David Bowie) kidnaps her little brother. She has only limited time to correct a major mistake.

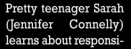

Various labyrinth entities help Sarah in her desperate quest to rescue kid brother Toby from Jared's eager clutches.

LEFT: Froud's conceptual painting.
RIGHT: On set with the manic "Firies"

TIME BANDITS 1981

-116- 1.85

WHO MADE IT:

HandMade Films/Avco Embassy Pictures (U.K./U.S.). Director: Terry Gilliam. Producers: Terry Gilliam, George Harrison, Denis O'Brienn, Neville C. Thompson. Writer: Michael Palin & Terry Gilliam. Cinematography (Technicolor): Peter Biziou. Music: Mike Moran. Starring John Cleese (Robin Hood), Sean Connery (King Agamemnon/Fireman), Shelley Duvall (Dame Pansy/Pansy), Kenny Baker (Fidget), Craig Warnock (Kevin), Katherine Helmond (Mrs. Ogre), Ian Holm (Napoleon), Michael Palin (Vincent), Ralph Richardson (Supreme Being), Peter Vaughan (Winston the Ogre), David Warner (Evil Genius), David Rappaport (Randall), Malcolm Dixon (Strutter), Mike Edmonds (Og), Jack Purvis (Wally), Tiny Ross (Vermin).

WHAT IT'S ABOUT:

A little boy named Kevin finds his boring life with clueless parents dramatically interrupted by the sudden arrival of the Time Bandits. He follows these tiny tykes, who are guided by a map they've stolen from the Supreme Being, as they slip through portals into ages past and make off with untold riches. Eventually they tangle with the devilish Evil Genius, who intends to remake Creation, before all is set straight and Kevin is returned home… only to face a different kind of challenge.

WHY IT'S IMPORTANT:

A wacky romp through the ages, *Time Bandits* allows director Terry Gilliam another splendid opportunity for reality-challenging visuals and snarky satiric jabs. Young Kevin's adventure with a gaggle of lovable mini-thieves is mostly an excuse to skewer legendary figures such as Napoleon (played with whiney petulance by Ian Holm), Robin Hood (John Cleese is "jolly good"), and even Lucifer and the Supreme Being himself (affording David Warner another opportunity to sneer demonically, and Ralph Richardson to be letter-perfect as a benevolent if slightly overworked gentleman Creator). Coming off best is rough-and-tumble King Agamemnon (Sean Connery), a strangely ideal father figure for needy orphan-to-be Kevin (Craig Warnock) during a respite in ancient Greece.

Of course, even for a comedic fantasy, the fact that all encountered historical characters speak understandable English is a bit hard to swallow. That said, Michael Palin's central premise is clever enough to sustain this movie for nearly two hours of picturesque flapdoodle. It seems the creation of the universe was something of a "botched job," with inviting time holes scattered through the ages. Using a map stolen from Mr. Being himself, Fidget (*Star Wars*' Kenny Baker) and his motley minions enter these door-like anomalies, gather treasures from countless time periods, and than promptly vamoose, endlessly pursued by their ticked-off Creator. In the even more fanciful Time of Legend, some of Gilliam's most audacious fantasy characters shine in their respective set-pieces, an ogre with a backache (Peter Vaughan) and a marching giant who wears a ship for a hat (Ian Muir) among them. Everything builds to a no-holds barred special effects climax, as reinforcements from myriad time periods join forces to take on the glowering Warner.

Generally speaking, youthful protagonists of most fairy tale epics wind up learning a valuable lesson by final fade, with their own real-world troubles cleverly paralleled in the fanciful adventure they endure. It's not especially clear what befuddled Kevin gets out of his breathless trip through Earth's history, other than a burned-down house and the violent death of his thoroughly annoying parents (does a wink from Sean Connery's fireman really compensate?). Still, satire and wild visuals aside, a palpable bond clearly emerges among the misbehaving bandits, who are genuinely concerned about each other's safety. Honor among thieves? Yes, especially those who are kind to attention-deprived children. When all's said and done, even the exhausted Supreme Being gives these lovable, light-fingered opportunists a pass.

TOP: the film's most iconic image, shot in super-slow motion with a miniature ship donned by "giant" actor Ian Muir. RIGHT: Wily Time Bandits pose with their stolen map as an off-screen Kevin immoralizes them on Polaroid film. BELOW: The Supreme Being (Ralph Richardson) gets his house in order.

The worlds visited by Kevin and his bandit pals include ancient Greece, where King Agamemnon (Sean Connery) proves his mettle by vanquishing a fierce minotaur-like creature. Eventually the time travelers must face demonical evil in the form of an Evil Genius (played with customary venom by David Warner), who wants the stolen map so he can reshape the universe to his liking.

LEFT: Kenny Baker as an Ewok in *Return of the Jedi*. RIGHT: Director Terry Gilliam on location.

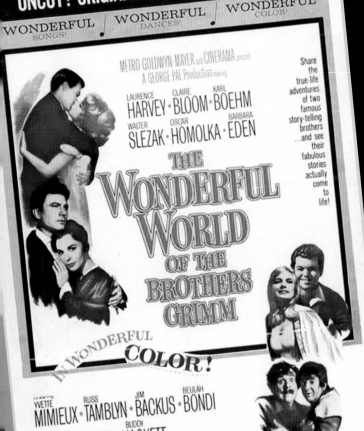

WHO MADE IT:

Metro-Goldwyn-Mayer (U.S.). Directors: Henry Levin, George Pal. Producer: George Pal. Writers: David P. Harmon, Charles Beaumont, William Roberts, based on "Die Bruder Grimm" by Dr. Hermann Gerstner. Cinematography (Metrocolor): Paul Vogel. Music: Leigh Harline. Special Visual Effects: Tim Baar, Wah Chang, Robert Hoag, Gene Warren, Jim Danforth. Starring Laurence Harvey (Wilhelm Grimm/The Cobbler), Kal Boehm (Jacob Grimm), Claire Bloom (Dorothea Grimm), Walter Slezak (Stossel), Barbara Eden (Greta Heinrich), Oscar Homolka (Duke), Arnold Stang (Rumpelstiltskin), Martita Hunt (Anna Richter), Yvette Mimieux (Princess), Russ Tamblyn (Woodsman/Tom Thumb), Jim Backus (King "Dancing Princess"), Beulah Bondi (The Gypsy), Terry-Thomas (Ludwig), Buddy Hackett (Hans), Otto Kruger (King "The Singing Bone").

WHAT IT'S ABOUT:

Brothers Wilhelm and Jacob Grimm are writers; but while bachelor Jacob spends his days chronicling history, family man Wilhelm would rather lose himself in wondrous fairy tales, which are so much more enchanting than real life. He amuses the locals with these inspired tales, but antagonizes his no-nonsense employer, the Duke. Returning from one of his story-scouting expeditions, Wilhelm falls into a river, catches a fever and loses all the valuable work he and his brother were preparing. Despite this setback, the Grimms manage to get on their feet again, and are soon satisfying both adults and children with their respective writings.

WHY IT'S IMPORTANT:

Sense of wonder specialist George Pal spent much of his Hollywood career leapfrogging from science fiction subjects (*Destination Moon*, *The War of the Worlds*) to full-fledged fantasies (Oscar-winning Puppetoons, *Tom Thumb*). Following his success with *The Time Machine* and sword and sandal-inspired *Atlantis the Lost Continent*, Pal embarked on the most ambitious project of his career: a star-studded biopic of the Brothers Grimm, complete with stop-motion adaptations of three engaging fairy tales, all to be filmed in the ultra-prestigious Cinerama process.

Although Pal had produced a successful screen biography of Houdini nine years earlier, *Grimm* posed a far greater challenge, starting with an ambitious, budget-busting shooting schedule in Europe. Just as daunting, all fx sequences needed to be carefully designed for Cinerama's unique and ultimately impractical widescreen system. Shrugging off enormous pressure, Pal somehow rose to the occasion; *The Wonderful World of the Brothers Grimm* is arguably his most impressive mainstream movie, a charming blend of pseudo-reality (the Grimms are lightened up a bit for family consumption) and three expertly-crafted, self-contained fairy tales.

The usually austere Laurence Harvey is inexplicably perfect as fantasy-obsessed Wilhelm, a charming and adoring family man who dazzles local kids, including his own, with fanciful tales. The conflict with no-nonsense writing partner Jacob is enough to hang this scenario on; will irresponsible Wilhelm's preoccupations cost them their well-paying research job? It's pretty much that simple. Although the reality-based sequences are fine (bolstered by a first-rate supporting cast), *Wonderful World* truly comes to life whenever Grimm's fairy tales are depicted. These three stories perfectly match the breezy tone of the biographical material, suggesting that Wilhelm's life itself is enchanted because of his vast imagination and childlike sense of wonder (an angle director Terry Gilliam would re-explore half a century later). Indeed, the movie ends with a title stating "And they lived happily ever after," neatly summing up George Pal's

In the film's most audacious sequence, a gravely ill Wilhelm Grimm (Laurence Harvey) is visited by the various fairy tale characters he has championed, who will vanish if his poor health prevents their creation in the books he's yet to write. Tom Thumb (Russ Tamblyn, reprising his 1958 portrayal) is among Wilhelm's callers.

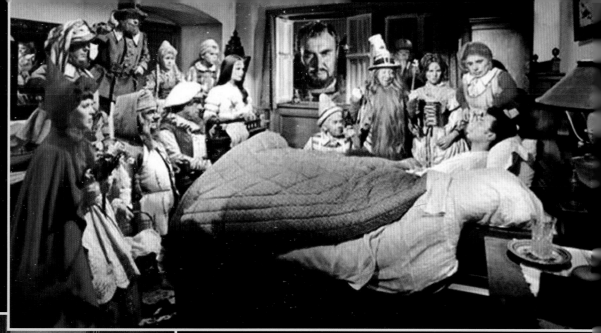

LEFT: Wilhelm captivates local kids with one of his stories as publisher Stossel (Walter Slezak) looks on. RIGHT: Jacob Grimm (Karl Boehm) tries to win the affection of lovely Greta Heinrich (Barbara Eden).

Three meticulously-crafted fairy tales highlight Pal's movie, the first (BELOW) featuring his famous Puppetoons.

LEFT: On location in Europe. RIGHT: Jim Danforth animating the dragon miniature.

Three self-contained fairy tales added luster to George Pal's *The Wonderful World of the Brothers Grimm*, originally produced in the grandiose three-screen Cinerama process. LEFT: That's Laurence Harvey under the brush with some lovable puppet pals in "The Cobbler and the Elves." ABOVE: Woodsman Russ Tamblyn waltzes off with princess Yvette Mimieux as King Jim Backus gives the bride away in "The Dancing Princess." BELOW: Brave squire Buddy Hackett squares off against a fire-breathing dragon while ignoble knight Terry-Thomas shouts instructions from a safe distance in "The Singing Bone."

Subtitle: The Lion, The Witch and The Wardrobe

WHO MADE IT:

Walt Disney Pictures/Walden Media (U.S./U.K.). Director: Andrew Adamson. Producers: Andrew Adamson, Perry Moore, Mark Johnson, Philip Steuer. Writers: Christopher Markus & Stephen McFeely, Ann Peacock, Andrew Adamson, based on a book by C.S. Lewis. Cinematography (color): Donald McAlpine. Music: Harry Gregson-Williams. Starring Georgie Henley (Lucy Pevensie), Skandar Keynes (Edmund Pevensie), William Moseley (Peter Pevensie), Anna Popplewell (Susan Pevensie), Tilda Swinton (White Witch), James McAvoy (Mr. Tummus). Jim Broadbent (Professor Kirke).

WHAT IT'S ABOUT:

Four young members of the Pevensie family flee imperiled London during WWII and take refuge in a countryside estate. They soon stumble upon a wardrobe closet that leads to another dimension known as Narnia, where the evil White Witch and her minions threaten all. Much to their surprise, the kids learn that they are part of an ancient prophecy and are destined to rule this magical realm. Soon they'll need to overcome fear, along with other personal negatives, as they boldly ally themselves with the mighty lion Aslan and his freedom-loving forces.

WHY IT'S IMPORTANT:

There have been various versions of C.S. Lewis' seminal children's classic, but this adaptation, spawned by the mega-success of *The Lord of the Rings* and *Harry Potter* films, is probably the most satisfying. Author Lewis had been inspired by a real-life incident during WWII, as children being evacuated from London during the blitz found refuge in his countryside estate. From this came a wondrous, conflict-heavy fantasy-adventure alive with thankfully subtle religious symbolism – the child heroes are the "Sons of Adam" and the "Daughters of Eve," while mighty leader Aslan, who dies for human sins only to be gloriously resurrected, is Jesus mixed with the imperiled but eternal British lion. There is an interesting irony at work here as the children flee one kind of battleground to be key participants in another. "This is not your war," they are told by sly, vicious four-footed servants of the merciless White Witch (Tilda Swinton, who is positively chilling). Characters are coerced into 'not getting involved,' and betrayal to save one's own skin becomes a significant plot point that threatens to divide our little family group. So the potent symbols writer Lewis and filmmaker Andrew Adamson are playing with are not only parallel to classic Greco-Roman/Judeo-Christian religious mythology but to the moral imperatives and regrettable social weaknesses that defined the second World War.

Although clearly a commercial enterprise, *The Chronicles of Narnia* is made with meticulous care and benefits from an enormous budget, boasting a special effects credit list that goes on forever. Director Adamson tells his story straightforwardly, with little time for poetic or artistic flourishes – this is an easy to grasp family-friendly confection, not a self-consciously arty rendering. Only in the climactic battle set-piece does the wholesome Disney agenda clash with inevitable logic, as mighty swords flash and bodies go flying without a single drop of blood being shed on screen (red-feathered arrows and crimson costumes help suggest the carnage). With a plucky cast of youngsters, an impressive budget and a director who knows how to shoot an intimate epic, *The Chronicles of Narnia* satisfied both viewers and critics back in the day, out-performing Peter Jackson's highly-anticipated remake of *King Kong*. Followed by less persuasive sequels (and abandoned by Disney after #2 faltered), this franchise never quite attained *Harry Potter* levels of boxoffice power, but remains the third most successful mass market foray into the fanciful realms of enchanted creatures and monstrous supernatural adversaries

ABOVE: Little Lucy (Georgie Henley) discovers the entrance to an enchanted realm in a mysterious clothes closet. RIGHT: The Pevensie children meet Narnia's noble leader and protector, Aslan, voiced by Liam Neeson.

Susan (Anna Popplewell) uses her proficiency with bow-and-arrow to defend freedom from the forces of darkness.

ABOVE: The White Witch (Tilda Swinton) orders her monster army to destroy Aslan's warriors in a violent confrontation.

ABOVE: Aslan receives some aerial assistance. RIGHT: The mighty lion himself, roaring in righteous defiance.

Finely-detailed production painting of the fearsome White Witch (based on Swinton's likeness) in her bear-driven chariot.

ENCHANTED 2007

107   1.85

WHO MADE IT:

Walt Disney Pictures (U.S.). Director: Kevin Lima. Producers: Barry Sonnenfeld, Chris Chase, Barry Josephson, Sunil Perkash, Ezra Swerdlow. Writer: Bill Kelly. Cinematography (Technicolor): Don Burgess. Music: Alan Menken. Starring Amy Adams (Giselle), Patrick Dempsey (Robert Philip), James Marsden (Prince Edward), Timothy Spall (Nathaniel), Idina Menzel (Nancy Tremaine), Rachel Covey (Morgan Philip), Susan Sarandon (Narsissa), Julie Andrews (Narrator).

WHAT IT'S ABOUT:

A charmingly naïve fairy tale princess named Giselle is plunged into the real world by her wicked stepmother-to-be, fearsome Queen Narcissa. Now trapped in New York City, poor bewildered Giselle is taken in by a young lawyer and his daughter, all the while awaiting her heroic Prince Edward to arrive for the big rescue. But during her eventful stay in Manhattan, the young princess reads about emancipated women and develops a backbone. As Giselle begins to wonder about who her true Prince is, the evil Narcissa arrives to slay her hated rival with trickery… and a poisoned apple.

WHY IT'S IMPORTANT:

Every now and then Disney hits the jackpot with a live-action fantasy that rivals their best animated offerings. While this light-hearted romp is high concept from start to finish, it's also a sharp, super-charming love rectangle with enough humor, sweetness and colorful special effects to satisfy both kids and their jaded parents. At the heart of it all is Amy Adams' irresistible performance as Princess Giselle, literally in over her head and out of her element. Adams is forced to play the princess as something of a dippy dope at first, specifically a sweet but banal take-off on Disney's very own Snow White, to allow for her eventual growth into "a real person." Her best scene may be that unexpected outburst of anger following an argument, which both titillates and frightens her; it's a "crossing over the threshold" moment that is funny for audiences and a little sad at the same time. The cartoon princess has lost her fairy tale virginity, becoming a genuine woman in the process. We know Enchanted's working the way it's supposed to when viewers already charmed by Giselle's innocence and sweetness, adore her all the more now that she's evolved into a true, fully-dimensional human being. This mirrors co-star Patrick Dempsey's feelings as well; like all "straight men" in fantasies of this kind, Robert's the pragmatic disbeliever (at first) whose dry down-to-Earth responses earn their share of titters. He's also a divorced dad and a lawyer who presides over the separation of once loving couples, putting his jaded view of relationships on a collision course with Adams' "happily ever after" mindset. In a way, he's a male version of Maureen O'Hara's character from *Miracle on 34th Street*, turned into a gentle cynic after becoming disillusioned with love, his little girl (well played by youngster Rachel Covey) encouraged to see the world "the way it really is" instead of channeling it through fairy tale propaganda. Excellent as these principals are, they are ably supported by a colorful and engaging ensemble: James Marsden plays his displaced Prince Charming (Edward, actually) to the scene-stealing hilt, Idina Menzel as Dempsey's fiancée and Adams's rival deserves and gets her own happy ending, while amusing toadie henchman Timothy Spall learns the meaning of self-respect after a turgid TV soap opera opens his eyes. Most deliciously delightful of all is Susan Sarandon's turn as *Enchanted*'s resident evil stepmother-witch, mostly a variation of Disney's Malefecent from *Sleeping Beauty* (she even transforms into a dragon to enable Nuevo-feminist Giselle some feisty moments), briefly becoming the old hag from *Snow White* to deliver that inevitably-poisoned apple.

With a game cast, sustained fun throughout, some wonderful new songs by Alan (*Little Mermaid*) Menken and even imaginative "pop-up" storybook credits, director Kevin Lima's *Enchanted* is never anything less than a Disney delight.

LEFT: Tricked by the evil Queen Narsissa, sweet Princess Giselle (Amy Adams) is plunged down a well and up a man-hole into the three-dimensional reality of New York City. She finds a friend in separated divorce lawyer Robert Philip (Patrick Dempsey), RIGHT, who helps her adjust to the 21st Century.

Following his beloved Giselle, hand-some suitor Prince Edward (James Marsden) also pops up in the Big Apple as agog work-men look on.

Thanks to Giselle, the joy-ous balm of singing infects young and old alike in Central Park. Alan (*The Little Mermaid*) Menken pro-vides the catchy musical score.

Dragon-transformed Narcissa re-veals her true venomous nature.

The elaborate production number and musical centerpiece of *Enchanted* was shot on location in New York's Central Park.

Aka March of the Wooden Soldiers

WHO MADE IT:

Metro-Goldwyn-Mayer/Hal Roach Studios (U.S.). Directors: Gus Meins, Chares Rogers. Producer: Hal Roach. Writers: Frank Butler & Nick Grinde, based on the book by Glen MacDonald. Cinematography (b/w): Francis Corby, Art Lloyd. Music: Victor Herbert, Glen MacDonough. Starring Stan Laurel (Stannie Dum), Oliver Hardy (Ollie Dee), Charlotte Henry (Little Bo-Peep), Henry Klienbach aka Henry Brandon (Silas Barnaby), Felix Knight (Tom-Tom Piper), Florence Roberts (Mother Widow Peep).

WHAT IT'S ABOUT:

Stannie Dum and Ollie Dee try to borrow money from their boss, an unsympathetic toymaker, in order to pay off the mortgage on the house-like shoe belonging to their friend, Mother Peep. Otherwise the hovel will be claimed by evil landlord Barnaby, leaving the old woman, her needy brood, and Little Bo Peep herself without a roof over their heads. Infuriated by efforts to trick him (Stannie substitutes for unhappy bride Bo Peep in a wedding gone awry) Barnaby finally unleashes a horde of monstrous bogeymen to destroy Toyland... and only human-sized wooden soldiers activated in the nick of time by Stannie and Ollie, can save the day.

WHY IT'S IMPORTANT:

Hal Roach was a genius. In the 1930s, his thoroughly engaging semi-surreal brand of comedy defined Hollywood humor as much as Lubitsch or Chaplin's work did, although his target audience was a tad less sophisticated. If nothing else, Roach was the producer who showcased Laurel and Hardy at their very best, with several classic shorts and a few feature gems establishing their status as the most beloved comedy duo of all time. By 1934, Stan and Ollie had become so iconic – almost living cartoon characters – that they fit perfectly into the fantastic, childlike universe of Roach's fanciful *Toyland*. Stannie Dum and Ollie Dee are two good-hearted citizens who retain L&H's famous personas (inoffensive ignorance and lovable pomposity) as they attempt, often clumsily, to rescue Mother Peep and her daughter from the clutches of resident villain Silas Barnaby (Henry Brandon under his original moniker, Henry Klienback). Sweet Charlotte Henry, who played the title role in Paramount's star-studded *Alice in Wonderland* one year before, is imperiled damsel Bo-Peep this time around, adored by Felix Knight as romantic interest Tom-Tom Piper. Also memorable in a cameo appearance is a hale and hearty Santa Claus himself, reminding viewers that *Babes* functions quite nicely as a Christmas confection (Indeed, children's paradise Toyland plays like a logical extension of Santa's workshop at the North Pole).

Everything in this delightful fable builds toward the much-anticipated climax. A combination of stop-motion animation and striking dutch camera angles celebrates the Wooden Soldiers' awakening and inevitable march into battle, where (as decidedly less interesting stuntmen-in-costumes) they rout Barnaby's nefarious forces. This finale is nicely set up with the introduction of the man-sized soldiers as an ordering mistake of Stannie's – they were supposed to be toy-sized – involving our comedy duo directly in their enemy's downfall and the ultimate liberation of Toyland. So connected to this property were Laurel and Hardy that Walt Disney paid homage to their indispensable presence in his 1961 color remake with Annette Funicello.

More expensive than usual for Hal Roach but worth every penny, *Babes in Toyland* is a perennial delight, not exactly in the class of *Wizard of Oz* but reasonably close. The elaborate sets and costumes are appropriately outrageous, Victor Herbert's music is rousing (especially during the climax), and Stan and Ollie, at the peak of their unique comedic powers, were never more appealing. It's all happens in the engaging, audacious never-never land devised by one of Hollywood's genuine comedy wizards.

Laurel and Hardy become unlikely heroes as they attempt to help the widow Peep (Florence Roberts).

LEFT/BELOW: Man-sized wooden soldiers, the result of a Stannie ordering mistake, are called into action (via stop motion) to stop Barnaby's foul schemes.   RIGHT: Santa Claus pays a call. RIGHT/BELOW: Evil-minded Barnaby (Henry Brandon) and his fiendish bogeymen.

BELOW: Walt couldn't have been too happy with this Mickey knock-off!

Built on a Hollywood sound stage, the Toyland set was enormous.

77 A GUY NAMED JOE 1943

120   1.37

Poster/photos:©1943 Metro-Goldwyn Mayer Renewed by Warner Bros.

WHO MADE IT:

Metro-Goldwyn-Mayer (U.S.). Director: Victor Fleming. Producer: Everett Riskin. Writers: Dalton Trumbo, Frederick Hazlitt Brennan, Chandler Sprague, David Boehm. Cinematography (b/w): George Folsey, Karl Freund. Music: Herbert Stothart. Starring Spencer Tracy (Pete Sandridge), Irene Dunne (Dorinda Durston), Van Johnson (Ted Randall), Ward Bond (Al Yackey), James Gleason ('Nails' Kilpatrick), Lionel Barrymore (The General), Barry Nelson (Dick Rumney), Esther Williams (Ellen Bright), Don DeFore (James J. Rourke).

WHAT IT'S ABOUT:

During WWII, ace pilot Pete Sandrige is killed in action, leaving fiancée Dorinda and several close friends behind. But Pete is returned to Earth as an invisible heavenly messenger, assigned to help novice pilots "win their wings." He winds up advising brash young Ted Randall, who soon becomes smitten with still-in-mourning Dorinda. Ultimately, everyone must put aside fear and personal concerns for the greater good of a nobler calling.

WHY IT'S IMPORTANT:

Although very much a part of the 'afterlife' fantasy genre that proliferated in 1940s Hollywood, *A Guy Named Joe* is decidedly more somber and thoughtful than most variations on this venerable theme. "Anyone in the American Air Force is a good chap, a guy named Joe," an enthused British youngster explains to his pals early on. Given what was at stake at this particular moment in history, no one can deny how inspiring the U.S. entry in WWII was for battered European nations. This movie and others from the period spell that out quite nicely. Fortunately, Dalton Trumbo's screenplay is patriotic but never overbearing, taking a fearless amount of time to establish gruff but good-hearted protagonist Pete Sandridge (Tracy) and those in his orbit before his fatal crash and spiritual return. The wartime-influenced "call to duty" theme resonates throughout, as it should, but Trumbo and director Fleming deftly balance righteous propaganda with some solid, surprisingly unsentimental characterizations – even feisty love interest Dorinda (Irene Dunne), initially the obligatory dirt-smudged tomboy pal, winds up facing some agonizing adult challenges with courage and poise. Newbie pilot Ted Randall (played nicely by superstar-to-be Van Johnson) also matures, evolving from callow grandstander to a relatively dignified veteran.

Given the uncertainty of humanity's future, the reassuring balm of an orderly universe where good souls are not only rewarded, but have a hand in all future goodness, struck exactly the right chord with war-weary audiences of the day. Our hero, downed and deceased flyer Sandridge, emerges from smoky nothingness only to be informed by "The General" (Lionel Barrymore) that his service to mankind is only beginning. It seems a vigilant Soldier of Freedom's work is never done, in this world or the next. Along the way, an amusing plot twist forces grumpy ghost Sandridge to play matchmaker between still beloved but now lonely Dorinda and annoying flyboy Randall, his headstrong "student." But, as *Casablanca*'s Rick Blaine once said, the lives of three little people don't amount to a hill of beans in this crazy world, especially since, in the case of *Joe*, one of them is already dead. When the movie ends wistfully with vanishing Tracy passing the torch, there's little doubt that, with real-world sacrifices being just as noble and selfless, a guy named Joe can enter the Great Beyond justified.

Spencer Tracy in the M-G-M motion picture "A Guy Named Joe" • Painting by Harry Anderson

"What's it like up there, Pete?"

"WHEN *you're up there* . . . everything's kinda still, and you've got a feeling you're half-way to heaven. You don't even seem to hear your own motors—just a kind of buzz far off . . . like the sky was calling you . . . like the sky was singing you a song. . . .

"And somehow it's never eight o'clock up there . . . it's always now. The earth's so far below you don't care about it any more. It's the sky that's important. The sky is your pal. You feel like nudging the sky and saying, 'Hello sky—how are *you* today, sky —and how was the moon last time you saw him?'. . . The wind-draft comes straight off the morning star, and the clouds float toward you like old friends you never want to say goodbye to. . . . And you say to yourself, 'Boy, oh boy—this is the only time a man's ever alive—it's the only time he's really free!' And the old sky, he smiles back and says, 'You're right, brother—you're right!'"—*Excerpt from script of motion picture "A Guy Named Joe"*

Is air travel something that fits into your life? Add to Spencer Tracy's word-picture the practical advantages of flight—its revolutionary saving in time, its basic economy, its restful comfort, its "go when you want to go" schedules. There are few travelers, indeed, who will not prefer it to any other . . . few who will not find in it new and unsuspected value to themselves. *Air Transport Association, 1515 Massachusetts Avenue, N. W., Washington 5, D. C.*

This advertisement is sponsored by the nation's airlines and leading manufacturers in the aviation industry

THE AIRLINES OF THE UNITED STATES
LEADING THE WORLD IN AIR TRANSPORT

Poster/photos: © 1999 Warner Bros. Pictures

WHO MADE IT:

Warner Bros. Pictures/Castle Rock Entertainment (U.S.). Director: Frank Darabont. Producers: Frank Darabont, David Valdes. Writer: Frank Darabont, from the novel by Stephen King. Cinematography (Technicolor): David Tattersall. Music: Thomas Newman. Starring Tom Hanks (Paul Edgecomb), Michael Clarke Duncan (John Coffey), David Morse (Brutus 'Brutal' Howell), Bonnie Hunt (Jan Edgecomb), James Cromwell (Warden Hal Moores), Michael Jeter (Eduard Delacroix), Graham Greene (Arlen Bitterbuck), Doug Hutchison (Percy Wetmore), Harry Dean Stanton (Toot-Toot), Dabbs Greer (Old Paul Edgecomb).

WHAT IT'S ABOUT:

In charge of the lawful execution of murderers in a remote prison known as The Green Mile, Paul Edgecomb is confronted by an enigma that seems to defy all reason. It appears that a convicted child killer named John Coffy possesses the miraculous power to heal, somehow absorbing the physical pain of others into his own body, then vomiting it out. Ultimately, a guilt-ridden Edgecomb is forced to execute John, in spite of confirming this man's innocence and learning the true nature of the murders he was convicted of.

WHY IT'S IMPORTANT:

Just as *The Curious Case of Benjamin Button* is forever in the shadow of *Forrest Gump*, Frank Darabont's movie version of Stephen King's *Green Mile* must contend with the whole-hearted embrace of his previous King adapation, 1995's *The Shawshank Redemption*. But *Mile* is an important work in its own right, an astute parable of hope and redemption with its fantasy content smartly kept around the edges. Tom Hanks as Paul Edgecomb dominates the film just as he does the poster, his decent "Boss" of an execution camp carrying us through this unlikely spiritual experience, with aged counterpart Dabbs Greer masterfully bringing Paul up-to-date for an unexpected, fanciful conclusion. Other key characters also register strongly: Michael Clarke Duncan's performance as the miracle man is mostly physical, but he's a fine actor with several opportunities to demonstrate his craft, most notably in his hopeful ramblings on the way to the electric chair. Some have criticized King and Darbont for revisiting the "Uncle Remus" school of magical and benign black stereotypes with selfless healer John Coffey, especially since he's always coming to the aid of white people with little or no reward for his services. But Coffey actually transcends this pigeon-holing; he is, as Edgecomb points out, a "force of nature," a vessel for God to work His wonders, even if love is often twisted and misunderstood by most of the human species. Given the location of this story and the function of its primary characters, it's inevitable that the horrors of capital punishment would be dramatized, and never more horrifically than in the sabotaged electrocution of Eduard Delacroix (Michael Jeter). *Mile's* resident villain, sadistic guard Percy Wetmore (Doug Hutchison) may be something of a prison movie cliché, but his cosmic comeuppance is so logical and satisfying that the use of this familiar device is understandable. Never condescending to religious belief, *The Green Mile* employs fantasy to chart some of life – and death's – most important questions. There is an undisguised darkness in Coffey's sad view of the world, mixed with his unflinching desire to ease human suffering whenever and wherever possible. Edgecomb accepts the "punishment" of prolonged existence for destroying a living miracle, but will nevertheless end his days knowing he has lived and loved well. This is an unusual moral lesson unusually well told, courtesy of one of the century's most gifted novelists and a filmmaker of rare sensitivity and multiple creative skills.

75 BLITHE SPIRIT 1945

96 1.37

WHO MADE IT:

Noel Coward-Cineguild (U.K.)/United Artists (U.S.). Director: David Lean. Producer: Noel Coward. Writers: Noel Coward, based on his play; David Lean, Ronald Neame, Anthony Havelock-Allan. Cinematography (Technicolor): Ronald Neame. Music: Richard Addinsell. Starring Rex Harrison (Charles Condomine), Constance Cummings (Ruth Condomine), Kay Hammond (Elivira Condomine), Margaret Rutherford (Madame Arcati), Hugh Wakefield (Dr. George Bradman), Joyce Carey (Violet Bradman), Jacqueline Clarke (Edith), Noel Coward (Narrator Voice).

WHAT IT'S ABOUT:

Flustered Englishman Charles Condomine is suddenly visited by the feisty spirit of his former wife, an eccentric young woman named Elvira. Her mischievous, unseen (for the most part) presence makes life difficult for him, and proves to be somewhat perplexing for Charles' current spouse, Kay, as well. Instigator of this supernatural mishap and perhaps capable of reversing it is local spiritualist Madame Arcati. But before poor Charles knows what's happened, he has two wifely spirits to contend with!

WHY IT'S IMPORTANT:

It's fascinating to compare David Lean's film version of Noel Coward's wildly popular play *Blithe Spirit* with American-made fantasies dealing with marriage, low-simmering personal dissatisfaction and supernatural intervention. Coward's approach is so British that the author actually found fault with debonair Rex Harrison's spot-on performance. Coward also rather famously despised the movie as a whole, actually using the "f" word to describe what colleague Lean did to his material. In truth, *Blithe Spirit* is a first rate adaptation, retaining the play's wit, sense of perverse imagination, and scathing commentary about life among England's upper-middle class. *Spirit* also functions as a bawdy domestic farce, with two (ultimately three) ghosts forming a dysfunctional family unit. While it's no surprise that Charles' eccentric first wife Elvira (Kay Hammond) is colorful and mischievous, the fussy intolerance of second wife Ruth (American actress Constance Cummings) is even funnier. Whether she's chastising Charles for his latest misstep or griping to scatterbrained medium Madame Arcatii (Margaret Rutherford in a career-making role) about the irresponsibility of invoking malignant spirits, Cummings' matter-of-fact sarcasm is exactly what this fantastical confection requires.

But Coward clearly has more on his mind than a whimsical bedroom comedy with magical gimmicks. "You invite mockery, Charles," a resigned Elvira dryly tells her unsmiling husband. "Something to do with your personality, a certain seething grandeur." If love is an illusion and marriage inevitably hopeless, let's be sharp enough to laugh at our pomposity and see the entertainment value of dithering pride, *Spirit* seems to be suggesting. The film's three principals are as selfishly immature dead as they are alive; each is so consumed with his/her petty differences that the profound mysteries of eternity seem of little interest. From Coward's agreeably harsh perspective, nothing but nothing can distract the working British gentleman from innocuous priorities.

Although *Blithe Spirit* rarely escapes its stage play origins, Lean relies on some rather unprecedented special effects to create visual interest. Instead of the usual double exposures and optical tricks to depict ghostly manifestations, he offers up actors literally painted a ghoulish green, with light trained on them for an other-worldly glow. This is welcome and effective, enabling the "dead" members of Lean's cast to smoothly interact with the "living" during robust conversation scenes, of which there are many.

BIG FISH 2003

WHO MADE IT:

Columbia Pictures (U.S.). Director: Tim Burton. Producers: Arne Schmidt, Richard D. Zanuck, Bruce Cohen, Dan Jinks. Writer: John August, based on the novel by Daniel Wallace. Cinematography (color): Philippe Rousselot. Music: Danny Elfman. Starring Ewan McGregor (Ed Bloom – Toung), Albert Finney (Ed Bloom – Senior), Billy Crudup (Will Bloom), Jessica Lange (Sandra Bloom – Senior), Helena Bonham Carter (Jenny – Young/Jenny – Senior/The Witch), Alison Lohman (Sandra Bloom – Young), Robert Guillaume (Dr. Bennett – Senior), Marion Cotillard (Josephine Bloom), Matthew McGrory (Karl the Giant), Steve Buscemi (Norther Winslow), Missi Pyle (Mildred), Danny DeVito (Amos Calloway), Deep Roy (Mr. Soggybottom).

WHAT IT'S ABOUT:

A young man named Will Bloom, preparing for the death of his aged father Ed, has a heartfelt emotional need to fill in the blank spaces of the old man's life, so that father-and-son can find some closure. But Will is irritated by the wild tall tales his father has told – and retold – over the years, and coming to grips with the truth is a lot harder than he thought.

WHY IT'S IMPORTANT:

Big Fish is a Tim Burton movie for viewers who generally dislike Tim Burton movies. Although the film provides a plethora of other-worldly creatures (witches, werewolves, giants, ghostly amphibians, and living trees among them), the sensitive father-son relationship at the heart of this drama is wisely grounded in reality. Burton's penchant for stylized sets and flamboyant visual flourishes would be wildly distracting in a movie like this; instead, he shoots in mostly realistic settings, allowing the tall tales spouted by amiable Ed Bloom (Albert Finney) to play as highly-unlikely but possibly true scenarios. Billy Crudup as Bloom's gently alienated son Will tries desperately to balance his father's colorful ramblings from the reality of past events, only to discover that they apparently fit hand-in-glove. "Not everything your father told you was a total fabrication," Will's savvy mom (Jessica Lange) reminds him, as the troubled young man begins to understand the importance of Edward's unique, all-encompassing gifts. Ed ultimately "becomes" his beloved tall tales, with a little help from Will's eleventh hour imagination, and achieves immortality through the re-telling of these endearing yarns by the grandchildren he'll never know. Not surprisingly, the true-or-false characters who inhabit Bloom's colorful universe are a carnival unto themselves, from self-conscious giant Karl (Matthew McGrory) to a milky-eyed witch with clairvoyant skills (Helena Bonham, in and out of old age makeup). After spending a whole movie watching them in tall-tale context, the viewer shares with Will a certain exhilaration at seeing them in the flesh at Ed's well-attended funeral – some are exactly as the old man described them, others are undeniably "normal," but no less magical, loving and inspiring. By eschewing fanciful and abstract storytelling for a more straightforward approach, Tim Burton proves himself an astute fantasy filmmaker capable of switching stylistic gears when the material requires it. Reality hangs by a slender thread in this fragile, low-key relationship story, with emotions like jealousy and resentment gently clashing with love and the deeply-rooted need for familial bonding. With gentle humor and a poet's eye for visuals, *Big Fish* reminds us that affection and imagination are the most important truths of all.

FROM THE IMAGINATION OF DIRECTOR TIM BURTON

AN ADVENTURE AS BIG AS LIFE ITSELF.

BIG·FISH

THIS HOLIDAY SEASON

DANIEL WALLACE

JOHN AUGUST

73

BEING JOHN MALKOVITCH 1999

 112 1.85

Poster/photos: © 1999 USA Films

WHO MADE IT:

Gramercy Pictures/Propaganda Films (U.S.). Director: Spike Jonze. Producers: Charlie Kaufman, Michael Kuhn, Steve Golin, Vincent Landay, Sandy Stern. Writer: Charlie Kaufman. Cinematography (Technicolor): Lance Acord. Music: Carter Burwell. Starring John Cusack (Craig Schwartz), Cameron Diaz (Lotte Schwartz), Ned Bellamy (Derek Mantini), Eric Weinstein (Father at Puppet Show), Mary Kay Place (Floris), Orson Bean (Dr. Lester), Catherine Keener (Maxine Lund), John Malkovitch (John Horatio Malkovitch), K.K. Dodds (Wendy), Charlie Sheen (Charlie).

WHAT IT'S ABOUT:

Craig Schwartz, a slightly weird street puppeteer, discovers an even weirder dimensional portal behind the filing cabinets in his office, which leads directly into the brain and living consciousness of actor John Malkovitch, for a fifteen minute stretch. This mega-phenomenon inspires a thriving cottage industry for Schwartz and a conniving office temptress, and soon Lotte Schwartz, Craig's wife and an over-the-top animal lover, becomes addicted to living through the consciousness of a heterosexual man. Somehow, all parties involved – including Mr. M himself – must find a way to cope with this bizarre pseudo-miracle.

WHY IT'S IMPORTANT:

With the possible exception of John Malkovitch and a monkey, there is absolutely no one to root for in director Spike Jonze's striking directorial debut. Although the concept of seeing life through somebody else's eyes fuels the plot, what screenwriter Charlie Kaufman is more interested in is the chronically amoral nature of humankind. Sad little street puppeteer Craig Schwartz (John Cusak) may be our put-upon protagonist, but he's just as shallow, selfish, and manipulative as everyone in this story. It's no great shocker that *Being John Malkovitch* ends with Schwartz, the ultimate insecure control freak, having his way with unsuspecting sex object Maxine (the quintessential bitch), whether it's happening in his mind or through her own "portal" that he's discovered. It's significant that Kaufman has his anti-hero talk about the profound

importance of the mind-link he's stumbled upon, so that the grotesque immorality of transforming this miracle into a tawdry money-making scheme is all the more pronounced. Malkovitch himself, an exploited innocent and the human vessel for aging would-be immortals, has the rare opportunity to see the world through his own parallel mind, and it turns out he's just as self-obsessed as everyone else (the man's an actor, after all). Looked at from a different perspective, *Being John Malkovitch* functions very nicely as a wacky parody of romantic comedies. Experiencing the opposite sex from an insider's perspective provides an orgasmic rush like no other for Schwartz's pet-obsessed wife Lotte (arguably Cameron Diaz's best performance). And Orson Bean is hilarious as the dirty old man who sets poor Malkovitch's ordeal in motion, whether sharing his joys with kindred spirit Craig or welcoming a distraught Lotte into the communal invasion of their victim's rattled psyche.

Super-cynical and a ruthless mirror to our selfish obsessions, *Being John Malkovitch* is a rollicking good time at the movies. You may hate yourself after watching it, and rightly so, but they'll probably be a sick smile on your face as you pathetically relate to the actions depicted. Malkovitch, Malkovitch, Malkovitch...?

A little man with giant talents in Pal's endearing fable...

TOM THUMB 1958

98 | 1.85 |

MGM presents A GEORGE PAL PRODUCTION

"tom thumb"

The Wonderful Musical Adventure

He's only 5½ inches high but he's terrific!

...it's colorsome!

RUSS TAMBLYN · ALAN YOUNG · TERRY-THOMAS · PETER SELLERS · JESSIE MATTHEWS
Starring JUNE THORBURN · BERNARD MILES and the PUPPETOONS with Stan Freberg Screen Play by LADISLAS FODOR Based On a Story From the Pen of the BROTHERS GRIMM
Songs by PEGGY LEE and FRED SPIELMAN · JANICE TORRE · KERMIT GOELL Photographed in EASTMAN COLOR · A GALAXY PICTURE · Directed by GEORGE PAL

WHO MADE IT:

Metro-Goldwyn-Mayer (U.S./U.K.). Director: George Pal. Producers: George Pal, Dora Wright. Writer: Ladislas Fodor, based on a story by Jacob and Wilhelm Grimm. Cinematogarphy (Eastmancolor): Georges Perinal. Music: Douglas Gamley, Ken Jones. Starring Russ Tamblyn (Tom Thumb), Alan Young (Woody), June Thorburn (Forest Queen), Terry-Thomas (Ivan), Peter Sellers (Antony), Bernard Miles (Jonathan), Jessie Matthews (Ann), Ian Wallace (The Cobbler), Peter Butterworth (Kapellmeister), Peter Bull (Town Crier), Stan Freberg (Yawning Man – voice).

WHAT IT'S ABOUT:

Woodsman Honest John is given three wishes by the Forest Queen for his kindness in sparing a mighty oak. Although he and his wife manage to waste these wishes, they are nevertheless sent a miniscule son – Tom, as big as his mother's thumb. Greeted gleefully by a roomful of living toys, Tom also befriends frustrated musician Woody; he happens to be in love with the comely Forest Queen, but won't commit to their romantic relationship until his career prospects improve. Fooled into committing crimes by a pair of nefarious hoods, little Tom Thumb finally manages to set things straight, proving his accused parents innocent of wrongdoing and playing a key role in his pal Woody's wedding.

WHY IT'S IMPORTANT:

George Pal's *Tom Thumb* is a noteworthy film for a number of reasons. It was the amiable producer's first endeavor for MGM after his long tenure at Paramount (where he was "Mr. Science Fiction" during the first half of the 1950s). It's also sandwiched between Jack Arnold's *The Incredible Shrinking Man* (1957) and the special effects perfection of Walt Disney's *Darby O'Gill and the Little People* (1959), all three movies part of a mini-trend involving mini-people. Popular tastes changed significantly as the '50s wore on, with fantasy experts like Pal and Ray Harryhausen retiring their spaceships and aliens for colorful genies, fairies and steely-eyed sorcerers. Pal would go on to produce *The Wonderful World of the Brothers Grimm* for Metro (with Russ Tamblyn reprising his Tom Thumb role) and *Atlantis the Lost Continent*, along with *The Time Machine*, which straddled both related genres.

But *Tom Thumb* got there first. Never quite igniting the way it should, this nevertheless diverting fairy tale has much in common with Disney's *Pinocchio*, as total innocent Tom is duped into criminal activity by a pair of nefarious and funny villains, before heroically coming to the rescue of his imperiled loved ones. True, Tom never transforms into a full-size person by story's end, but he is given a cute, girlfriend-like toy figure to keep him company atop pal Woody's wedding cake. With several opportunities to demonstrate his extraordinary dancing skills, Russ Tambyn shines in a role originally intended for Donald O'Conner, who would have been great in his own right. Equally endearing is future *Time Machine* co-star Alan Young as Woody, prideful Second Woodwind-player of the local band, who is featured in a romantic subplot with magical forest sprite (lovely June Thorburn). Finally, British comics Terry-Thomas and an uncharacteristically fat Peter Sellers have a ball chewing up make-believe scenery as Tommy's knotty manipulators, Ivan and Antony.

Show-stopping sequence: The welcoming 'party' number, as all the toys Tom's childless foster parents have purchased dance and frolic upon his arrival, the little man's inherent magical properties somehow bringing them to life. It's a delightful showcase for both the multi-talented Tamblyn and Pal's celebrated Puppetoons, stop-motion scene stealers ported over from their original home at Paramount.

ABOVE: An elated Tom in his new mother's hand. LEFT: The animated Yawning Man (voiced by Stan Freberg) has his own song to sing, one of the movie's highlights.

Miniature Tom (Russ Tamblyn), dressed in little more than his birthday suit, is an unexpected but welcome addition to the household of Honest John (Bernard Miles).

LEFT: Tom tries to hide from nasty villains Antony and Ivan (Peter Sellers, Terry-Thomas).

Ambitious musician Woody (Alan Jones), smitten with the lovely Forest Queen (June Thorburn), risks life and limb to rescue his friend Tom.

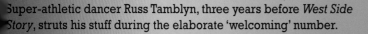

Super-athletic dancer Russ Tamblyn, three years before *West Side Story*, struts his stuff during the elaborate 'welcoming' number.

71 A MIDSUMMER NIGHT'S DREAM 1935

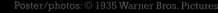

WHO MADE IT:

Warner Bros. (U.S.). Directors: William Dieterle, Max Reinhardt. Producers: Henry Blanke, Hal B. Wallace, Jack L. Warner – all uncredited. Writers: Charles Kenyon & Mary C. McCall Jr., based on the play by William Shakespeare. Cinematography (b/w): Hal Mohr. Music: Erich Wolfgang Korngold. Starring: Dick Powell (Lysander), Olivia de Havilland (Hermia), Mickey Rooney (Puck), James Cagney (Bottom), Ian Hunter (Theseus), Victor Jory (Oberon), Anita Louise (Titania), Frank McHugh (Quince), Joe E. Brown (Flute), Hugh Herbert (Snout), Ross Alexander (Demetrius), Billy Barty (Mustard-Seed).

WHAT IT'S ABOUT:

Unsuspecting mortals become entangled in a benign supernatural war between the mighty fairy demigods, Oberon and Titania. To compel Titania to relinquish a child under her protection and guidance, angry Oberon casts a love spell that has far-reaching, often absurd consequences. Joining various young lovers in the woods are a group of actors, one of whom, Bottom, undergoes a bizarre metamorphosis. Ultimately, with the coming of dawn, Oberson's spell is lifted and normalcy returns to one and all.

WHY IT'S IMPORTANT:

More interesting as a visually-rich fantasy film than as an especially sharp adaptation of Shakespeare's classic (though Will himself would have probably applauded Mickey Rooney's preternaturally energetic performance), *A Midsummer Night's Dream* is more like auteur Max Reinhardt's personal feverdream run amok... and we're all the better for its outlandish excesses. So good was the 'trick' cinematography (Hal Mohr), that, when an Oscar nomination somehow eluded it, an industry write-in campaign forced the Academy's grudging re-consideration; it would go on to claim the well-earned award, even if write-ins were verboten forever after. Second DP on the project, Mohr goes wild with soft lenses, uncanny light refractions, sweeping optical vistas... a veritable catalogue of dream imagery that is gaudy and magnificent at the same time.

Predating *Wizard of Oz* by four years, *Dream* also provides a plethora of bizarre-looking nether world entities, ranging from luminous fairies and benevolent gnomes to leather-winged bat-people. The latter are nightmarish hench-creatures belonging to Oberon (Victor Jory), Lord of Darkness, most astonishing-looking of all in his black, sequin-reflecting body suit and twisted Lovecraftian crown. As for the other performers, James Cagney is terrific as egotistical Bottom, even if critics of the time had problems with his perceived miscasting ("I don't know what the hell they want," groused Cagney). Equally fun and thoroughly committed are other members of Bottom's wily troupe, including former vaudevillians Joe E. Brown, Hugh Herbert and Frank McHugh of the hyena laugh. Elsewhere, Olivia de Havilland makes her screen debut with customary aplomb, easily outclassing "lead" Dick Powell, who begged not to be in this movie, but was overruled by Jack Warner (in all fairness, Powell does his best and is inoffensive). Ian Hunter is a convincing Theseus, and future *Oz* inhabitant Billy Barty, playing diminutive sprite Mustard-seed, even manages to amuse self-obsessed Bottom. As mentioned, rascally Rooney steals this extravagant show from various co-stars, reciting his difficult dialogue flawlessly, and with an infectious charm that only an actor of his youth and enormous talent can manage.

Big, crazy, showy to a fault some critics say, *A Midsummer Night's Dream* clearly isn't for all tastes. But if you're up for a trip to willowy realms beyond imagining, with a game cast, splendiferous music score (the renown Erich Wolfgang Korngold) and no-expense-spared production values, mad Max Reinhardt's take on the Bard's most outrageous play may be just your cup of rum-spiced java.

Warner Bros. contract players (Dick Powell and Olivia de Havilland among them) were recruited as the bewildered young lovers of Shakespeare's fantasy.

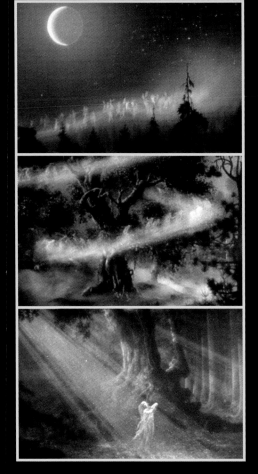

BELOW: Under Oberon's spell, Fairy Queen Titania (Anita Louise) finds herself inexplicably drawn to a humanoid donkey (Jimmy Cagney beneath the mask).

ABOVE: Mesmerizing, innovative optical effects dominate *Midsummer*. BELOW: Mickey Rooney makes an unforgettable Puck.

Victor Jory as the glowering Oberon, generally shot with vaseline-smeared star lenses.

This movie was a big deal for Warner Bros., which promoted its product in an elaborate campaign. Most Hollywood adaptations of Shakespearian works were star-studded ensembles.

70 · WHO FRAMED ROGER RABBIT 1988

 104   1.85

WHO MADE IT:

Buena Vista Pictures/Touchstone Pictures/Amblin Entertainment (U.S.). Director: Robert Zemeckis. Producers: Steven Spielberg, Kathleen Kennedy, Frank Marshall, Robert Watts. Writers: Jeffrey Price & Peter S. Seaman, based on the novel "Who Censored Roger Rabbit?" by Gary K. Wolf. Cinematography (color): Dean Cundey. Music: Alan Silvestri. Starring Bob Hoskins (Eddie Valiant), Christopher Lloyd (Judge Doom), Joanna Cassidy (Dolores), Charles Fleischer (Voice for Roger Rabbit, Benny the Cab, Greasy, and Psycho), Kathleen Turner (Voice of Jessica Rabbit), Stubby Kaye (Marvin Acme), Alan Tilvern (R.K. Maroon).

WHAT IT'S ABOUT:

In Hollywood of the 1940s, cartoons and humans co-exist. Barely. Eddie Valiant, hard-boiled gumshoe with a personal grudge against these irritating life forms, finds himself embroiled in a mystery that starts out as a possible frame-up of superstar Roger Rabbit, but ultimately involves shady real estate schemes and the cultural metamorphosis of the city's approach to mass transit. Not everyone is who or what they appear to be, and this is especially true of both Jessica Rabbit (a good girl drawn "bad") and the nefarious Judge Dread, actually a closeted, self-hating 'toon.

WHY IT'S IMPORTANT:

There have been a number of live-action/animated combo movies over the years, Disney's controversial *Song of the South* pretty much establishing the format back in the '40s. But *Who Framed Roger Rabbit* is more than just a kitschy, eye-popping gimmick flick for kids. Based on a sharp novel, it suggests that animated characters are first-rate performers and second class citizens in sun-baked Los Angeles, who co-exist peacefully (more or less) with vaguely disgruntled humans. By ingeniously combining the film noir detective genre with '40s cartoon mayhem, *Rabbit* embraces West Coast pop mythology with unrestrained glee and rampant imagination. Audiences of the day were more than receptive.

Hard-boiled, no-nonsense dick Eddie Valiant (Bob Hoskins) doesn't care much for "'toons" of any stripe after a traumatic event from his past, but a job is a job, and soon he's embroiled in a challenging mystery that involves screen star Rabbit (Charles Fleischer's voice) and his apparently unfaithful wife Jessica (Kathleen Turner's sultry tones). Eventually revealed as the real culprit behind grandiose business deals that will change Tinseltown forever and spell doom for 'toons is ultra-bizarro Judge Doom (a role made for Christopher Lloyd)… a crazed animated self-loather, in disguise. Eventually our heroes foil Dread's plans and manage to set things straight, more or less. Valiant, for all his surly impatience, winds up adopting oddball 'toon psychology and methods, forgetting his grudge and gaining a new respect for his Techni-'colored' friends in the process. *In the Heat of the Night* couldn't have handled it better.

As this animated race is presented as real, cartoon characters are carefully computer-shaded to suggest dimensionality. It's a nifty technique that's both logical and aesthetically pleasing. Finally, as if 'toons interacting with real humans in Hollywood settings wasn't outrageous enough, director Bob Zmeckis and company up the ante in Act III with a breathless visit to surreal ink-and-paint ghetto Toontown, successfully reversing the central gimmick.

Fast and funny, practically bubbling over with imaginative ideas and groundbreaking fx techniques, *Who Framed Roger Rabbit* comes complete with a subtext ('toons as victims of prejudice, clandestine business arrangements and local corruption). Still, more thoughtful implications aside, this is first and foremost a grand entertainment from Spielberg's family-friendly fantasy factory, and another solid movie by Robert Zmeckis (*Back to the Future*, *Death Becomes Her*).

Toontown provides its share of pleasures and perils, with Jessica Rabbit embodying both extremes.

RIGHT: Resident villain Judge Doom (Christopher Lloyd) is no fan of excitable toon hero Roger Rabbit.

LEFT: Pals in a jam during the movie's frenetic climax. ABOVE: Bob Hoskins shares the frame with superstars Mickey Mouse and Bugs Bunny. That's all, folks!

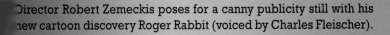

Director Robert Zemeckis poses for a canny publicity still with his new cartoon discovery Roger Rabbit (voiced by Charles Fleischer).

CABIN IN THE SKY 1943

At Last on the Screen! The Musical Comedy Sensation!

CABIN IN THE SKY

Starring
★ **ETHEL WATERS** ★ Eddie **"ROCHESTER"** Anderson
(Famed Torch Singer) *(Funnier Than Ever)*

LENA HORNE
(Gorgeous Song-Bird)

with ★ **LOUIS ARMSTRONG** ★ **REX INGRAM** ★ **DUKE ELLINGTON AND HIS ORCHESTRA**

★ **THE HALL JOHNSON CHOIR**   SCREEN PLAY BY JOSEPH SCHRANK Directed by VINCENTE MINNELLI Produced by ARTHUR FREED

A Metro-Goldwyn-Mayer PICTURE

WHO MADE IT:

Metro-Goldwyn-Mayer (U.S.). Directors: Vincente Minnelli; Busby Berkeley ("Shine" sequence). Producers: Arthur Freed, Albert Lewis. Writer: Joseph Schrank, based on a play by Lynn Root. Cinematography (b/w): Sidney Wagner. Music: George Bassman, Roger Edens. Starring Ethel Waters (Petunia Jackson), Eddie 'Rochester' Anderson (Joseph 'Little Joe' Jackson), Lena Horne (Georgia Brown), Louis Armstrong (The Trumpeter), Rex Ingram (Lucifer Jr./Lucius Ferry), Kenneth Spencer (The General/Rev. Greene), Oscar Polk (The Deacon/Fleet-foot), Willie Best (Second Idea Man), Butterfly McQueen (Lily).

WHAT IT'S ABOUT:

A good but occasionally reckless fellow, "Little" Joe Jackson is shot at a local club for an outstanding gambling debt. His wife, god-fearing Petunia, prays for both his life and his equally endangered eternal soul. Approached by agents of both God and Lucifer, Joe is given six additional months on Earth to either shape up or face eternal damnation. He finds

temptation in the seductive form of sweet Georgia Brown; but Petunia is determined to save her man, no matter what it takes.

WHY IT'S IMPORTANT:

A Faustian morality play with music and dance, *Cabin in the Sky* was based on the extremely successful Broadway stage production that caught the attention of talent-on-the-rise Vincente Minnelli, who was anxious to begin his movie career at MGM with something noteworthy. Hollywood's *Cabin*, like its inspiration, offers an all-black cast, boasting the most significant performers of its era under one relatively lavish roof. Not surprisingly, racial stereotypes go hand-in-hand with striking musical numbers and flamboyant, plot-driven camera virtuosity, Minnelli proving himself a master of cinematic staging and artful visual design right out of the gate. Although many members of the black community rightfully cringe at some of the character depictions, the premise of *Cabin in the Sky* actually transcends race. Like all Faust variations, it's a universally-understood parable about "taking the easy way out" rather than earning one's rewards through hard work and loving relationships. Eddie "Rochester" Anderson is exactly right as the movie's resident everyman, his amusingly befuddled Little Joe torn between the seductive appeal of devil's agent Georgia Brown (Lena Horne at her most alluring) and the grounded, no-nonsense embrace of his wise and pious wife Petunia (famed torch singer Ethel Waters, who practically stops the show with her rendition of "Taking a Chance on Love."). A la MGM's *Wizard of Oz*, characters

from Joe's everyday experience turn up in his life-changing feverdream as either devils or saints, depending upon their real-world personas. It's hardly surprising that the sly baddies are extremely entertaining and comical, their colorful, almost nonstop banter an urban riff on traditional folklore whimsy. Also borrowed from *Wizard*: that Godzilla-sized twister, which literally brings the house down in Act III.

Sassy and reverent, broadly comedic yet peppered with gunplay and violence, *Cabin in the Sky* teaches a familiar moral lesson in decidedly offbeat terms. It launched Mr. Minnelli's career as a film director and deftly provides a spectacular showcase for some of the greatest musical performers in American history.

82 | 1.37 |

WHO MADE IT:

Universal International (U.S.). Directors: William A. Seiter; Gregory La Cava (uncredited). Producers: Lester Cowan, William A. Seiter, John Beck. Writers: Harry Kurnitz, Frank Tashlin, based on the book by S.J. Perelman and Ogden Nash and the novel "The Tinted Venus" by F. Anstey. Cinematography (b/w): Frank Planer. Music (songs): Kurt Weill. Starring Robert Walker (Eddie Hatch), Ava Gardner (Venus), Dick Haymes (Joe Grant), Eve Arden (Molly Stewart), Olga San Juan (Gloria), Tom Conway (Whitfield Savory II).

WHAT IT'S ABOUT:

Eddie Hatch is a handsome but slightly loopy young window decorator in a bustling city department store. One day, he's ordered to fix a stuck curtain surrounding the soon-to-be-displayed statue of Venus, a priceless artifact which is on loan. In a whimsical moment, he kisses the statue and somehow brings Venus to life. Not surprisingly, having a genuine Goddess alive in the 20th Century causes all kinds of outlandish mayhem for Hatch and his friends. When all's said and done, the Goddess is back in her world of immortals… but fortunately, Eddie doesn't have to wait long to find true love again.

WHY IT'S IMPORTANT:

Not exactly a musical (although the mesmerizing "Swing Low" became a super-hit), *One Touch of Venus* re-imagines *Pygmalion* as a nebbish department store window dresser, with Galetea the statue of Venus who comes to life after his fateful kiss. Fortunately, this particular Venus has arms, so a David Lynch film ahead of time is avoided. Universal's acquired property certified Ava Gardner as a major star, after the same studio blasted her to fame with *The Killers* two years earlier. Playing a role like this isn't easy (just ask Rita Hayworth, who pretty much embarrassed herself in an imitation *Venus* vehicle, *Down to Earth*). But Gardner pulls it off effortlessly, her cool, all-knowing Goddess of Love a nice foil for well-meaning but bumbling resurrector Eddie Hatch (Robert Walker). Although the movie deals with immortality, time shifting, and the loss of love, it's a decidedly light confection, lacking even the relatively profound sentiments of Universal's parallel romantic fantasy of the same year, *Mr. Peabody and the Mermaid*. Interestingly, *Venus* provides a supporting cast that is so interesting on its own terms that it threatens to divide our attention. Eve Arden cracks wise with typical ironic aplomb as Molly Stewart, personal secretary to store owner/ladies' man Whitford Savory II (best named character in the movie); he pursues Venus while Stewart secretly pursues him, although the unflappable Goddess of Love is on to her agenda and finds all these entanglements highly entertaining. The third romantic couple of *Venus'* dizzy mix is Hatch's best friend Joe Grant (crooner Dick Haymes) and ambitious co-worker Gloria (Olga San Juan), who is initially smitten with forever-flustered Eddie. It's significant that neither one of these rival females harbors jealousy or resentment toward beautiful Venus; rather, all three women bond and support each other. There is no real villain in this story at all, even with the glowering Savory serving as Big Boss (will he or will he not fire Eddie for "stealing" his statue?) and funny, befuddled cops all over the place. Perhaps because of Venus' legendary status as the charming manipulator all things romantic, every likeable main character winds up with a mate, including Eddie. Light and unchallenging, but as smooth as Ava Gardner's undraped limbs, *One Touch of Venus* is an endearing 82 minutes of madcap comedy and at least one beautiful song. The same can't be said for the 1980s TV movie remake, offering Vanna White (!) in Gardner's signature role. As no-nonsense Mr. Savory would put it, the results were decidedly less than satisfying.

Gorgeous Ava Gardner was a contract player for MGM when Universal borrowed her for two important projects – *The Killers* and *One Touch of Venus*. She emerged from both smash movies a newly-minted superstar with a "temptress" persona. The stunning, life-cast statue created for *Venus* turned up six years later in another defining Ava Gardner film, Joseph Mankiewicz's *The Barefoot Contessa*. RIGHT: Director William A. Seiter offers a suggestion to his Orry-Kelly-clad Venus during production.

67 THE JUNGLE BOOK 1942

(108) 1.37

THE JUNGLE FIRE! A whole world ablaze as the jungle strikes back at those who would violate its secret code!

"I'LL SHOW YOU THE MYSTERIES... THE WONDERS OF THE JUNGLE'S SAVAGE HEART!"

JEWELLED SECRET CITY.. guarded by the jungle's fiercest denizens!

Alexander Korda
PRESENTS

"Rudyard KIPLING'S JUNGLE BOOK" in TECHNICOLOR

MOWGLI, HALF-BOY, HALF WOLF... armed only with a knife and the love of a girl, meets the challenge of Shere-Khan, the Killer Tiger!

It's Out of this World!

Directed by ZOLTAN KORDA • Screenplay and Dialogue by LAURENCE STALLINGS

WHO MADE IT:

United Artists (U.S.). Director: Zoltan Korda. Producer: Alexander Korda. Writer: Laurence Stallings, based on the novel by Rudyard Kipling. Cinematography (Technicolor): Lee Games, W. Howard Greene. Music: Miklos Rozsa. Starring Sabu (Mowgli), Joseph Calleia (Buldeo), John Qualen (The Barber), Rosemary De Camp (Messua), Frank Puglia (The Pindit), Patricia O'Rourke (Mahala), Ralph Byrd (Durga), John Mather (Rao), Faith Brook (English Girl), Noble Johnson (Sikh).

WHAT IT'S ABOUT:

Raised in the jungle by wolves, teenager Mowgli is adopted by the loving Messua, his surrogate mother, and introduced to the "civilized" ways of an Indian village. He learns human language, and also learns to be wary of an influential merchant named Buldeo, who hates the boy and thinks of him as a wild beast. Meanwhile, Buldeo's pretty daughter finds herself attracted to Mowgli, and he shows her his amazing jungle paradise, where animals talk and magical riches reside. Once this becomes known to the villagers, greed threatens to transform the jungle into a raging inferno.

WHY IT'S IMPORTANT:

The perfect vehicle for newly-minted Indian star Sabu (who played the title role in *Thief of Bagdad*), *The Jungle Book* is a lavish Technicolor fantasy-adventure helmed stateside by *Thief* producer Alexander Korda. Unlike MGM's semi-realistic approach to Burrough's *Tarzan* series, Korda embraces outlandish, fanciful concepts that would prove a challenge to any filmmaker: Johnny Weissmuller's jungle man may shout commands to various animals, but Sabu's Mowgli enjoys casual chats with his non-human acquaintances... which we as audience members hear. In some ways, *Jungle Book* almost plays like a male version of *Alice in Wonderland*, with idiosyncratic animals chattering away like self-absorbed human beings much of the time.

One of the more intriguing aspects of Laurence Stallings' screenplay is the structure: everything is told in glorious flashback by a seemingly benign native named Buldeo (played with customary panache by Joseph Calleia), whom we assume is a friend of the jungle boy he's describing. But as Buldeo gets into his story, it's clear that he's not only a self-centered felon, but an aggressive would-be murderer... Mowgli's most dangerous enemy, more treacherous than any animal. We can't help wondering if time has brought wisdom to our colorful narrator, but that, as he so sagely points out, "is another story."

Enriched by Korda's production values and Sabu's irreplaceable presence, *The Jungle Book* is generally considered the best movie adaptation of Kipling's tricky novel. Disney tackled it twice, with animation in 1967, then with a game but uneven live-action version in the 1990s, directed by Stephen (Van Helsing) Sommers and featuring overly-buffed Jason Scott Lee as Mowgli. But this original '42 Technicolor adventure, boasting an transplendent musical score by Miklos Rosza, stands the test of time extremely well, with even CGI-spoiled kids of the 21st Century mesmerized by its sparkling look and audacious fantasy sequences.

Tidbit: Sabu became a Hollywood star in the '40s based on his wonderful Korda movies, but mostly in support of Maria Montez and Jon Hall in a series of campy, serial-style adventure flicks for Universal that typed him forever. He returned to respectable form in *Black Narcissus* (1948, Powell and Pressburger), seduced by a wanton, ring-nosed Jean Simmons.

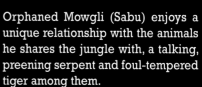

Orphaned Mowgli (Sabu) enjoys a unique relationship with the animals he shares the jungle with, a talking, preening serpent and foul-tempered tiger among them.

ABOVE: The only way to travel in the jungle, by elephant! RIGHT: Mowgli befriends a pretty village girl named Mahala (Patricia O'Rourke), and the two soon find themselves in mortal danger.

Mowgli does his best to protect these majestic, treasure-filled ruins from greedy villagers, tale-teller Buldeo among them.

ABOVE: Denizens of the jungle in fierce conflict. That's a real tiger and a prop croc.

Walt Disney produced a new live-action version of *Jungle Book* in 1994, with Mowgli transformed into a buffed-up action hero (Jason Scott Lee).

Poster/photos: © 1937 Metro-Goldwyn-Mayer

90 ROARING MINUTES OF LAUGHS!

ROACH presents

CONSTANCE BENNETT
CARY GRANT
in
TOPPER

WITH

Roland **YOUNG** Billie **BURKE**
(as Mr. and Mrs.)

ALAN MOWBRAY · EUGENE PALLETTE

ASSOCIATE PRODUCER · MILTON H. BREN
SCREEN PLAY BY JACK JEVNE, ERIC HATCH and EDDIE MORAN

DIRECTED BY NORMAN Z. McLEOD

A Metro-Goldwyn-Mayer PICTURE

WHO MADE IT:

Hal Roach Studios/Metro-Goldwyn-Mayer (U.S.). Director: Norman Z. McLeod. Producer: Hal Roach. Writers: Jack Jevne, Eric Hatch, Eddie Moran, based on the novel by Thorne Smith. Cinematography (b/w): Norbert Brodine. Music: Marvin Hatley (uncredited). Starring Constance Bennett (Marion Kerby), Cary Grant (George Kerby), Roland Young (Cosmo Topper), Billie Burke (Clara Topper), Alan Mowbray (Wilkins), Eugene Pallette (Casey), Hedda Hopper (Grace Stuyvesant).

WHAT IT'S ABOUT:

George and Marion Kerby are free spirits – in more ways than one. In life, they entertained themselves by befuddling good-natured but hopelessly conservative banker friend Cosmo Topper... and in death, they are exactly the same way. After an automobile accident results in the young couple's untimely demise, they return as ghosts to drive poor Mr. Topper crazy and his wife Clara crazy (she's halfway there already). Ultimately, Topper becomes as reckless and foolhardy as the Kirby's, and suffers a similar fate. But at least this mild-mannered gentleman has company on the ghostly plane.

WHY IT'S IMPORTANT:

Ghosts during Hollywood's pre-war heyday were generally funny sprites, using their invisibility for childlike mischief. This frequently resulted in outrageous sight gags, or maybe anti-sight gags might be more accurate. MGM's *Topper*, presented by comedy ace Hal Roach, originated from a popular Thorne Smith novel; the title refers not to the dashing and debonair Cary Grant character George Kerby, killed in an auto crash with his equally madcap spouse Marion, but to the befuddled living soul both Kerbys wind up haunting, dull, quietly frustrated banker Cosmo Topper (Roland Young, most recently *The Man Who Could Work Miracles*). Playing "free spirits" George and Marion against so conservative a protagonist is where the fun of this screwball farce comes from, since, as the title implies, it's really the banker's story. Even as Kerby-inflicted shenanigans take center stage, Cosmo quietly evolves from bore to reckless dabbler, a loosening up that ultimately costs him his life (and hastens an afterlife with George and Marion, which certainly won't be conventional – even for a ghost).

It's fascinating to watch producer Hal Roach handling this kind of material years before Columbia and other studios jumped on the heavenly bandwagon. In some ways, Roach's sensibilities are closer to those of James Whale, another auteur of the 1930s; indeed, what was Whale's *The Invisible Man* if not a scientifically-created phantom, wickedly toying with comedy-relief supporting characters and eliciting big laughs from audiences with each new gag? Most significant is Roach's deft use of musical scoring, his trademark approach from both Laurel and Hardy and *Our Gang* shorts: carefree background tunes play incessantly like natural source 'elevator' music, going along their merry way without actually commenting on specific visual actions. The ironic counterpoint this technique invariably produces is always hilarious.

No where near as sophisticated as *Blithe Spirit* but still classy enough for MGM, *Topper* was an immediate boxoffice hit, inspiring an interesting-in-its-own-right sequel minus Grant and Constance Bennett. It also sparked a popular TV sitcom in the late '50s, with Leo G. Carroll taking over for Young, Robert Sterling and Anne Jeffries as small screen Kerbys, and a beer-guzzling ghost dog named Neil thrown in for additional invisible gags.

65 PLEASANTVILLE 1998

124 1.85

WHO MADE IT:

New Line Cinema (U.S.). Director: Gary Ross. Producers: Steven Soderberg, Jon Kilik, Michael De Luca, Mary Parent, Gary Ross. Writer: Gary Ross. Cinematography (b/w and color): John Lindley. Music: Randy Newman. Starring Tobey Maguire (David), Reese Witherspoon (Jennifer), William H. Macy (George Parker), Joan Allen (Betty Parker), Jeff Daniels (Bill Johnson), J.T. Walsh (Big Bob), Don Knotts (TV Repairman), Marley Shelton (Margaret Henderson), Jane Kaczmarek (David's Mom), Giuseppe Andrews (Howard).

WHAT IT'S ABOUT:

A teenage brother and sister are suddenly catapulted into a retro-TV world via a strange new remote control device given to them by an equally strange TV repairman. Now trapped in a black-and-white parallel universe, they must unleash the emotions of a '50s era TV community to discover their own full potential and set things straight.

FROM THE CO-CREATOR OF "BIG" AND "DAVE"

PLEASANTVILLE

Nothing is as simple as Black and White.

WHY IT'S IMPORTANT:

Pleasantville is something of a spiritual cousin to Joseph Losey's *The Boy with Green Hair*, although the films are more than half a century apart. Both make striking use of color – the very idea of it – to fuel their respective fantasy concepts and teach unsuspecting viewers a warm-hearted civics lesson. *Pleasantville* takes on conformity and embraces the inevitability of change, suggesting that those maintain the status quo are "colorless" entities who are squandering their personal potential. Although the set-up resembles what we've come to expect from lesser movies with a high concept (spoiled teens are zapped into an old-fashioned TV world), it isn't long before that red rose blooms in this colorless community and it's pretty obvious that writer-director Gary Ross has a bit more on his mind than adolescent hi-jinks. The teens in question are amusing but real and ultimately heroic, with brainy geek David (Tobey Maguire, a few years before *Spider-Man*) and semi-ditsy sister Jennifer (pre-*Legally Blonde* Reese Witherspoon) earning full color after "growing up" in their own unique way (Jennifer does it by donning glasses and completing a book she's started, David by finally defying his beloved retro-world and standing up to local bigots).

Does *Pleasantville* play fair with its TV inspiration? Not entirely. The worlds presented in old TV shows like *Father Knows Best* and *The Donna Reed Show* are not the limited cookie-cutter prisons where the sun always shines and people don't question authority; many episode plots are fueled by gentle conflicts on real issues. Moreover, Ross' subtext (conservative values must succumb to progressive left-wing change) is cheated somewhat by conducting this petri-dish social experiment in an unreal community ("What is sex?" asks mom earnestly; the local library is filled with blank-paged books). Finally, if the villainous major can be goaded into literally revealing his true colors, why wouldn't the newly-minted haters and book burners be flush with vibrant hues themselves (mostly red, I'd imagine). After all, it's complacency that's being targeted as the great color-drainer in this scenario, not intense emotion.

Even so, *Pleasantville* makes a worthwhile point and conveys it with style to spare. Kudos to some very talented actors (William H. Macy is brilliant as clueless husband George, Joan Allen perfectly cast as his newly-awakened wife), a heartfelt music score by Randy Newman, and a brief but welcome appearance by TV legend Don Knotts as the catalyst for all this craziness.

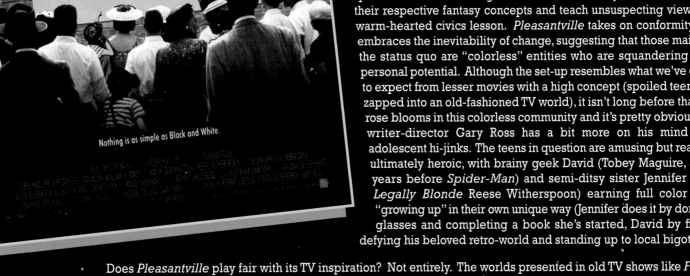

WHO MADE IT:

Warner Bros. (U.S.). Director: Alfonso Cuaron. Producers: Chris Columbus, David Heyman, Michael Barnathan, Callum McDougall, Tanya Seghatchian. Writer: Steve Kloves, based on the novel by J.K. Rowling. Cinematography (color): Michael Seresin. Music: John Williams. Starring Daniel Radcliffe (Harry Potter), Gary Oldman (Sirius Black), Rupert Grint (Ron Weasley), Emma Watson (Hermione Granger), Alan Rickman (Professor Severus Snape), Maggie Smith (Professor Minerva McGonagall), Tom Felton (Draco Malfoy), Matthew Lewis (Neville Longbottom), Richard Griffiths (Uncle Vernon), Pam Ferris (Aunt Marge), Michael Gambon (Dumbledore), David Thewlis (Lupin).

WHAT IT'S ABOUT:

Harry Potter must contend with escaped felon Sirius Black, a foul betrayer who apparently murdered Potter's parents and is now coming for their surviving son. Instructors at Hogwarts do everything in their power to protect the students, but the noctural activities of recently-hired Professor Lupin begin raising eyebrows. Using a cloak of invisibility, a magic map, and eventually Hermione's time turner, Harry begins to put the pieces of this perplexing puzzle together, learning more about his slain parents while discovering the true, benevolent character of Sirius Black.

WHY IT'S IMPORTANT:

No one can deny the impact J.K. Rowling's fanciful creation has made, with extremely popular young adult novels launching a string of equally popular movies. Unfortunately, the first two entries in the big screen series, directed by Chris Columbus, were efficiently mounted but pedestrian, both running out of steam by their third acts and proving a tad much for youthful, inexperienced actors to carry on their little shoulders. This all changed with *The Prisoner of Azkaban*, which actually gets better as it goes along. Thirteen is still pretty young, but it's old enough for our trio of wizards-in-training to be a little more interesting as human beings, and they seem delighted with the challenge.

In all fairness to Columbus, the *Azkaban* storyline is a bit meatier than what came before; Harry is growing up, which means difficult questions will be raised, and the answers may prove not only disheartening, but possibly deadly-dangerous. More importantly, the evolution of escaped madman Sirius Black (great as always Gary Oldman) from murderer of Harry's parents to their unfaltering friend and beloved ally has a profound effect on young Potter; he does a substantial amount of maturing in this adventure. Rowlings and director Alfonso Cuaron up the ante by tossing in lycanthropically-challenged Professor Lupin (smoothly played by David Thewlis), who helps and hinders the youthful heroes during their quest for the truth. The battle between wolfed-out Lupin and the feral dog Black transforms into is one of the movie's CGI highlights.

Not that the other special effects creations are any less impressive. The terrifying, shrouded Dementors who haunt extra-sensitive Harry are hair-raising throughout, those living portraits are as charming as ever, avian ally Buckbeak has his moments, and that enormous tree used to signal the changing of the seasons proves to be quite a formidable challenge for our trio of snoopers.

But ultimately, it's the down-to-Earth life lessons provided by *The Prisoner of Azkaban* that stay with viewers, and Harry Potter himself. He learns rather directly that people, even trustworthy people, aren't always what they seem, that passion and a hunger for justice are indeed admirable qualities, but clarity of vision is just as important. And we don't always have a magic map – and caring loved ones – to help us on our way.

ABOVE: Obnoxious Aunt Marge (Pam Ferris) gets her just desserts when an insulted Harry loses control and magically inflates her. RIGHT: Harry (Daniel Radcliffe) bonds with new friend Buckbeak during an outdoor class.

ABOVE, LEFT & RIGHT: There's more to both escaped "killer" Sirius Black (Gary Oldman) and Professor Lupin (David Thewlis) than meets the eye. LEFT: The usually cold-hearted Professor Snape (Alan Rickman) instinctively defends his students from harm when they are imperiled by a werewolf. LEFT: Fed-up Hermione (Emma Watson) has had enough nasty cracks from Malfoy (Tom Felton), but ultimately chooses a right cross over magical retribution. RIGHT: Harry and Hermione retrace their steps in a time loop.

Award-winning director Alfonso Cuaron (*Great Expectations*, *Children of Men*), born in Mexico City, gives actor Daniel Radcliffe some helpful pointers.

WHO MADE IT:

Paramount Pictures (U.S.). Director: John Farrow. Producer: Endre Bohem. Writer: Jonathan Latimer, based on a story by Mindret Lord. Cinematography (b/w): Lionel Lindon. Music: Franz Waxman. Starring Ray Milland (Nicholas 'Nick' Beal), Audrey Totter (Donna Allen), Thomas Mitchell (Joseph Foster), George Macready (Rev. Thomas Garfield), Fred Clark (Frankie Faulkner), Henry O'Neill (Judge Hobson), Darryl Hickman (Larry Price), Nestor Paiva (Karl), King Donovan (Peter Wolfe).

WHAT IT'S ABOUT:

Honest DA Joseph Foster decides to run for governor in order to rid his city of the gangsters who infest it. He receives help from a mysterious stranger known as Nick Beal, who seduces him with easy money and an alluring young woman. Although Foster is elected, he is now corrupted by Beal and is no better than the villains he vowed to fight. With some assistance from a local minister, Governor Foster sees the profound

error of his ways and resigns. But Beal, in truth the Devil, fades into the fog, awaiting his next trusting victim…

WHY IT'S IMPORTANT:

Like its country cousin *The Devil and Daniel Webster*, *Alias Nick Beal* is a fantasy film with horror overtones, or a horror film with fantasy overtones, flip a coin. Either way, this postwar take on the Faust legend manages to make the material fresh for a generation that experienced genuine evil first hand. Star Ray Milland's smooth-as-silk Nick Beal foreshadows his famous turn in Hitchcock's *Dial M for Murder*, while target of choice Thomas Mitchell (originally set to play Daniel Webster in *Devil and…*) is completely believable as decent everyman Joe Foster, led to moral ruin through Nick's manipulations and his own very human fallibility. Almost stealing the show from these showy pros is Audrey Totter, veteran femme fatale of Hollywood's noir era. Here she delivers an Oscar-worthy performance as the tainted, sad-faced siren Beal enlists to seduce his prey. Adding to a sharp screenplay and top-tier cast is an approach in direction that is classy, economical and rather uncommon for any era. John Farrow's career as a director is decidedly uneven, but he's in top form with *Alias Nick Beal*, casually providing ingenious modern takes on classically horrific events with a confidence that is sometimes startling. Beal emerges from and disappears into hellish fog, pops into rooms out of nowhere and can even murder on the Earthly plane… But reality-obsessed Farrow is careful never to employ optical effects or camera tricks to depict magical events, placing his devil directly behind another character (who then moves out of the way) to imply a sudden manifestation. He even frames figures to suggest their symbolic power struggle (in-control Beal close-up vs. tiny Foster in extreme long shot). This kind of cinematic creativity gives a unique edge to *Alias Nick Beal*, elevating it from diverting drawing-room morality play to one of the best semi-forgotten films of its era.

Special credit should also be given to Franz Waxman's discomforting score, which makes eerie

She'll change your life.

Amélie

A film by **JEAN-PIERRE JEUNET**

WHO MADE IT:

Miramax Films/UGC (U.S./France/Germany). Director: Jean-Pierre Jeunt. Producers: Claudie Ossard, Jean-Marc Deschamps. Writers: Guillaume Laurant, Jean-Pierre Jeunet. Cinematography (b/w and Duboicolor): Bruno Delbonnel. Music: Yann Tiersen. Starring Audrey Tautou (Amelie Poulain), Flora Guiet (Young Amelie), Mathieu Kassovitz (Nino Quincampoix), Amaury Babault (Young Nino), Andre Dussollier (Narrator), Rufus (Raphael Poulain), Serge Merlin (Raymond Dufayel), Lorella Cravotta (Amandine).

WHAT IT'S ABOUT:

A beautiful young girl named Amelie lives mostly in her make-believe world, a far more wonderful and much safer place than reality. Ignored by her cold fish father, Amelie loses herself in fanciful projects and willowy escapades, even playing matchmaker for a time with unsuspecting co-workers. Along the way, a caring and concerned parent-like neighbor tries to prevent this pretty pixie from making a "mess" of her life, particularly in her offbeat relationship with a handsome stranger who collects rejected photographs from a public picture-taking machine.

WHY IT'S IMPORTANT:

So much more than just *Walter Mitty* with a French accent, *Amelie* charmingly suggests that fantasy and reality co-exist in our lives, and need to be balanced correctly for maximum results. As so directly pointed out by her wise old neighbor (and who better than an artist to comprehend such personal truths?), winsome young Amelie is using her vast imagination primarily to run away from life. The result of an "iceberg" father and a "neurotic" mother, this painfully shy creature sublimates with every breath she takes, turning her day-to-day existence into a magical adventure… a clever, twisty game, and one that eventually inspires another needy player, Nino (Mathieu Kassovitz).

Interestingly, the fantasies on display are not exclusively from our heroine's imagination. Nino is awakened by jolly living photographs (all of the same guy, and they argue with each other), while heavenly light envelops those fortunate souls aided by Amelie during her "do-gooder" phase (resulting in a brief but significant Zorro interpretation). It's almost as if life itself has a good-natured sense of wonder. That's certainly apparent in the mixed-up personal relationships our self-appointed guardian angel giddily sets in motion, most of which gloriously backfire. Not that all of Amelie's unexpected deeds are blithely benevolent. She uses her puckish brain cells to punish a deserving local bully, and drives her disinterested father bonkers by stealing his beloved gnome figure and sending it on a bogus international journey through a series of faked photos. Typical of this film's sense of bright irony, he's finally inspired to take a trip himself.

At the heart of this heartwarming and gentle love tale is Amelie herself, played with bright-eyed hopefulness and post-adolescent angst by the lovely Audrey Tautou. Whether probing into past lives to return some priceless childhood artifacts or teasing Nino as a provocative

WHO MADE IT:

Lux Film (Italy)/Paramount Pictures (1955 U.S.). Directors: Mario Camerini; Mario Bava (uncredited). Producers: Dino De Laurentiis, Carlo Ponti. Writers: Franco Brusati, Mario Camerini, Ennio De Concini, High Grey, Ben Hecht, Ivo Perilli, Irwin Shaw, based on the poem by Homer. Cinematography (Technicolor): Harold Rosson. Music: Alessandro Cicognini. Starring Kirk Douglas (Ulysses), Silvana Mangano (Circe/Penelope), Anthony Quinn (Antinoos), Rossana Podesta (Nausicaa), Jacques Durmesnil (Alicinous).

WHAT IT'S ABOUT:

The Greek hero Ulysses finds himself a stranger in a strange land, the victim of amnesia. Gradually, his memory lifts: He remembers his life as a noble king, with his beloved and beautiful wife, Penelope, dutifully awaiting his return. He also recalls his fantastic exploits outwitting the monstrous Cyclops Polythemus, and defying the icy will of Circe, who transforms his crew into swine. Ultimately Ulysses returns to his own land and vanquishes those hungry for his throne, including formidable opponent Antinous.

WHY IT'S IMPORTANT:

The precursor to Steve Reeves' *Hercules* and all that followed in its wake, Dino De Laurentiis' *Ulysses* is a grand example of vintage Italian cinema at its most creatively flamboyant. Kirk Douglas and Anthony Quinn would re-team two years later as Van Gough and Gauguin in Minnelli's *Lust for Life*, and the star power of this duo helped transform *Ulysses* into an international hit. Also key is the film's legitimate artistic pleasures, ranging from a fanciful style of cinematography (the great Mario Bava is an uncredited resource) to a man-eating Cyclops every bit as memorable as Ray Harryhausen's horned semi-satyrs. Dominating these proceedings is Douglas in the title role, and it's hard to imagine anyone else playing it as well. Hollywood's future Spartacus embodies Ulysses: the character is audacious, foolhardy, uncompromising in battle, alive with the joy of being alive... traits the frequently combative Kirk clearly identifies with. Whether outfoxing his one-eyed captor or refusing wax in his ears so he can experience the Siren's devastating song, he is a figure of brash vitality like no other. It's easy to understand why wife Penelope (Silvana Mangano) waits indefinitely for his return, especially considering the greedy, drunken suitors who hover about her palace like bothersome moths. The most memorable sequence in the film is our hero's famous encounter with towering Cyclops Polyphemous, son of Neptune, the offended god who curses Ulysses for his blasphemous acts. As usual, the adventurer's reckless decisions place himself and his men in mortal danger, but a clever ploy with wine and a freshly-sharpened club handle vanquish the unsuspecting giant as he sleeps off a drunken binge. Instead of employing stop motion techniques to realize Polythemus, the actor wears an elaborate hydraulically-engineered facemask, remote-controlled so that his single, glowering eye can shift about quite realistically (Italy would go on to produce an excellent *Minotaur* in 1961, using a similar approach, and eventually Carlo Rambaldi's *King Kong* and *E.T.* would take

LEFT: Suffering from amnesia after washing ashore, mighty king Ulysses (Kirk Douglas) befriends the lovely Nausicaa (Rossana Podesta), who soon falls in love with this energetic, risk-embracing stranger. ABOVE: Ulysses and his men in the cave of the Cyclops, facing one of their deadliest (and hungriest) adversaries.

One-eyed giant Polythemus makes a snack of "stringy Greeks," but is ultimately vanquished by Ulysses' ingenuity… and an outsized club handle.

American actors Kirk Douglas and Anthony Quinn would co-star two years later in the prestigious Van Gough biopic, *Lust for Life.*

LEFT: Early, rejected Cyclops make-up design. RIGHT: Silvana Mangano enjoys a laugh with Kirk Douglas on set.

ANGELS IN THE OUTFIELD 1951

  99 1.37

Poster/photos: © 1951 Metro-Goldwyn-Mayer Renewed by Warner Bros

WHO MADE IT:

Metro-Goldwyn-Mayer (U.S.). Director/Producer: Clarence Brown. Writers: Dorothy Kingsley & George Wells, based on a story by Richard Conlin. Cinematography (b/w): Paul Vogel. Music: Daniele Amfitheatrof Starring Paul Douglas ('Guffy' McGovern), Janet Leigh (Jennifer Paige), Keenan Wynn (Fred Bayles), Donna Corcoran (Bridget White), Lewis Stone (Arnold P. Hapgood), Spring Byington (Sister Edwitha), Bruce Bennett (Saul Hellman), Ellen Corby (Sister Veronica).

WHAT IT'S ABOUT:

Loud-mouthed baseball manager 'Guffy' McGovern is saddled with both a losing team and an unpleasant personality, challenges novice reporter Jennifer Paige must contend with. All this changes unexpectedly when an angel arrives on the scene to set McGovern straight with some much-needed heavenly advice. A reformed Guffy's team begins winning big time, and all is going well until a young orphan girl

spots real angels in the outfield. This results in a major rhubarb with Guffy finally defending his cosmic connections in court. But goodness wins out in end, in more ways than one.

WHY IT'S IMPORTANT:

Baseball fantasy films are something of a genre onto themselves Damn Yankees!, Rhubarb, It Happens Every Spring, Field of Dreams, The Natural (sort of), and, of course, MGM's original Angels in the Outfield. Green-lit by the studio after the success of The Stratton Story, a James Stewart ballpark biopic Angels is blessed by a cast to die for: Paul Douglas hits his customary mark as a crabby-lovable lug of a manager for a losing team that can really use some divine intervention Janet Leigh is fresh-faced loveliness personified as a reporter with a lot to learn about both the game and Douglas (her occasional lapses into East Coast-accented frustration are hilarious), and little Donna Corcoran avoids being cloying as the earnest, unassuming orphan who spots the ball-playing phantasms. As every parable requires a villain, Keenan Wynn fits the bill as an obnoxious, trouble-provoking sportscaster who endures one well-deserved black eye after another

Save for a stray feather or an occasional water cooler belch, director Clarence Brown never shows us angels, unlike the CG-dominated 1990s remake. An ethereal note of music signals their presence, and only Douglas' Guffy actually hears the Heavenly chatter of his personal watchdog, a former ballplayer and literal kindred spirit (James Whitmore, who humbly listens to God talking on the radio in the same year's The Next Voice You Hear…, also from MGM). The other recurring "special effect" is the electronically-garbed voice track used whenever Guffy loses his temper and launches into a four-letter word tirade on the field.

Funny and more sophisticated than one might imagine, with a serious side (the Bruce Bennett character's implied fate) that nicely compliments feel-good whimsy, Angels in the Outfield scores a solid creative homerun, making use of America's almost preternatural obsession with its national pastime to provide an enduring, and endearing, family classic.

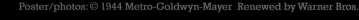
59 THE CANTERVILLE GHOST 1944

97 1.37

WHO MADE IT:

Metro-Goldwyn-Mayer (U.S.). Director: Jules Dassin. Producer: Arthur Field. Writer: Edwin Blum, based on the story by Oscar Wilde. Cinematography (b/w): Robert Planck, William H. Daniels – uncredited. Music: George Bassman. Starring Charles Laughton (Sir Simon de Canterville/The Ghost), Robert Young (Cuffy Williams), Margaret O'Brien (Lady Jessica de Canterville), William Gargan (Sergeant Benson), Reginald Owen (Lord Canterville), Rags Ragland (Big Harry), Una O'Connor (Mrs. Umney), Donald Stuart (Sir Valentine Williams), Frank Faylen (Lieutenant Kane), Lumsden Hare (Mr. Potts), Mike Mazurki (Metropolus).

WHAT IT'S ABOUT:

Cowardly Sir Simon is walled up inside his hiding place by an intolerant father, who places a curse upon him: Simon shall remain a wandering spirit and haunt his estate until a descendent, or clansman, proves himself courageous. That person turns out to be Cuffy Williams, an American staying at the Simon castle with his platoon at the invitation of pint-sized Lady Jessica de Canterville. Both soldier and girl wind up becoming good friends with the ghost and are

sensitive to his plight, but when Cuffy's moment to prove his valor arrives, he falters. Can he turn this around and help both himself and his ectoplasmic relative?

WHY IT'S IMPORTANT:

There have been various film versions of Oscar Wilde's bemusing fantasy, each with its own commendable charms. But the MGM take, filmed at the height of World War II, has a special resonance that subtly transcends its playful persona; as with the same studio's *A Guy Named Joe*, the film's themes of valor, death and well-earned redemption in the afterlife held special meaning for audiences members in 1944, especially if they had recently lost loved ones in the finally-subsiding conflict. At the heart of this tale is acclaimed thespian/famed over-the-topper Charles Laughton, Quasimodo himself, having a ball with Edwin Blum's canny screenplay. *The Canterville Ghost* deftly combines a heartfelt parable about cowardice and responsibility with slapstick comedy of the broadest kind. Laughton, robust king of perverse playfulness, happened to be a huge fan of Abbott and Costello, and the comedy duo's *The Time of Their Lives* (1946) owes a certain debt to the wild fantasy notions on display here. Shiny and showy MGM special effects enable the Ghost to appear in some curious forms as he tries to spook his American interlopers, the inevitable headless (and head-spinning) routine managing to be funny and genuinely disturbing at the same time. As the ghostly Sir Simon's two best friends, Robert Young (Cuffy) and Margaret O'Brien (young Lady Jessica) follow their success in the similarly war-themed *Journey For Margaret* with a perfect showcase for their charms, and the movie fades out on both of them practically rubbing noses. Also lending Laughton worthy support are familiar character players Una O'Connor (a tad more restrained than usual, without James Whale to goad her), Reginald Owen as Canterville's damning dad and even a young Peter Lawford as the rotund boaster's dashing sibling.

But clever story and MGM production benefits aside, this is Mr. Laughton's movie from beginning to end, an ideal opportunity for some laughs, perhaps a few tears, feel-good wisdom and maybe even a genuine scare or two. Sir Simon may not be the first benevolent ghost in literature, but he's certainly the most enduring, and in the hands of a great actor, lovable as a teddy bear. A very BIG teddy bear...

58 DARBY O'GILL AND THE LITTLE PEOPLE 1959

WHO MADE IT:

Walt Disney Productions (U.S.). Director: Robert Stevenson. Writer: Lawrence Edward Watkin, suggested by "Darby O'Gill" stories by H.T. Kavanagh. Cinematography (Technicolor): Winton C. Hoch. Music: Oliver Wallace. Visual Effects: Peter Ellenshaw, Eustace Lycett, Joshua Meador. Starring Albert Sharpe (Darby O'Gill), Janet Munro (Katie O'Gill), Sean Connery (Michael McBride), Jimmy O'Dea (King Brian), Kieron Moore (Pony Sugrue), Estelle Winwood (Sheelah Sugrue), Walter Fitzpatrick (Lord Fitzpatrick), Denis O'Dea (Father Murphy), Jack MacGowran (Phadrig Oge), J.G. Devlin (Tom Kerrigan).

WHAT IT'S ABOUT:

Old codger Darby O'Gill has a unique relationship with the legendary leprechaun King Brian, who lives in an enchanted kingdom deep below a misty mountain of ancient ruins. The two scalawags outwit each other on an ongoing basis, and Brian is often carried about the local village by O'Gill in an old flour sack. When Katie, Darby's comely daughter, tries to aid her imperiled father and is engulfed by the powers of darkness, only a noble sacrifice can save her life. Fortunately for Darby O'Gill, kindred spirit Brian proves to be a true friend in the end.

WHY IT'S IMPORTANT:

A grand fantasy best remembered for its striking visual effects, *Darby O'Gill and the Little People* was a project Walt Disney had been trying to hatch for quite some time. It came along during a significant period for his live-action unit, with well-polished confections like *Swiss Family Robinson*, *Pollyanna*, and *The Absent-Minded Professor* impressing both audiences and critics. With picture-perfect Albert Sharpe in the lead and a gaggle of fine Irish players lending support, including a very young Sean Connery (under contract to Fox at the time) and winsome Janet Munro as the charming lovers, *Darby* delivers the sense-of-wonder goods with a smile on its Celtic face. It's a simple tale of pride, friendship (Darby and local leprechaun monarch Brian are best pal adversaries) and ultimately love, with old codger O'Gill finally offering his own life to protect the daughter his antics so foolishly endangered.

Disney's house director Robert Stevenson (with *Mary Poppins* a few years away) is an old hand at culling pleasing performances and maintaining an ingratiating tone. But for this full-out fantasy opus, he shares the spotlight with special effects wizard Peter Ellenshaw. Together these filmmakers devise an ingenious succession of visual wonders that amaze even in this cynical age of CGI. Matte paintings and forced perspective enable King Brian's kingdom to come alive most convincingly, with mini-figures smoothly sharing the frame with a full-size Darby (Harryhausen would combine these techniques with stop-motion animation a year later in *The Three Worlds of Gulliver*). And if the antics of Brian and his dancing minions aren't enough to dazzle young viewers, Disney rather mischievously tries to scare their pants off with some truly horrific third act creations: the grotesque, taloned Banshee and the equally frightening Death Coach, which descends from stormy heavens to claim a repentant Darby.

Not the best of Disney's live-action fantasies, but a wonderful excursion into fanciful Irish mythology (shot convincingly in California). *Darby O'Gill and the Little People* is as fresh today as it ever was. Along with George Pal's semi-cousin *Tom Thumb*, it established this colorful genre as a formidable force at the box office in the late '50s, paving the way for even more ambitious productions.

ABOVE: Darby (Albert Sharpe) captivates his drinking cronies with tales of the wee folk. RIGHT: In truth, O'Gill does have a chatty relationship with magical King Brian, who (briefly) grants the old man's wish for a fabled pot of gold. Unfortunately, the desire for a fourth wish undoes the first three.

Sean Connery, three years before becoming 007, is the handsome young leading man of this endearing fable, in love with winsome Janet Munro and a rival for upstart Keiron Moore.

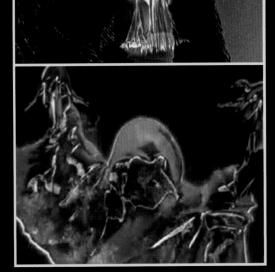

ABOVE: Spirited fiddle music spurs a dancing extravaganza in Brian's underground kingdom. RIGHT: Darby and King Brian (Jimmy O'Dea) share a drink together in this forced perspective fx set-up. EXTREME RIGHT: The wraith-like banshee comes for the soul of Katie O'Gill.

The surviving crown prop worn by Jimmy O'Dea in the film, now on display in Burbank, California as part of the Disney Studio's official archives.

WHO MADE IT:

United Artists (U.S.). Director: Rene Clair. Producers: Arnold Pressburger, T.W. Baumfeld. Writers: Dudley Nichols, Rene Clair, Helene Fraenkel, based on a play by Lord Dunsany & Hugh Wedlock, and a novel by Howard Snyder. Cinematography (b/w): Eugen Schufftan, Archie Stout. Music: Robert Stolz. Starring Dick Powell (Lawrence 'Larry' Stevens), Linda Darnell (Sylvia Smith/Sylvia Stevens), Jack Oakie (Uncle Oscar Smith/Cigolini), Edgar Kennedy (Mulrooney), John Philliber (Pop Benson), Edward Brophy (Jake Shomberg), George Cleveland (Mr. Gordon), Sig Ruman (Mr. Beckstein).

WHAT IT'S ABOUT:

Eager to scoop the competition, ambitious young newspaperman Larry Stevens wishes he knew about future events before they actually happened. This wish is granted by a mysterious old man who cautions him about inevitable consequences. Now able to predict the news 24 hours ahead of time, Stevens turns his paper into an overnight sensation, picks sure-fire winners at the race track, and squeezes the most out of life in general. Only when he reads about his own upcoming death does Stevens begins to understand the pitfalls of his miraculous new power.

WHY IT'S IMPORTANT:

The ability to see into the future is a ripe subject for whimsical morality plays, allowing characters to discover their inherent pros and cons when temptation inevitably strikes (who wouldn't take a little time to bet on winning race horses under the circumstances?). In place of a traditional crystal ball, *It Happened Tomorrow* provides the effective gimmick of an evening newspaper retrieved 24 hours in advance, revealing key events that can easily be misinterpreted but never actually prevented. Caught smack in the middle of this time-bending conundrum is reporter Larry Stevens (Dick Powell), who receives tomorrow's tips from a little old man named Pop Benson (John Philliber), something of a mascot at the paper where Stevens works. It is benevolent, soft-spoken Pops who sets up the film's pragmatic philosophy of time to a roomful of sympathetic if patronizing journalists. When Larry sees him several times later in the story, he doesn't realize that the old fellow had died in the interim… that's how he's able to provide Larry with tomorrow's scoops. Other-worldly Pops is always presented as a benevolent soul (quite literally), but his after-death appearances come with hellish mist and a sense of impending mystery… an evocative tip-off that what's going on here isn't quite right.

It Happened Tomorrow was director Rene Clair's well-received follow-up to his equally bizarre *I Married a Witch*. Once again an outlandish premise is given class and style by sophisticated scripting (how many ways can "truth" be misinterpreted?) and first-rate performances across the board, including a hilarious turn by Jack Oakie as fake nightclub seer Cigolini aka Uncle Oscar (fresh from his career-making parody of Mussolini in Chaplin's *The Great Dictator*). Still, it's pretty much Dick Powell's show, and he's never less than perfect… just enough of an ambitious newshound that we accept his logical advantage-taking, but ultimately a decent Joe who wisely rejects this potentially chaotic foresight ("I can live without it," he eventually says with significance). So can we all, because what's here in the demanding but emotionally

WHO MADE IT:

Paramount Pictures (U.S.). Director: Mitchell Leisen. Producers: E. Lloyd Sheldon, Emanuel Cohen – both uncredited. Writers: Maxwell Anderson, Gladys Lehman, based on the play by Alberto Casella and an adaptation by Walter Ferris. Cinematography (b/w): Charles Lang. Music: Bernhard Kaun, John Leipold, Milan Roder – all uncredited. Starring Fredric March (Prince Sirki/Death), Evelyn Venable (Grazia), Guy Standing (Duke Lambert), Katharine Alexander (Alda), Gail Patrick (Rhoda), Helen Westley (Stephanie), Kathleen Howard (Princess Maria), Kent Taylor (Corrado), Henry Travers (Baron Cesarea).

WHAT IT'S ABOUT:

Death, posing as the aristocratic Prince Sirki, takes a holiday from his regular role as depopulator of Earth's creatures to learn why the human race fears him so. He spends three days at the state of Duke Lambert, interacting with a number of guests who at first find him fascinating, but are ultimately frightened and repelled when they begin to suspect the truth. It is only beautiful young Grazia, originally engaged to Lambert's son, who loves this mysterious stranger for himself alone, in spite of the dark inevitability he represents.

WHY IT'S IMPORTANT:

One of Mitchell Leisen's earliest features for Paramount, *Death Takes a Holiday* clearly betrays its stage origins (it's based on an obscure Italian play) and creaks into melodrama more often than not, possibly too often for a modern audience. But even with these early '30s drawbacks, the film makes a strong impression, providing some intriguing and surprisingly timely ruminations about life, death, and (a favorite theme of fantasy cinema), the transcendent power of love. Semi-restrained Fredric March heads a fine ensemble, a microcosm of humanity that his Reaper alter-ego, Prince Sirki, can test and observe. Some of March's best lines refer to the foolhardy, "death-defying" behavior of his new-found friends, subtle asides that go over the heads of these unsuspecting characters, but register slyly with viewers. Original author Casella's main thesis concerns Death's need to understand why mankind fears the sweet caress of oblivion, why his very essence frightens the hell out of people. Love and the inevitable loss of it proves to be the definitive answer Sirki is searching for. Humans cling to life because existence without mutual adoration is unbearable. The final choice made by Grazia (Evelyn Venable) courageously reverses this idea – life without Death to cherish is equally impossible – and the darker implication of this ending has the power to unnerve even the most jaded contemporary audience. Remade twice (a '70s TV-flick; *Meet Joe Black*), *Death Takes a Holiday* benefits from polished studio production values at a time when young Hollywood was beginning to define itself as the popular missing link between art and commerce. The magnificent Italian villa set is almost a living character, its extended hallways allowing Leisen to experiment with fluid tracking shots. In keeping with Death's sinister persona, ominous shadows eventually congeal into his dramatic shrouded figure, a striking special effect accomplished on-set, utilizing in-camera techniques. And even *Holiday*'s opening titles are novel, actor and player names superimposed over each cast member after the narrative has already started. Dated perhaps by today's overblown standards, this thoughtful exercise in existentialism still has the power to affect and disturb and probably will for all eternity.

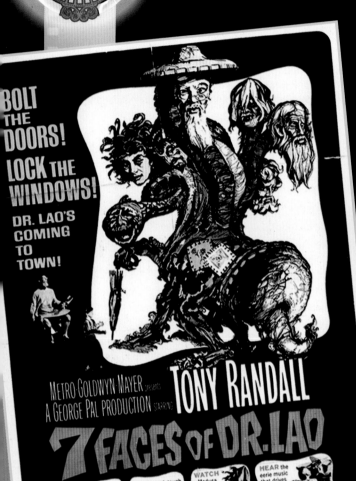

WHO MADE IT:

Metro-Goldwyn-Mayer (U.S.). Director: George Pal. Producer: George Pal. Writer: Charles Beaumont, based on the novel "The Circus of Dr. Lao" by Charles G. Finney. Cinematography (Metrocolor): Robert Bronner. Music: Leigh Harline. Visual Effects: Paul Byrd, Wah Chang, Jim Danforth, Robert Hoag, Ralph Rodine. Starring Tony Randall (Dr. Lao/The Abominable Snowman/Merlin/Appollonius/Pan/Giant Serpent/Medusa/Audience Member), Barbara Eden (Angela Benedict), Arthur O'Connell (Clint Stark), John Ericson (Ed Cunningham), Noah Beery Jr. (Tim Mitchell), Lee Patrick (Mrs. Cassin), Kevin Tate (Mike Benedict), John Qualen (Luther), Frank Kreig (Peter Ramsey), Royal Dano (Carey), John Douchette (Lucas), Argentina Brunetti (Sarah Benedict), Frank Cady (Mayor James Sargent).

WHAT IT'S ABOUT:

Dr. Lao, a strange little Asian man, arrives in a small western town, where a local businessman named Stark lords it over the rest of the population. With the help of a crusading newspaperman and a lovely widow, Lao manages to open the eyes of locals who have become accustomed to the status quo in just about everything. Lao's magical circus is an astonishing collection of strange, helpful creatures, all of them extensions of the doctor's will and personality. Ultimately, even Stark sees the error of his selfish ways, and Lao, work finished, vanishes as mysteriously as he appeared.

WHY IT'S IMPORTANT:

After the success of *The Time Machine* and *The Wonderful World of the Brothers Grimm*, producer/director George Pal happily unveiled this oddball parable set in the old west, boasting a tour-de-force multi-performance by Tony Randall and some of the wildest fantasy visuals ever presented in a sound movie. Charles Finney's philosophical novel is a fun starting point for scripter Chuck Beaumont, enabling him to wax profound and tickle the funny bone a few seconds later… much as Dr. Lao himself gleefully changes accents whenever wisdom starts sounding like speech-making. In addition to the effervescent Randall, MGM also dishes up contract player John Ericson as a gung-ho newspaperman, luminous Barbara Eden (who previously worked with Pal on the Grimm biopic) as Marion the librarian – whoops, sorry; schoolteacher Angela Benedict, and a cigar-chomping Arthur O'Connell as scheming land developer Clinton Stark, resident villain of the piece… although Dr. Lao knows better. Adding their own brand of comfortable familiarity are a troupe of reliable character actors, Frank Cady, Royal Dano and Noah Berry Jr. among them.

So, with clever writing and some sparkling performers, a solid production and fanciful special effects (from *The Time Machine* team!), what could possibly keep viewers away? Simply put, moviegoers couldn't get their brains around what kind of picture *7 Faces* was supposed to be. Many heard the title, took one look at that disturbing still of O'Connell staring at his reptilian alter-ego, assumed the whole thing was some kind of weird horror flick, and stayed home. As is frequently the case, *7 Faces of Dr. Lao* became a beloved cult classic years later, after countless showings on television. A younger, sharper audience had no problem accepting the film as a colorful parable with charming actors and some nifty visuals. Even better, the Chinese fortune-cookie philosophy of *7 Faces* plays especially well with idealistic Baby Boomers, who make a habit of finding profundity in what their head-scratching parents consider obvious. Come to think of it, that's exactly the sort of spirited response Dr. Lao is hoping to cull from us mortals… no matter which of his seven faces he

Actor Tony Randall has a field day with his multiple roles, wearing exotic make-ups created by MGM's in-house pros-thetic wizard, Bill Tuttle. RIGHT: Medusa Lao turns an obnoxious wife to stone.

LEFT: Semi-villain Clint Stark (Arthur O'Connell) chats with a self-amused serpent who seems disturbingly famil-iar. RIGHT: romantic leads Angela (Bar-bara Eden) and Ed (John Ericson).

All seven faces make a dramatic appearance via stop-motion animation.

Producer George Pal shares an amusing moment with the Abominable Snowman, a grotesque but benevolent incarnation of Lao played mostly by a stuntman.

The Great Broadway Stage Hit Reaches The Screen

WITH *Lionel* **BARRYMORE** *Sir Cedric* **HARDWICKE**

Beulah **BONDI** *Una* **MERKEL** *Bobs* **WATSON**
Nat **PENDLETON** *Henry* **TRAVERS** *Grant* **MITCHELL**
A Metro-Goldwyn-Mayer PICTURE

WHO MADE IT:

Metro-Goldwyn-Mayer (U.S.). Director: Harold S. Bucquet. Producer Sidney Franklin. Writers: Alice D.G. Miller & Frank O'Neill, Claudine West, from the play by Paul Osborn and the novel by Lawrence Edward Watkin. Cinematography (b/w): Joseph Ruttenberg. Music: Franz Waxman. Starring Lionel Barrymore (Julian Northrup 'Gramps'), Sir Cedric Hardwicke (Mr. Brink), Beulah Bondi (Nellie Northrup 'Granny') Una Merkel (Marcia Giles), Bobs Watson (Pud), Nat Pendleton (Mr Grimes), Henry Travers (Dr. Evans), Grant Mitchell (Mr. Pilbeam), Eily Malyon (Demetria Riffle), James Burke (Sheriff Burlingame), Charles Waldron (Reverend Murdock).

WHAT IT'S ABOUT:

A wheelchair-bound man and his loving grandson Pud manage to outwit Mr. Brink, the gentle spirit of Death itself, who has come calling for the old gentlemen. They mange to trap this fellow in their backyard tree, which now brings swift oblivion to any unfortunate being who dares to touch it. Eventually the resourceful and wily Mr. Brink lures precocious Pud to his own demise, and both elderly man, who can now walk, and loving child enter the next world happily together.

WHY IT'S IMPORTANT:

Revisiting a theme previously explored in Paramount's *Death Takes a Holiday*, *On Borrowed Time* adds some philosophical weight while going right for the heartstrings... and once this charmer of a movie has the innocent viewer, he's under its spell for the rest of his life. And beyond, possibly. This time Death, aka Mr Brink (perfect moniker) is personified as a gentle, aristocratic Englishman (Sir Cedric Hardwicke, laid back in more ways than one), casually matching wits with a cantankerous old Gramps and his adoring grandchild (Barrymore and Watson). In spite of the full-blown MGM Hollywood treatment (this was the same year as the studio's *Wizard of Oz*), *Time* never loses a uniquely personal quality that makes dated performance style irrelevant Director Harold S. Bucquet strikes precisely the right note for this family-friendly but slightly disturbing parable, using melodramatic set-pieces and visuals effects sparingly. More characteristic is the passing of Beulah Bondi's character, Granny compassionately taken over the threshold in her bedroom by Mr. Brink as subtle lighting shifts and music cues (her favorite tune "Beautiful Dreamer," on the radio) signal the old woman's serene passing. One can only hope our real moment of truth is as gentle and comforting as this. Bobs Watson's performance as Pud is remarkable, somehow making '30s-style child overacting work in a way that seems to defy logic at times. His full-out crying scenes are devastatingly real, and director Bucquet sustains them for long takes, forcing viewers to live through this little boy's ongoing pain. As for brilliant-as-always, wheelchair-bound Barrymore he's Mr. Potter from *It's a Wonderful Life* reborn nine years earlier as a lovable cuss. We really believe these two people have a special bond and truly love each other, making their final fate heartbreaking and heartwarming at the same time. It's easy to understand why a tale like this works so perfectly in any culture, and in any period. For the record, a stunt double is used for revitalized Gramps' walking scene, and a standing Barrymore does his best to simulate the steady

53 GABRIEL OVER THE WHITE HOUSE 1933 · 86 · 1.37

WHO MADE IT:

Metro-Goldwyn-Mayer (U.S.). Director: Gregory La Cava. Producers: William Randolph Hearst, Walter Wanger (both uncredited). Writers: Carey Wilson, Bertram Bloch, from the novel "Rinehard" by T.F. Tweed. Cinematography (b/w): Bert Glennon. Music: William Axt. Starring Walter Huston (Judson Hammond), Karen Morley (Pendola Molloy), Franchot Tone ('Beek' Beekman), Arthur Byron (Jasper Brooks), Dickie Moore (Jimmy Velter), C. Henry Gordon (Nick Diamond), David Landau (John Bronson), Samuel S. Hinds (Dr. H.L. Eastman), Jean Parker (Alice Bronson).

WHAT IT'S ABOUT:

Judson Hammond, a typically corrupt and uncaring politician, seems to perish when he accidentally crashes his car. Instead, Hammond returns to life a new man, perhaps literally. Instead of playing ball with special interests, he takes them on and defeats them. Even more astonishing, Hammond becomes nothing less than a populist dictator, getting things accomplished without Washington's traditional red tape. Some suspect that the angel Gabriel is inhabiting this man's body, pushing a powerful, other-worldly agenda. After whipping the world itself into shape, America's awesome super-President mysteriously collapses and dies... his all-important domestic and global efforts finished.

WHY IT'S IMPORTANT:

Films from the early '30s are a curious lot, exploring offbeat ideas with pre-code tenacity before Hollywood began defining itself as a family-friendly juggernaut. *Gabriel Over the White House* cannot help but astonish modern viewers, partially because it pushes its bizarre premise to the max, but also because it appears to be a harrowing mirror to the real problems of its era... which oddly reflect 21st Century concerns. Indeed, camps of disgruntled 1932 out-of-workers provide an eerie parallel to the Occupy Wall Street protestors of 2011. Director La Cava is dead-on in his portrayal of oblivious politicians and rich folks who ignore the public's agony until the very democracy they support is imperiled... and ultimately overthrown. A populist dictator for the United States? Uncle Sam with an iron fist and little patience for selfish fat-cat squabbling, whether at home or abroad? It all happens here, with a straightforwardness and implied endorsement from the filmmakers that is downright terrifying. Ultimately, *Gabriel Over the White House* is a possession story as much as it is a political call to arms. Subtly and economically, Walter Huston's corrupt President is inhabited by the windy spirit of – is it really the angel Gabriel, an instigator of conflict in addition to being God's messenger, that inhabits the comatose body of Judson Hammond after he recklessly drives his car off the road? It's only speculation by female aide/moderate love interest Pendola Molloy (Karen Morley), but clearly some sentient force is possessing this once-corrupt man. After "saving the world" with a new peace treaty instigated by constructive coercion (there is a bit of Michael Rennie's Klaatu in President Hammond), this new and triumphant global dictator falls dead on the document. The spirit departs, leaving us mortals to either move forward into a grand new world of mutual cooperation, or screw things up all over again. Any bets?

A frightening look at how the best of intentions can result in the loss of human freedom, even if the moviemakers themselves are oblivious to the danger of their own scenario (dictators rarely give up their power or exit so conveniently), *Gabriel Over the White House* is both shocking and admirable, an earnest attempt to deal with real social issues and point an accusing finger at the corrupt and all-too comfortable movers and shakers of our civilization. Thanks for the audacious eye-opener, La Cava and MGM.

BEWITCHED, BOTHERED AND BAMBOOZLED is James Stewart, a New York book publisher suddenly hexed by local antique shop owner and witch-about-town Kim Novak.

52

BELL, BOOK AND CANDLE 1958

Poster/photos: © 1958 Columbia Pictures Corporation

GETTING HERE IS
HALF THE
FUN...

WHO MADE IT:

Columbia Pictures (U.S.). Director: Richard Quine. Producer: Julian Blaustein. Writer: Daniel Taradash, based on the play "Bell, Book and Candle" by John Van Druten. Cinematography (Technicolor): James Wong Howe. Music: George Duning. Starring James Stewart (Shepherd 'Shep' Henderson), Kim Novak (Gillian 'Gil' Holroyd), Jack Lemmon (Nicky Holroyd), Ernie Kovacs (Sidney Redlitch), Hermione Gingold (Bianca de Passe), Elsa Lanchester (Aunt Queenie Holroyd), Janice Rule (Merle Kittridge).

WHAT IT'S ABOUT:

During the Christmas season, a New York City book publisher named Shep Henderson is suddenly beset by a trio of offbeat witches who live in his building... and one of them, the beautiful Gillian, puts a love spell on him using her cat-familiar. This wreaks havoc with Shep's personal life, destroys his wedding plans with former fiancée Merle, and finally causes him to seek out a most unusual "cure." Even so, Gillian gets caught in

her own romantic trap, falling in love for the first time and losing her supernatural powers.

WHY IT'S IMPORTANT:

Although it's based on a play, *Bell, Book and Candle* comes off quite nicely as a movie, with inventive director Richard Quine (he of the little figurine in the opening titles) using the widescreen medium with considerable aplomb. Romantic comedies involving broom-riders weren't exactly new in the '50s (Rene Claire's *I Married a Witch* pretty much introduced the genre to movie audiences), but John Van Druten's play, set in ultra-hip New York City (and at least partially in Greenwich Village), consciously or unconsciously links the witch and warlock community to other abused minority groups who must remain in the closet while living in less enlightened times. How much of this social subtext informs the performances we're seeing? I suspect Jack Lemmon was in on the "alternate meanings" of Van Druten's careful dialogue, although homespun Stewart was probably just as oblivious as his semi-intolerant book publisher character.

Either way, what emerges is a whimsical and somewhat daring for its day romantic farce, benefiting from its luminous star leads (Stewart and Novak just finished shooting Hitchcock's *Vertigo* a few weeks earlier) and some welcome on-location photography – yep, that hat really does go flying off the Flatiron Building in a single extended super-shot, courtesy of cinematographer James Wong Howe. Also quite startling for 1958 audiences: a skinnier-than-usual Jimmy Stewart as observed through the Siamese cat eyes of Gillian's pet familiar, Pyewacket.

Apart from these gimmicky visual pleasures, the Pulver-era Lemmon is perfectly cast as an immature jazzy warlock, vets Elsa Lanchester and Hermione Gingold chew scenery with customary panache, and Ernie Kovacs threatens to steal the entire show as a drunken historian who writes about the very entities he winds up breaking bread – and busting streetlamps – with. Also worth praising is George Duning's whimsical, often romantic main theme, which is impossible to forget after seeing the movie a few times, or even once. Maybe it's witchcraft...

51 | BRIDGE TO TERABITHIA 2007 96 1.85

DISCOVER A PLACE THAT WILL NEVER LEAVE YOU, AND A FRIENDSHIP THAT WILL CHANGE YOU FOREVER.

WALT DISNEY PICTURES AND WALDEN MEDIA

BRIDGE TO TERABITHIA

THE BELOVED NOVEL COMES TO LIFE

WHO MADE IT:

Buena Vista (U.S). Director: Gabor Csupo. Producers: Hal Lieberman, Lauren Levine, David Paterson, Alex Schwartz. Writers: Jeff Stockwell and David Paterson, based on the book by Katherine Paterson. Cinematography (color): Michael Chapman. Music: Aaron Zigman. Starring Josh Hutcherson (Jess Aarons), AnnaSophia Robb (Leslie Burke), Zooey Deschanel (Mrs. Edmunds), Robert Patrick (Jack Aarons), Bailee Madison (May Belle Aarons), Kate Butler (Mary Aarons), Devon Wood (Brenda Aarons), Grace Brannigan (Joyce Aarons), Latham Gaines (Bill Burke), Judy McIntosh (Judy Burke), Patricia Aldersley (Grandma Burke).

WHAT IT'S ABOUT:

Fast-running youngster Jesse Aarons is upset when school newcomer Leslie Burke, a city girl, beats him and everyone else in a much-anticipated race. But Leslie pursues a friendship with him, and soon the two are off in the woods, imagining that they are king and queen of an enchanted kingdom filled with monsters and trolls. Sadly, an unexpected tragedy forces Jesse to grow up in a hurry, but his brief experience has an effect that will last him the rest of his life.

WHY IT'S IMPORTANT:

Bridge to Terabithia is a surprise, although not necessarily a pleasant one. Kid viewers most likely expecting the latest variation of *NeverEnding Story* are instead subjected to a semi-torturous re-enactment of their day-to-day anxiety at home and in school, all part of a harsh world filled with misunderstanding, insecurity, and finally tragic loss. Promotional images of various entities conjured by hyper-imaginative Leslie Burke (AnnaSophia Robb) suggest a movie filled with exotic adventures in amazing vistas populated by outlandish, whimsical life-forms. Instead, Act III had many grown-up critics sniffling. This difficult journey wraps itself around viewer heartstrings the minute super-adorable Leslie enters sad young Jesse's (Josh Hutcherson) world. A misfit in a conservative family, he draws pictures of fantastic creatures even as his conventional, financially-strapped father (Robert Patrick) is either ignoring him or berating him for simply having an imagination. But dad is no ogre, or even a black-shrouded phantasm who materializes from time to time in the boy's dark fantasies; he's a decent, caring, ultimately mature man who tells his son exactly the right thing when the distraught kid needs it most. *Terabithia* becomes almost a catalogue of pre-teen trauma, but rightly counters every obnoxious bully (male and female) with a hip, caring teacher, or a best friend's smart and knowledgeable dad. Director Gabor Csupo is clearly interested in real life, how to come to terms with it and what you need to do to retreat from it, with fantasy sequences amounting to less than ten minutes of actual screen time.

Most of the bizarre inhabitants of Terabithia are semi-generic with zero character development, as befits their function as momentary escapes for needy Jesse and Leslie (and finally little sis May Belle, nicely played by Bailee Madison). An exception is the giant troll, who is given a verbal set-up, ominous footprints, an enigmatic full-body initial view, and the best fantasy entrance in the whole movie, as what appear to be tree trunks are revealed as his enormous legs. When this "monster" finally does step into the sunlight, he's preternaturally benign... a weird-looking but wonderful benefactor, a la Boo Radley. Maybe that's why the minds behind this fascinating oddity of a Disney flick saw fit to give the giant an actual line of dialogue. "Hey," he says to his human friends with a gentle smile. And they get the message. So do we, at least most of us, and we're very much the better for it... even with all the emotional exhaustion.

ABOVE: Terabithia in all its glory. LEFT: Leslie (AnnaSophia Robb) beats the tar out of soon-to-be best pal Josh (Jess Aarons) in a race during their first encounter at school.

An exotic land, Terabithia has its share of fantastic, often dangerous creatures!

ABOVE: Leslie and Josh are regular visitors to a world where fantasy and reality co-exist. Kindred spirits, they come from entirely different backgrounds.

Director Gabor Csupo checks out a shot on location. Katherine Peterson's popular novel was also adapted into a 1985 TV-movie produced by the BBC.

50 THE 5,000 FINGERS OF DR. T 1953

WHO MADE IT:

Columbia Pictures (U.S.). Director: Roy Rowland. Producer: Stanley Kramer. Writers: Dr. Seuss, Allan Scott. Cinematography (Technicolor): Frank Planer. Music: Frederick Hollander. Starring Peter Lind Hayes (August Zabladowski), Mary Healy (Heloise Collins), Hans Conreid (Dr. Terwilliker), Tommy Rettig (Batholomew Collins), John Heasley (Uncle Whitney), Robert Heasley (Uncle Judson), Noel Cravat (Sgt. Lunk).

WHAT IT'S ABOUT:

A fatherless boy named Bart Collins has a nightmare in which he is tormented by his arch, no-nonsense piano teacher, Dr. Terwilliker. Bart finds himself within a colorful fantasy universe of musical madness, making friends with paternal plumber Mr. Zabladowski, a perfect mate for mom, while eluding Dr. T's uber-eccentric clutches. After countless chases and captures, boy triumphs over teacher with an atomic concoction that accidentally goes off – ending Bart's wacko nightmare.

WHY IT'S IMPORTANT:

"Message" producer Stanley Kramer seemed to enjoy flying in the face of Hollywood convention, usually benefiting from his audacious thematic gambles. One of his rare missteps is *The 5,000 Fingers of Dr. T*, an ambitious attempt to bring Dr. Seuss' peculiar sensibilities to the screen. Loudly despised by the very artist whose imagination it celebrates, this Technicolor fantasy was unleashed upon a pragmatic 1950s viewing audience to disastrous results. For many years it was a handy metaphor for total commercial and critical meltdown at the movies, the *Ishtar* or *Gigli* of its day.

Then, perhaps not surprisingly, this tarred-and-feathered megaflop made a comeback after countless showings on television. A hipper, sharper generation, far more open to abstraction, saw in *Fingers* an irreverent re-working of *The Wizard of Oz* formula, given added coolness by a touch of self-aware parody and just a little zany sadism. Once seen, the mad, singing Elevator Operator's crossed-eyes are never forgotten.

And that musical score! Frederick Hollander's songs, boasting precious lyrics by Dr. Seuss himself, were celebrated by Hollywood's inner circle, even garnering an Oscar nomination (no easy trick for a movie this hated). Hitting all the right notes, the soundtrack is often satiric, occasionally sentimental, always clever and lush – this tale is all about music, after all, enabling Hollander and Seuss to fully embrace orchestral creativity in the context of a child's wild dream. As Dr. T keeps musicians of every stripe imprisoned in his colorful catacombs (except for pianists, of course), the potential for some astonishing, imaginatively-staged performances is literally built into the film's premise. The good doctor's "Dress Me Up" ditty, a showcase for star Hans Conreid's offbeat talents, was eventually embraced and parodied on *The Simpsons*. This is no great surprise, as creator Matt Groening counts himself among *Dr. T*'s many latter-day fans. In addition to picture-perfect Conreid, little Tommy Rettig of *Lassie* fame is a believable Bart Collins (his named reworked from "brat'), while real-life husband and wife Peter Lind Hayes and Mary Healy are just fine as sympathetic parental figures.

Deranged yet delightful, a Hollywood mega-flop that continues to win over admirers in the 21st Century, *The 5,000 Fingers of Dr. T* should never be remade. It's simply not necessary, Tim and Johnny. The amazing experience we already have is a testament to endearing strangeness, so just leave 'weird enough' alone.

TOP, LEFT: Young Bart (Tommy Rettig) must endure piano lessons insisted upon by his widowed mom (Mary Healy). Meanwhile, friendly plumber August Zabladowski (Peter Lind Hayes) makes a fine dad for Bart, whether in dreams or humdrum reality. ABOVE, RIGHT: The massive super-piano of Dr. T requires five thousand cooperative little fingers to play, all subservient to their demanding instructor.

Bart battles nightmarish dream entities in the very first scene, setting up this fatherless boy's imaginative subconscious before his Dr. T fantasy begins.

ABOVE: Supreme Ruler Terwilliker (Hans Conreid) is thwarted by the off-beat tactics of his pint-sized enemy, Bart Collins (ABOVE, INSERT). RIGHT: Captive musicians in T's dungeon play for all they're worth.

Director Roy Rowland shows storyboards for *5,000 Fingers of Dr. T* to the film's co-screenwriter, children's book writer supreme Dr. Seuss.

49 — THE FABULOUS BARON MUNCHAUSEN 1961

126 | 1.85

Aka Baron Prasil

Poster/photos: © 1962 Filmove Studio Gottwaldov (Czech)

WHO MADE IT:

Ustredni Pujcovna Filmu (Czecholslovakia). Director/Producer: Karel Zeman. Writers: Karel Zeman, Jiri Brdecka, Josef Kainar. Cinematography (Color): Jiri Tarantik. Music: Zdenek Liska. Starring Milos Kopecky (Baron Munchausen), Rudolf Jelinek (Tonik), Jana Brejchova (Princess Bianca), Karel Hoger (Cyrano), Rudolf Hrusinsky (The Sultan), Zdenek Hodr (Nicole), Miroslav Holub (Enemy General), Eduard Kohout (General Ellenmerie), Frantisek Slegr (Captain).

WHAT IT'S ABOUT:

Landing on the moon in his spacecraft, a star traveler from Earth is astounded to find several distinguished gentlemen in striking period costumes... including the wildest tale teller of all, Baron Munchausen. Soon, the spaceman makes a return trip to Earth, following Baron M on a fantastic, colorful, highly improbable journey. After several crazy escapes and equally mad retaliations, Munchausen and the modern man of science come to appreciate each other's unique gifts.

WHY IT'S IMPORTANT:

At a time when American producers like Disney, Pal and Schneer where rolling out lavish widescreen adaptations of fantasy classics, Czech filmmaker Karel Zeman dared to look backward for cinematic inspiration. Recalling the childlike simplicity of George Melies' groundbreaking works, Zeman often makes remarkable use of Gustav Dore's 19th Century engravings to tell his stories, a striking and unusual fx approach that charmed sophisticated viewers but infuriated mainstreamers (his seminal *The Fabulous World of Jules Verne* was booed at the Walker theater in Bensonhurst Brooklyn, with angry patrons yelling "fake" and "phony" in response to the movie's deliberately non-realistic visuals). Needless to say, a surreal treatment of this magnitude wasn't exactly in vogue at the time, at least not in the U.S.

More of an art house confection, *Baron Prasil* (aka *The Fabulous Baron Munchausen*) is the innovative director's most ambitious undertaking, a fanciful potpourri of grandiose melodramatic flourishes and striking graphic oddities. The good Baron, granddaddy of all super-colorful braggarts, is one of the most adapted characters in film history, with everyone from the Nazis to Terry Gilliam weighing in with a take. Matching up the experimental Zeman with this material was nothing short of lightning in a bottle. From the opening moon-landing to poetic Cyrano's tossing of his hat into the starry heavens, *Baron Prásil* is an astounding, one-of-a-kind movie wonder, even given Mr. Zeman's past efforts. Bringing space exploration into the Munchausen mythos somehow puts everything in perspective, with straight-faced, unflappable cosmonaut Tonik (Rudolf Jelinek) a perfect foil for the flamboyant Baron. A succession of absurd miracles Tonik is exposed to during and after his return trip to Earth push the filmmaker's bizarre predilections to the max: beyond his beloved Dore-style imagery, every kind of fx visual trick seems weirdly appropriate in this unbridled universe of the exaggerated, from preposterous naval battles to Jonah-like visits within enormous, brazenly-impossible sea monsters. Rapid-editing flourishes and sudden color filter changes add to the general disorientation, transforming the awed viewer into a confused but enriched participant in Munchausen's extended tall tale.

The debate about how best to convey fantasy on the screen is an old one, with many scholars favoring subtlety (as in Cocteau's films) over an unrestrained, jam-on-jam avalanche of outrageous special effects depicting equally outrageous concepts. Less is more? Sometimes, depending upon the material. But with a genius like Zeman calling the shots and a liar like Munchausen providing the inspiration, fabulous *Baron Prásil*, dedicated to the very idea of human imagination, is a precious gem to be cherished.

TOP, LEFT: On the lunar surface, Baron Munchausen (Milos Kopecky) and some distinguished friends toast a visiting cosmonaut (Rudolf Jelinek). TOP, RIGHT: The good Baron's unique approach to space travel. LEFT: Princess Biana (Jana Brejchova) prepares for her escape. RIGHT, BOTTOM: Our heroes venture inside the belly of an amazingly huge aquatic beast.

iconic image of Munchausen atop a cannonball, as rendered by Zeman.

LEFT: It's Hans Albers on the ball in a 1943 Nazi-produced epic. RIGHT: Terry Gilliam tried his hand in a 1988 incarnation starring John Neville and Robin Williams.

48 MARY POPPINS 1964

(139) 1.66

WHO MADE IT:

Buena Vista/Walt Disney Productions (U.S.). Director: Robert Stevenson. Producer: Walt Disney, Bill Walsh. Writers: Bill Walsh & Don DaGradi, based on the books by P.L. Travers. Cinematography (Technicolor): Edward Colman. Music: Irwin Kostal. Starring Julie Andrews (Mary Poppins), Dick Van Dyke (Bert/Mr. Dawes Senior), David Tomlinson (Mr. Banks), Glynis Johns (Mrs. Banks), Hermione Baddeley (Ellen), Reta Shaw (Mrs. Clara Brill), Karen Dotrice (Jane Banks), Elsa Lanchester (Katie Nanna), Arthur Treacher (The Constable), Ed Wynn (Uncle Albert), Reginald Owen (Admiral Boom), Jane Darwell (The Bird Woman), Arthur Malet (Mr. Dawes Junior).

WHAT IT'S ABOUT:

Two darling but precocious young children require a special kind of governess, and they get more than they ever bargained for in the delightful form of Mary Poppins. This charming young woman descends from the heavens via umbrella and proceeds to shake up not only the Banks family, but the entire local business establishment as well. She receives able support from her old friend Bert, a kindred spirit, as they visit colorful worlds-within-worlds with the little charges in tow.

WHY IT'S IMPORTANT:

A full decade after launching himself into live-action movies, Walt Disney hit the jackpot with *Mary Poppins*, an inspired, beautifully-produced Hollywood adaptation of P.L. Travers' popular books. *Poppins* was the *Harry Potter* of its day – only better, as it doesn't require comic book-influenced apocalyptic peril to maintain the interest of young viewers. What it offers is screen newcomer Julie Andrews as Mary (she won a well-deserved Oscar right out of the gate) and Dick Van Dyke as lovable street vendor Bert, who, equipped with a thick Cockney accent, is eccentric enough to hobnob with Mary's other-worldly entities at the drop of a hat. Together these two are absolute magic on film, whether chatting nonchalantly or performing in outlandish special effects sequences that pop into the movie at regular intervals. Often these set-pieces combine live-action musical choreography with colorful cartoon animation, a la Walt Disney's groundbreaking *Song of the South* (1946) and the more recent non-Disney *The Incredible Mr. Limpet* (1962).

Fundamentally, this is a story about a pair of cute toddlers inadvertently ignored by their loving but on-the-move parents – Daddy Banks is a fuddy-duddy businessman, mom Winifred a preoccupied Suffragette. Enter brand new nanny Mary Poppins (always identified by her full name), who vows to fill this void "until the wind changes." Wind itself actually plays a significant, ongoing role in *Poppins*, first sweeping its umbrella-brandishing heroine into the neighborhood, then literally blowing away her competition for Banks' nanny position. And when things and people aren't being tossed around they're levitating from the joy of pure laughter, best epitomized by Ed Wynn's chortling Uncle Albert (and eventually "villain" Mr. Dawes Senior, played with gusto by a mostly unrecognizable Dick Van Dyke, after this aged money-grubber undergoes a Scrooge-like transformation).

A huge critical and popular success, *Mary Poppins* is charming and sentimental without being cloying, even with two picture-perfect kiddies sharing much of the screen time. The fact that Broadway singing sensation Andrews is more attractive than the usual storybook nanny gives this modern fairy tale some buoyancy, her youth and freshness matching Van Dyke's surreal level of energy throughout. Also making the most of small roles are screen vets Reginald (*A Christmas Carol*) Owen as the appropriately named Admiral Boom and Jane (*Grapes of Wrath*) Darwell as downtown London's much-beloved Bird Lady.

TOP: Mary Poppins descends from the heavens. LEFT, MIDDLE: Mr. Banks (David Tomlinson) and his kids (Mathew Garber, Karen Dotrice). RIGHT & BOTTOM: Local chimney-sweep Burt (Dick Van Dyke) knows how to show Mary Poppins a good time, in this or any other world!

Disney pioneered the use of live-action and animated footage combined, one of the major pleasures of *Mary Poppins*.

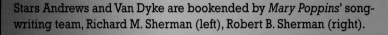

Stars Andrews and Van Dyke are bookended by *Mary Poppins*' songwriting team, Richard M. Sherman (left), Robert B. Sherman (right).

An enchanting stranger (Julie Andrews) descends from the heavens to bring merriment and awe to everyone in her orbit, including jack-of-all-trades boyfriend Bert (Dick Van Dyke). *Mary Poppins* was a smash hit for Walt Disney Productions, boosting Van Dyke's movie career and making a superstar of Broadway sensation Andrews.

WHO MADE IT:

Warner Bros. (U.S.). Director: Edward A. Blatt. Producers: Mark Hellinger, Jack L. Warner. Writers: Daniel Fuchs, based on the play "Outward Bound" by Sutton Vale. Cinematrography (b/w): Carl Guthrie. Music: Erich Wolfgang Korngold. Starring John Garfield (Tom Prior), Paul Henried (Henry Bergner), Sydney Greenstreet (Reverend Tim Thompson, Examiner), Eleanor Parker (Ann Bergner), Edmund Gwenn (Scrubby), George Tobias (Pete Musick), George Coulouris (Mr. Lingley), Faye Emerson (Maxine Russell), Sara Allgood (Mrs. Midget).

WHAT IT'S ABOUT:

A group of diverse people find themselves on a mysterious ship bound for an equally mysterious port. It becomes clear before very long that they are all dead, suspended between worlds, awaiting judgment from a white-coated, heavy-set messenger from above. He finally arrives to do his job, sending the resigned passengers one-by-one to their final destinations. But two of these desperate souls, suicides who love each other profoundly, are spared and returned to life when a case is dramatically made for them.

WHY IT'S IMPORTANT:

A remake of primitive talkie *Outward Bound*, *Between Two Worlds* never quite overcomes its stagey origins, but still registers as a dark and disturbing metaphor. Throughout human history belief in an afterlife has persisted, arguably to give hope to the hopeless and something wonderful to look forward to when reality doesn't quite measure up. Will we really be judged for our "good" and "evil" acts after we die, or is this abstract form of justice merely a desperate, therapeutic conceit? *Outward Bound/Between Two Worlds* opts for the former theory, using the metaphor of a moody ship voyage to suggest a kind of waiting room scenario for recently deceased souls. Although the premise has merit in any era, it is especially poignant during WWII's more intense years, with the loss of loved ones uppermost in the thoughts of most homefront families. Like all such tales, *Worlds* presents a microcosm of humanity in its ensemble, with clueless passengers ranging from ruthless businessman (Coulouris, perfectly cast) to lovable lug (George Tobias, ditto). Top-billed John Garfield offers another of his angry, street-smart young rebel characterizations, Isobel Elsom is appropriately obnoxious as a selfish society woman, and Edmund Gwenn is most sympathetic of all as ship steward Scrubby, doomed to sail these purgatory waters forever as punishment for his suicide. The same sad fate awaits distraught protagonist Paul Henried and loving wife Eleanor Parker; but God, or at least white-suited emissary Sydney Greenstreet, finds extenuating circumstances in their particular case (due in no small part to Scrubby's heartfelt plea) and gives them a second chance on the Earthly plane. In addition to this fine ensemble and the usual first-rate Warner Brothers production values, *Between Two Worlds* benefits from Erich Wolfgang Korngold's memorable music score. The celebrated composer of *Adventures of Robin Hood* and *King's Row* delivers his usual thundering themes and lush romantic passages, but is also quite adept at subtle touches, most notably those icy piano notes that signify the Henried characters' final moments.

Talky, semi-pretentious and frequently obvious, *Between Two Worlds* received mixed reviews in its day, and really hasn't been elevated to classic status. But it is still a story worth experiencing, as it gently taps into the universal dream-wish of all humanity.

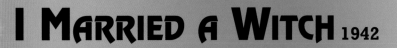

WHO MADE IT:

United Artists, produced by Paramount (U.S.). Director: Rene Clair. Producers: Rene Clair, Buddy DeSylva, Preston Sturges – all uncredited. Writers: Robert Pirosh & Marc Connelly, Norman Matson, based on a story by Thorne Smith. Cinematography (b/w): Ted Tetzlaff. Music: Roy Webb. Starring Fredric March (Jonathan, Nathaniel, Samuel, and Wallace Wooley), Veronica Lake (Jennifer), Robert Benchley (Dr. Dudley White), Susan Hayward (Estelle Masterson), Cecil Kellaway (Daniel), Elizabeth Patterson (Margaret), Robert Warwick (J.B. Masterson).

WHAT IT'S ABOUT:

The irrepressible spirit of a beautiful young witch and her wily, wicked warlock father bedevil the ancestor of the sanctimonious Salem leader who condemned them. In modern times, this man is reborn as the gifted politician Jonathan Wooley, who finds his personal and professional routine turned upside down by the mischievous sprites. Jennifer the Witch gets caught in her own love trap, even as warlock Daniel gets himself bottled up (hiccup). But when all is said and done, Jonathan and Jennifer marry and produce a brood of formidable kids... with the little girl appearing especially troublesome.

WHY IT'S IMPORTANT:

Although whimsical romantic fantasy had worked before in mainstream movies (1937's *Topper* was a huge hit), Rene Clair's innovative *I Married a Witch* seemed to open the floodgates for a specific kind of adult fable, one with more sex appeal and sophisticated humor. Slightly unreal to begin with, pouty/sultry star Veronica Lake seemed destined to play an other-worldly heroine (Ava Gardner was also blessed in this department). Lake's the perfect fit for Jennifer, a petulant young witch who drinks her own love potion and falls for the guy she's trying to hex. Just as flawlessly cast is Cecil Kellaway as her scalawag warlock papa, whose gleeful amorality may be one of the reasons a nervous Paramount Pictures disowned the film (note the familiar "The End" studio title, superimposed over a UA logo). Once again, distinguished Fredric March finds himself in the midst of a brazenly fantastic scenario. His Jonathan Wooley is earnestness personified, the perfect foil for Jennifer's childlike passions (including revenge) and her father's oh-so-wicked ways. As is typical of this sub-genre, politics plays into the plot, with both personal and professional moral dilemmas frequently dovetailing. Still, it's the winning relationship between a slightly stuffy but virtuous man, and a charmingly girlish sprite, that dominates Thorne Smith's social satire. The pairing of March and Lake may have seemed a little strange at first, but it's actually just an early example of screwball romance, their "odd couple" flavoring matching the film's overall tone of madcap irreverence. Threatening to steal the movie entirely is Kellaway's impish, slightly perverse he-witch, Daniel. We can't help but adore this inherently lovable actor, even though his character is less trustworthy than Walter Huston's diabolical Mr. Scratch or Claude Rains' Nick. It's actually somewhat unsettling to watch him subject slightly-addled daughter Jennifer to surreal punishments, often unfair ones, with Kris Kringle-like cheeriness.

A case can probably be made that the producers of TV's *Bewitched* hijacked Thorne Smith's central idea and redesigned it as a family-friendly confection. But for tangy, semi-ribald fun and a nice opportunity to watch some Hollywood pros at the peak of their powers, supernatural or otherwise, *I Married a Witch* brings the magic home with a gleam in its mischievous eye.

45 | SWORD AND THE DRAGON 1956

80 | 2.35

Aka Ilya Muromets

Poster/photos: © 1956 Mosfilm (Russia)/1960 Valiant Films

WHO MADE IT:

Mosfilm (Russia)/Valiant Films (1960 U.S.). Director: Aleksandr Ptushko. Producers: Damir Vyatich-Berezhnykh, Joseph H. Harris, Sig Shore. Writer: Mikhail Kochnev. Cinematography (color): Yuli Kun, Fyodor Provorov. Music: Igor Morozov. Starring Boris Andreyev (Ilja Muromets), Shukur Burkhanov (Tsar Kalin), Andrikosov (Prince Vladimir/Vanda), Natalya Medvedeva (Princess Apraksia), Nelli Myshkova (Vasilisa/Vilya), Sergei Martinson (Mishatychka), Georgi Dyomin (Dobrynya Nikitich), Aleksandr Shvorin (Sokolnichek), Nikolai Glazkov (Plenchishye), Mikhail Pugovkin (Razumets).

WHAT IT'S ABOUT:

Burdened by a crippled body, Russian hero Ilja Muromets is given super-strength and a magical weapon to overcome various challenges and bring down his most-hated enemies, the Tugars. He is accepted into the service of Prince Vladimir of Kiev, the captured monster Nightingale being proof of Ilja's extraordinary strength and skill. A bond forms between Muromets and Vladimir's finest warriors, but treachery from a cowardly spy threatens this alliance. Eventually the Tugars launch an all-out attack, unleashing a fearsome, three-headed, fire-breathing dragon. Muromets and his soldier allies fight furiously, conquering their enemies and restoring peace to Vladimir's besieged kingdom.

WHY IT'S IMPORTANT:

The best of Russian director Ptushko's historical fantasies, *Sword and the Dragon* is an immense and unprecedented achievement. This mega-movie boasts spectacular special effects, ambitious musical numbers that compliment a grand background score, locations to die for (particularly in widescreen) and extravagant costuming. Seasoned performer Boris Andreyev, while a bit old to be playing this "young" warrior of legend, uses age to his advantage, embodying Muromets as a no-nonsense father figure (which, coincidentally, becomes a significant plot point in the third act). While portraying historical fantasy heroes "full out" runs the risk of making them seem corny or melodramatic for modern audiences, the approach works in this case; *Sword* is like an ancient tapestry come to life, grander than reality and filled with offbeat surprises. Whistling dwarf Nightingale (referred to as "The Wind Demon" in America's cut) is a special effects triumph, his cheeks bloating to *Exorcist*-like proportions via advanced fx hydraulics. When this weird creature blows, massive trees sway and hapless extras fly in every conceivable direction. Less spectacular but no less captivating are the cute little animals who help their mistress weave "a magic tablecloth" in a variety of whimsical ways during a show-stopping vocal. Through an optical process that predates CGI, thousands of marching Tugars (i.e., Mongols) are transformed into tens of thousands, all in a single frame. And if the title dragon seems a little artificial and a bit vulnerable (his heads are lopped off with single sword-swipes), he is nevertheless an impressive full-size prop, setting an armada of real ships ablaze with flame-thrower like precision.

Although some see a pro-Soviet message in Mikhail Kochnev's screenplay (the film was viewed as healthy propaganda by the government), *Sword and the Dragon*, like Siegfried or Gilgamesh, is a classical adventure that mostly transcends politics. Alive with imagination and colossal production values, it amounts to a movie experience not easily forgotten, and a source of pride for any culture.

Tidbit: Although produced in 1956, *Sword and the Dragon* didn't see a U.S. release until 1961. A colorful Dell comic book was officially licensed, wetting youthful viewers' appetites.

ABOVE: Ilja Muromets (Boris Andreyev) leads his people into spectacular battle. LEFT: Unlike Ray Harryhausen's creations, the Tugar Dragon was a full-scale prop that spewed fire like a flame thrower.

ABOVE: Nightingale (The Wind Demon) is about to blow.
BELOW: Men are but throne legs for the Tugar king.

TOP: Kiev's heroes and the Tugar's chief villains pose for this publicity still. RIGHT: Triumphant Ilja embraces his beloved Princess Apraksia (Natalya Medvedeva).

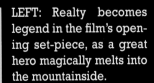

LEFT: Realty becomes legend in the film's opening set-piece, as a great hero magically melts into the mountainside.

Shooting on location in Russia. *Sword and the Dragon* boasted 106,000 extras and 11,000 horses in its cast, and was the first Soviet film filmed in CinemaScope.

44 MR. PEABODY AND THE MERMAID 1948 (89) [1.37]

UNIVERSAL INTERNATIONAL presents

WILLIAM POWELL ★ **ANN BLYTH**

in NUNNALLY JOHNSON'S

"Mr. Peabody and the Mermaid"

HERVEY · ANDREA KING · CLINTON SUNDBERG

Screenplay by NUNNALLY JOHNSON · From the novel "Peabody's Mermaid" by Guy and Constance Jones
Directed by IRVING PICHEL · Associate Producer Gene Fowler, Jr

WHO MADE IT:

Universal International/Inter-John Productions (U.S.). Director: Irving Pichel. Producers: Nunnally Johnson, Gene Fowler Jr. Writer: Nunnally Johnson, based on the novel "Peabody's Mermaid" by Guy Jones & Constance Jones. Cinematography (b/w): Russell Metty. Music: Robert Emmett Dolan. Starring William Powell (Mr. Peabody), Ann Blyth (Lenore the Mermaid), Irene Hervey (Mrs. Polly Peabody), Andrea King (Cathy Livingston), Clinton Sundberg (Mike Fitzgerald), Art Smith (Dr. Harvey), Hugo French (Major Hadley), Fred Clark (Basil).

WHAT IT'S ABOUT:

Bostonian Mr. Peabody, facing age 50, takes a Caribbean vacation with his wife. One day, while fishing alone, he snags a beautiful young mermaid and makes the mistake of bringing her to his hotel, where she lives happily in a pool. Mishaps ensue as Peabody tries to maintain a cozy relationship with his winsome prize catch, even as many of the locals come to think of his behavior as somewhat balmy. Held by the police following the sudden disappearance of his wife, Peabody dives into deep water after amphibious Lenore. He's rescued and the entire affair is dismissed as a delusion.

WHY IT'S IMPORTANT:

What kind of mermaid suits your regressive male fantasy? Tart and talkative, like Glynis Johns as *Miranda*, or mute and super-sweet, the way teenager Ann Blyth played Lenore in *Mr. Peabody*? Both approaches happen to be quite charming, and proved highly successful at the boxoffice in their respective venues. Of the two, however, Irving Pichel's movie is the more haunting and lyrical, content to spend most of its running time as a sitcom-style whimsy fest, until some mature, underlying themes of aging, personal fulfillment and mild mental illness begin to creep through. The result is a story that is both life-affirming and melancholy, almost accidentally paralleling Han Christian Anderson's *Little Mermaid* (the tragic, selfless aqua-heroine doesn't get the boy in that one, either). Not surprisingly, William Powell plays his by-the-book Bostonian with effortless perfection. "Fifty," he laments to the understanding notes of Robert Emmett Dolan's background score, "the old age of youth. The youth of old age…" A case can be made that this staid fellow's "affair" with an innocent-but-amorous teenage mermaid is a complicated delusion, a prelude to his ultimately life-threatening nervous breakdown. Indeed, the first time he sees this captivating creature, it's at so far a distance proper identification is clearly impossible. "It's not there now, but I saw it," Peabody explains to a confused gardener. "And what's more, it looked like a girl." The girl in question is absolutely adorable Ann Blyth, one year before she'd play the role of her career as Joan Crawford's daughter from hell in *Mildred Pierce*. Here, Ann's the answer to every married guy's daydreams: childlike, fully accepting and totally smitten. Unconditional love from a guileless sea siren? What self-respecting male wouldn't fall hook, line and sinker?

Amusing complications aside, the film builds to an unexpected, rather desperate life-and-death scenario, with "addled" Peabody jumping out of a boat so he can be reunited with his fish-tailed temptress. Lenore swims to his apparent rescue, then engulfs him in passionate, oxygen-transferring kisses… while at the same time, perhaps out of siren instinct, she drags her drowning lover down, deep into a black abyss. And oblivion. Somehow, Peabody survives to tell the tale (to his shrink, no less), realizing that the entire experience was in essence a bad reaction to middle age anxiety. Still, the blissful spirit of this youthful mermaid lives on, transferred to his understanding, decent-enough spouse (Irene Hervey). She's no Lenore of course, but then again, who could be?

THE MERMAID MAKERS: Lovely Ann Blyth is transformed from ingénue to golden-finned temptress by Universal's always enterprising makeup wizards. In the color image, Department head Bud Westmore helps Ms. Blyth into her cumbersome fishtail with some assistance from chief designer Jack Kevan.

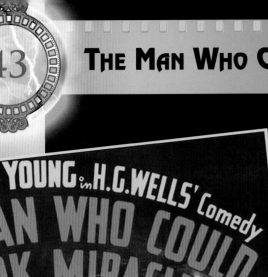

WHO MADE IT:

London Film Productions (U.K.)/United Artists (U.S.). Director: Lothar Mendes. Producer: Alexander Korda. Writers: H.G. Wells, Lajos Biro (uncredited), based on a short story by Wells. Cinematography (b/w): Harold Rosson. Music: Michael aka Mischa Spoliansky. Special Effects Director: Ned Mann. Starring Roland Young (George McWhirter Fotheringay), Ralph Richardson (Colonel Winstanley), Edward Chapman (Major Grigsby), Ernest Thesiger (Maydig), George Zucco (Moody), Wallace Lupino (Constable Winch), George Sanders (Indifference), Torin Thatcher (Observer).

WHAT IT'S ABOUT:

Mild-mannered Englishman George Fotheringay is suddenly given "powers beyond his means" by faraway deities who are experimenting with human behavior. He fends off countless selfish suggestions and tries his very best to use his new abilities intelligently, but is soon tripped up by his own character failings. A final, thoughtless command nearly rips the Earth apart and prompts cosmic forces to intervene, restoring all things as they were before the miracle worker was given his highly dangerous gift.

WHY IT'S IMPORTANT:

Author and eventual screenwriter H.G. Wells took a lot of heat for the heavy-handed polemics of *Things to Come* (1936), a film now generally regarded as a science fiction masterpiece. No such criticism marred his parallel project for Alexander Korda, *The Man Who Could Work Miracles*. Almost the antithesis of *Things*, this simple yet ingenious tale of absolute power leading to total disaster proved that pithy sociological studies could go down quite easily (and entertainingly) if the proper creative elements are in place. Element #1 was the inspired casting of Roland Young as the Man himself, one full year before this middle-aged Brit achieved Hollywood immortality as befuddled, ghost-ridden Cosmo Topper. Decent but not especially noble, fair-minded but never above indulging in some self-serving personal rewards, his George Fotheringay is humanity personified. And, thank goodness, we honestly like the guy.

As with similar parables like *An Enemy of the People* and *The Man in the White Suit*, Wells' scenario invites all of society's movers and shakers to make their case for how this world can best be run. These entrenched social/political "solutions" are presented to our increasingly frustrated protagonist, mankind's all-powerful new savior, who rightfully questions their built-in contradictions. The Right is raked over ideological coals (capitalism and militarism are mercilessly spoofed), but the Left doesn't fare much better, which is a tad surprising for a Wells diatribe. It's actually refreshing to hear Fotheringay questioning the ramifications of progressive Maydig's utopian visions, something the author himself failed to do in real life and in *Things to Come*.

It's ironic that Wells, an atheist, bookends *Miracles* with rather pompous Greco-Roman-style "Gods" influencing man's fate. But it's a picture-perfect device for this story, and one can only be grateful that the sentiments expressed about our inherent pros

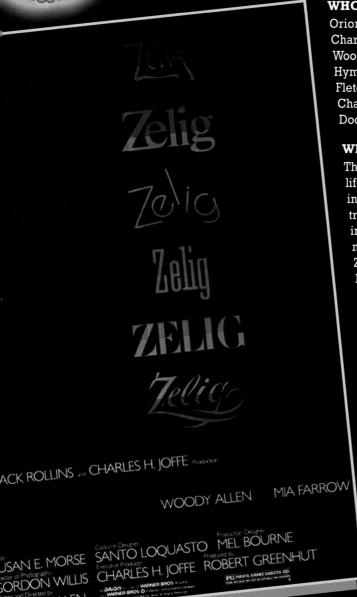

WHO MADE IT:

Orion Pictures Corporation (U.S.). Director: Woody Allen. Producers: Charles H. Joffe, Jack Rollins, Robert Greenhut, Michael Peyser. Writer: Woody Allen. Cinematography (b/w and color): Gordon Willis. Music: Dick Hyman. Starring Woody Allen (Leonard Zelig), Mia Farrow (Dr. Eudora Fletcher), Patrick Horgan (Narrator), John Buckwalter (Dr. Sindell), Marvin Chatinover (Gladular Diagnosis Doctor), Stanley Swerdlow (Mexican Food Doctor), Paul Nevans (Dr. Birsky).

WHAT IT'S ABOUT:

This feature-length "documentary" follows the life of Leonard Zelig, who astounded the world in the 20s and 30s with his uncanny ability to transform himself into the likeness of different individuals. Although exploited by family members during the early years of his life, Zelig is taken under the wing of sympathetic Dr. Eudora Fletcher, who helps him understand and ultimately come to terms with his unique condition. As events escalate, Zelig goes from hero to zero, then back again, but Fletcher's enduring love sustains him.

WHY IT'S IMPORTANT:

Over the years Woody Allen has experimented with angst-edged fantasy subjects, his most recent *Midnight in Paris* earning a Best Screenplay Oscar. More involving than *A Midsummer Night's Sex Comedy* and fresher than *Purple Rose of Cairo* is his 1983 pseudo-documentary *Zelig*, filmed at the height of Woody's first comeback (alongside *Broadway Danny Rose*). Realizing that his reality-based romantic comedies were beginning to repeat themselves, Allen plunged into creative territory he hadn't mined since his first feature, *Take the Money and Run*. But *Zelig* was something else again. Using the documentary structure for parameters, he invents a parallel reality for his unlikely hero. Allen's concept of a profoundly insecure person who physically changes into whatever he needs to be in order to fit in and be liked is pure genius, allowing for a variety of thematic interpretations (we are all French critics, in some ways). Because Zelig is such an inoffensive victim and, putting it mildly, a quick learner, he earns the affection of vaguely ambitious Dr. Eudora Fletcher (Mia Farrow) along with most of the viewing audience. So this really isn't the portrait of a wretched empty vessel hoping to blend in and disappear (although the Hitler sequence cannot help but underscore the connection). Rather, director Allen divides our interest between clever visual manipulations and the offbeat romantic relationship of Zelig and Dr. Fletcher, conveyed through documentary-style interviews and related material.

A clever overview of changing and unchanging human behavior, *Zelig* has stood the test of time well, although some viewers are still put off by a certain emotional distancing required by the documentary medium itself. In truth, director Allen manages to evoke pathos even under these artificially "objective" circumstances, touching the hearts of viewers while dazzling their eyes and challenging their minds at the same time. Now that's a good movie by anybody's standards. Just ask the French.

BERKELEY SQUARE 1933

84 1.33

WHO MADE IT:

Fox Film Corporation (U.S.). Directed by Frank Lloyd. Producer: Jesse L. Lasky. Writers: James L. Balderston, based on his play and the unfinished novel "The Sense of the Past" by Henry James. Cinematography (B/W): Ernest Palmer. Music: Peter Brunelli, Louis De Francesco, J.S. Zamecnik (all uncredited). Starring Leslie Howard (Peter Standish), Heather Angel (Helen Pettigrew), Valerie Taylor (Kate Pettigrew), Irene Browne (Lady Ann Pettigrew), Beryl Mercer (Mrs. Barwick), Colin Keith-Johnson (Tom Pettigrew), Alan Mowbray (Major Clinton), Ferdinand Gottschalk (Mr. Throstle), Samuel S. Hinds (American Ambassador).

WHAT IT'S ABOUT:

Dissatisfied with the modern world, American Peter Standish wills his way back to 18th Century England, a time he believes to be more civilized and dignified. Once there, he realizes that his imagined heaven is more of a hell, marked by ignorance, arrogance, and unsanitary conditions. His own betrothed believes him to be demonically possessed, but a cousin, Helen Pettigrew, empathizes with the distraught time traveler and comes to love him. A wiser Peter eventually returns to the 20th Century, realizing that he and Helen can only resume their relationship in God's time, not within their own respective eras.

WHY IT'S IMPORTANT:

The granddaddy of all personal time-travel stories, *Berkeley Square* was a lost film for many years. When it was finally found and restored, reactions were divided: some considered it a work of inspiration, while others were bothered by the movie's production limitations and staginess. Without question, *Square* is worth seeing for Leslie Howard's Oscar-winning performance alone, which is consistently interesting from start to finish. Unlike Tyrone Power's stoic interpretation in the 1951 remake *I'll Never Forget You*, Howard's Peter Standish wears emotions on his fringed sleeve. We watch his almost childlike sense of wonder degenerate into horror and pathos as the unique loneliness of time displacement turns day-to-day living in the 18th Century into an ongoing nightmare. Adding to his turmoil is the pressure of maintaining credibility (in both versions, verbose Standish makes one dumb mistake after another, revealing future events to astonished listeners) and enduring the pomposity, arrogance and chronic filthyness of an era he so coveted. Although he's smart enough to avoid changing past history too emphatically, a danger the '51 Standish seems oblivious to, his very presence in another time risks Lord knows what.

Sci-fi ramifications aside, *Berkeley Square* is first and foremost a star-crossed romance. We tend to view the past through rosy-colored glasses, Peter discovers, and only love makes existence in any era bearable. He finds his personal bliss through enchanting leading lady Heather Angel as Helen Pettigrew, whose passionate feelings for Peter transcend her logical fear of him. That fear extends to eventual accusations of demonic possession, a theory that sends the already incredulous Standish into a giddy fit. In a move that predates Peter Cushing in *Horror of Dracula*, resident villain Mr. Throstle crosses two candlesticks together to ward off Peter's diabolical power.

Production values for this early talky are understandably limited, but a full-fledged ball (complete with matte painted ceiling) is quite well-staged. And while Standish's entry into the past is handled with a first-person approach to a blurred-out door – he's literally struck by lightning in the Power version – there's a creepy simplicity to this approach that trumps conventional optical effects.

Somewhat creaky but full of passion, *Berekely Square* wound up being director Frank Lloyd's most cherished film. It was also greatly favored by none other than famed horror-fantasy writer H.P. Lovecraft, America's Poe. And although the final scenes of bittersweet farewell drag a bit more than they should, the movie overall is surprisingly potent, a semi-masterpiece worth experiencing.

A letter from the past is key to the "travel" plans of Peter Standish (Leslie Howard).

ABOVE, RIGHT: Reborn into the 18th Century, Standish unexpectedly falls in love with his lovely cousin, Helen Pettigrew (Heather Angel). ABOVE: At a ball, Peter finds his modern ways questioned by many guests, including old friend Major Clinton (Alan Mowbray). RIGHT: A portrait of Peter Standish plays an important part in his most unusual historical background. *Berekely Square* has inspired many imitations; TV's *Twilight Zone* weighed in with several variations, the Dana Andrews-starrer "No Time Like the Past" coming closest to Balderston's seminal romantic fantasy.

LEFT: Leading lady Heather Angel prepares herself for an upcoming shot. RIGHT: Director Frank Lloyd.

Time travel in fantasy films is more wish-fulfillment than science, usually with a great romance at the other end of the temporal rainbow. LEFT, in this beautiful publicity photo from *Berkeley Square*, disillusioned Leslie Howard hopes the 18th Century will be heavenly, but his horrified fiancée Kate Pettigrew winds up thinking he's possessed by demons (he winds up falling for Kate's sister instead). ABOVE: On the set of *Pandora and the Flying Dutchman*, James Mason is understandably gloomy as the accursed captain who must sail the seas throughout eternity until true love sets him free.

WHO MADE IT:

Dorkay Productions/Romulus Films (U.K.)/Metro-Goldwyn-Mayer (U.S.). Director/Writer: Albert Lewin. Producers: Joe Kaufman, Albert Lewin. Cinematography (Technicolor): Jack Cardiff. Music: Alan Rawsthorne. Starring James Mason (Hendrik van der Zee), Ava Gardner (Pandora Reynolds), Nigel Patrick (Stephen Cameron), Mario Cabre (Juan Montalvo), Marius Goring (Reggie Demarest), Pamela Kellino aka Mason (Jenny), Patricia Raine (Peggy), Abraham Sofaer (Judge).

WHAT IT'S ABOUT:

Setting: the Riviera. A selfish playgirl named Pandora Reynolds uses her great beauty to bend male admirers to her will. Recent conquests include an obsessive racing car owner/driver and a petulant, ultimately murderous matador. Bored and amoral, Pandora finally meets her match in a mysterious, enigmatic stranger, Hendrik van der Zee. He is in truth the legendary Flying Dutchman, cursed in another age for killing his innocent wife, whom he suspected of adultery, and renouncing God. Hendrik is now fated to roam the world eternally as captain of a ghost ship... unless he can find a woman who loves him enough to sacrifice her own life on his behalf. Ironically, he finds such a person in Pandora.

WHY IT'S IMPORTANT:

Frequently mistaken for a Powell/Pressburger offering, *Pandora and the Flying Dutchman* is actually Albert Lewin's follow-up to his 1945 Hollywood success, *The Picture of Dorian Gray*. Both films share an elegant sense of wonder that is vague and glass-boned, with a powerful time-crossed romance driving the plotline. It's a curious but somehow effective blend of well-known myths; both Pandora and the Flying Dutchman commit terrible sins and are forever incomplete, not worthy of love. That they find passion and redemption in each other's arms seems perversely logical, and with scenes viewed through the magical lens of cinematographer Jack Cardiff, soothingly poetic. For Ava Gardner, playing a beautiful temptress who leads men to ruin was hardly a stretch: she became a star in Robert Siodmak's *The Killers* doing just that, and would explore a variation of this routine in Joseph L. Mankiewicz's *The Barefoot Contessa* the following year, again with Cardiff as cameraman. Whether asking a beau to destroy his treasured possession as proof of his love for her, or giving up everything for a relative stranger who has touched her heart, Gardner's Pandora is an often unpredictable, always ethereal combination of seductiveness and sympathy. Co-star James Mason was also an old hand at playing doomed lovers, often with a Byronic bent, his quietly immortal Dutchman an irresistibly tragic figure who longs for both love and death. Taking us through this below-the-surface miracle with methodical class is Nigel Patrick as archeologist Stephen Cameron. Suspecting something "beyond nature, beyond reason," he confronts the Dutchman with his own hand-written diary from ancient times in what serves as a prelude to a period flashback. Mason, translating his own fatal words into English, finishes this reading without looking at the diary pages, the astonishing weight of his supernatural loneliness perfectly conveyed as a wide-eyed Patrick looks on.

Ultra-European in style and character, *Pandora* was nevertheless embraced by American audiences and remains a much-beloved oddity. Gardner had been semi-typed in amorous roles of this nature ever since Universal's *One Touch of Venus* put her on a pedestal in 1948, and Mason was just a few years away from even greater Hollywood success in *A Star is Born* ('55) and *Bigger Than Life* ('56). Together, working with an aggressively literate script enhanced by lush cinematography, this odd screen couple makes Lewin's fragile fantasy come to life, propelling willing viewers into an emotionally-satisfying, newly-minted romantic myth inspired by a couple of classical ones.

RIGHT: The affections of racing car enthusiast Stephen Cameron (Nigel Patrick) and the fate of his cherished vehicle (at first ordered off a cliff by an impulsive Pandora) set up the heroine's power over men. LEFT: Pandora meets van der Zee for the first time aboard his vessel; he is busy painting her portrait.

Pandora as seen by the Dutchman before she impulsively defaces his work.

In a flashback, we learn how van der Zee tragically slew his innocent wife, thinking her unfaithful.

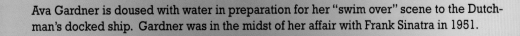

Ava Gardner is doused with water in preparation for her "swim over" scene to the Dutchman's docked ship. Gardner was in the midst of her affair with Frank Sinatra in 1951.

THE NEVERENDING STORY 1984

102 2.35

WHO MADE IT:

Bavaria Studios (Germany)/Warner Bros. Pictures (U.S.). Director: Wolfgang Petersen. Producers: John Hyde, Mark Damon, Bernd Eichinger, Dieter Geissler, Bernd Schaefers. Writers: Herman Weigel, Wolfgang Petersen, from the novel by Michael Ende. Cinematography (Eastmancolor): Jost Vacano. Music: Klaus Doldinger, Giorgio Moroder. Starring Barret Oliver (Bastian), Noah Hathaway (Atreyu), Gerald McRaney (Bastian's Father), Thomas Hill (Koreander), Alan Oppenheimer (Rockbiter/Falkor/G'Mork), Deep Roy (Teeny Weeny), Sydney Bromley (Engywook), Patricia Hayes (Urgi), Tami Stronach (Childlike Empress).

WHAT IT'S ABOUT:

A lonely little boy with an active imagination, chased by local bullies, takes refuge in a bookstore. He is soon introduced to a mysterious tome called The NeverEnding Story, which he borrows and promptly loses himself in. The boy begins to share this book's epic fantasy adventure and the exploits of its young hero in a way that startles him at first. But ultimately he realizes that book reading is a unique give-and-take experience, with his contribution ultimately making all the difference.

WHY IT'S IMPORTANT:

This movie came out of nowhere in 1984, rushed into release as a major summer offering after Warner Bros. took one look at Jeannot Swarc's *Supergirl* and promptly sold distribution rights to Tri-Star. Based on a popular novel, *The NeverEnding Story* offers agreeable widescreen spectacle along with an intimate 'lonely boy' real-world scenario, deftly blending both storylines into a satisfying whole. These worlds bleed into each other midway, as imaginative, bullied youngster Bastian (Barret Oliver), warned by his pragmatic dad to "keep both feet on the ground," loses himself in a mysterious book introduced to him by an equally enigmatic bookstore owner (Thomas Hill). Bastian channels his feelings through the story's noble boy-hero, Atreyu (Noah Hathaway, formerly little Boxey from TV's *Battlestar Galactica*), whose mission is to save the universe of Fantasia from the monstrous, all-consuming Nothing. Director Wolfgang Peterson cleverly captures the all-involving emotionalism of book-reading by having Bastian react directly to the story he's absorbing ("Good idea" says character Atreyu when he gets hungry and stops to eat; "No, that's a great idea!" responds Bastian in the real world, reaching for an apple as he reads.) Similarly, the boys shed parallel tears when Atreyu's valiant horse Artex sinks into quicksand, reinforcing the uniquely personal relationship between reader and read. It's only when this phenomenon starts happening in reverse, with Atreyu somehow hearing Bastian's heartfelt responses and finally requiring the real-world boy to contribute directly to the adventure's outcome, that the "dangerous" qualities of this mystical book become apparent. Dangerous, at least, in that deep emotions are tapped when opening one's mind to imaginative ideas, and little Bastian's naming of his own recently-deceased mother – a required new moniker for the empathetic Childlike Empress (Tami Stronach) – vanquishes the looming Nothing. Meanwhile, Peterson whips up a roster of fantasy creatures to die for, from the disillusioned, mountain-sized Rock Biter ("They look like good, strong hands, don't they?") to the lovable, doglike Luck Dragon who rescues the boy hero at his lowest ebb. FX master Brian Johnson's work has a distinctly European flavor, with a welcome air of unreality in the character designs belied by their charmingly moist noses and penetrating eyes. As for the two young leads, Barret Oliver is perfect as sad, friendless Bastian, just as Noah Hathaway seems born to play his adventurous alter-ego, Atreyu. Although these endearing actors never share a scene together (save for one super-long shot), their indispensible relationship registers strongly, forming the very backbone of *NeverEnding Story*. Also praiseworthy is the wonderful Doldinger-Moroder combo score, boasting both a catchy title song and an exhilarating racing/flying theme.

With the help of an engrossing book, bully-abused Bastian (Barret Oliver) finds solace in the enchanted, faraway realm of Fantasia.

Bizarre but helpful creatures abound in imperiled Fantasia.

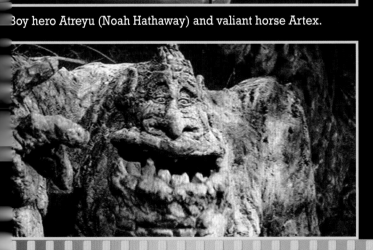

Boy hero Atreyu (Noah Hathaway) and valiant horse Artex.

LEFT: The Rock Eater has some of the film's most poetic lines. RIGHT: Bastian and the Childlike Empress (Tami Stronach).

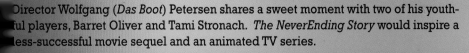

Director Wolfgang (*Das Boot*) Petersen shares a sweet moment with two of his youthful players, Barret Oliver and Tami Stronach. *The NeverEnding Story* would inspire a less-successful movie sequel and an animated TV series.

DREAM CHILD

Picked on by bullies, city waif Bastian (Barret Oliver, BELOW) uses a mysterious old book to retreat into the comforting universe of Fantasia, where he lives through the amazing adventures of courageous young hero Atreyu (Noah Hathaway, OPPOSITE PAGE), a kindred spirit. With fantastic landscapes and imaginative creatures that echo the creations of fantasy film pioneer Georges Melies, director Wolfgang Peterson's *The NeverEnding Story* became a surprise summer hit for Warner Brothers in 1984.

WHO MADE IT:

Columbia Pictures/Morningside Productions (U.S./U.K.). Director: Jack Sher. Producer: Charles H. Schneer. Writers: Arthur Ross, Jack Sher, based on the novel "Gulliver's Travels" by Jonathan Swift. Special Visual Effects: Ray Harryhausen. Cinematography (Eastmancolor): Wilkie Cooper. Music: Bernard Herrmann. Starring Kerwin Mathews (Dr. Lemuel Gulliver), Jo Morrow (Gwendolyn), June Thorburn (Elizabeth), Lee Patterson (Reldresal), Sherri Alberoni (Glumdalclitch), Gregorie Aslan (King Brob), Basil Sydney (Emperor of Lilliput), Charles Lloyd Pack (Makovan), Martin Benson (Flimnap), Mary Ellis (Queen of Brobdingnag), Peter Bull (Lord Bermogg), Alec Mango (Lilliput Minister).

WHAT IT'S ABOUT:

Dissatisfied with the world in general, young Dr. Gulliver is shipwrecked and awakens in a very different kind of environment – one where the inhabitants are miniscule. A giant in the remote kingdom of Lilliput, Gulliver uses his enormous strength to right various social wrongs. He even averts a war, but still cannot please the selfish and short-sighted desires of those he serves. Gulliver finds the same kind of intolerance in yet another world, this one dominated by giants. Reunited with his lost fiancee Elizabeth, the doctor finally finds his way home... where he intends to build a happy life based on their love.

WHY IT'S IMPORTANT:

Fresh from the startling success of *The 7th Voyage of Sinbad*, producer Charles Schneer and his fx impresario Ray Harryhausen swiftly became Columbia's answer to George Pal and Walt Disney, quality makers of robust color productions based on classic (i.e., "respectable") fantasy properties. Pal's upcoming *The Time Machine* and Fox's *Journey to the Center of the Earth* recently raised the bar for this sort of experience, although the colorful sub-genre really started with Disney's ambitious *20,000 Leagues Under the Sea* back in 1953. Regardless, the Morningside team was more than ready to take on those fanciful literary works we were all forced to read in high school. *Gulliver's Travels* by Jonathan Swift, previously incarnated as a Fleisher cartoon feature, provided Schneer and company with exactly what they needed at this juncture: a logical upgrade from *Sinbad* that would pave the way for more elaborate Verne and Wells adaptations of their own.

Reflecting the charm factor of *Journey*, former *Sinbad* star Kerwin Mathews is allowed an endearing personality with emotional range and a keen intellect, absolutely necessary for the mild social satire that follows. American actors Lee Patterson, Jo Morrow and especially Sherri Alberoni (as towering tot Glumdalclitch) acquit themselves nicely, but, as usual, it's a supporting cast of exceptional Brits that sells the more outrageous plot material. As for Harryhausen's celebrated special effects, there are fewer animated creatures than usual on display (an obnoxious squirrel and fierce alligator have their moments), with RH focusing on forced perspective rather than stop-motion thrills this time around. Also becoming part of Schneer's ongoing recipe for success: yet another wonderful Bernard Herrmann score, the famously cantankerous composer relishing such assignments (he'd remain on board for the next two RH epics).

Although designed as an audience-friendly confection, *Gulliver* soft-peddles but doesn't completely ignore its intellectual and social obligations, so inherent in Swift's thesis. In some ways, this is Harryhausen's deepest-thinking film, saying something significant about fickle, woefully insure and arrogant humanity while never losing sight of its primary obligation to entertain.

ABOVE, RIGHT: Castaway Dr. Gulliver (Kerwin Mathews) washes ashore on Lilliput, frightens the miniscule locals and is soon captured by same. BELOW: Gulliver tries to please his tiny masters, but their demands for death and destruction don't sit well with him. People are alike all over, it seems.

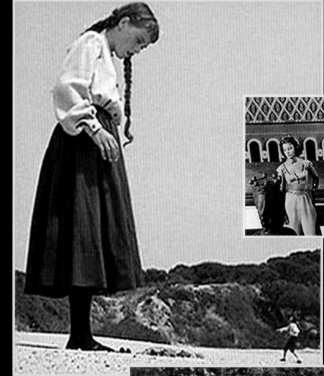

Glumdalclitch (Sherri Aberoni) befriends Gulliver in a land of giants.

ABOVE: The doctor is reunited with his lost fiancée (June Thorburn).

Man against monster: The doctor's most terrifying challenge in Brobdingnag is a ferocious dwarf alligator, prize possession of the King.

Everyday animals in giant form (courtesy of Ray Harryhausen's fx) threaten Gulliver and Elizabeth.

Master stop-motion animator Ray Harryhausen keeps his *Gulliver* 'gator in line. Most of the fx work in the film was accomplished with forced perspective techniques, just like *Darby O'Gill and the Little People*.

37 DREAMS 1990

119 1.85

WHO MADE IT:

Warner Bros. Pictures (U.S./Japan). Director: Akira Kurosawa. Producers: Hisao Kurosawa, Mike Y. Inoue, Steven Spielberg. Writer: Akira Kurosawa. Cinematography (Eastmancolor): Takao Saito, Shoji Ueda. Music: Shinichiro Ikebe. Starring Akira Terao ("I"), Chishu Ryu (Old Man), Martin Scorsese (Vincent van Gogh), Mitsunori Isaki ("I" as a Boy), Mieko Harada (Snow Fairy), Yoshitaka Zushi (Pvt. Noguchi), Mitsuko Baisho (Mother of "I"), Chosuke Ikariya (The Demon), Hisashi Igawa (Power Station Worker), Toshihiko Nakano ("I" as a Young Child).

WHAT IT'S ABOUT:

Eight mini-stories that have their origin in the dreams of acclaimed filmmaker Akira Kurosawa. The tales range from simple childlike experiences to bitter observations of mankind's less charitable pursuits. They place the protagonist, "I" (Kurosawa's alter-ego) in situations dealing with guilt and the joy of creativity, primal fear and the possibilities of a kinder world to come.

WHY IT'S IMPORTANT:

World-class filmmaker Kurosawa has dreams just like the rest of us, only his are artistically satisfying enough to warrant their own movie. Uneven as any anthology consisting of eight mini-tales would be, *Dreams* is nevertheless a unique screen experience, an ambitious, often extraordinary attempt to replicate the elusive qualities of our unconscious fantasies. The episodes involving "I" as a child are charming cautionary parables, complete with Kabuki interludes, while "Blizzard" allows Kurosawa the luxury of proceeding at a snail's pace like the snow-challenged expedition he tracks (a billowing-haired female apparition has echoes of *Kwaidan*). "The Tunnel" is a powerful denunciation of war and its consequences, as a guilt-ridden ex-commander is haunted by the grim specters of soldiers his negligence caused to be killed, with their incessantly marching feet drummed into his tortured brain. Martin Scorcese of all people portrays Vincent Van Gogh in a slight but endearing aside involving adult "I" (played as an agreeable open book by Akira Terao), now a student, somehow entering the great artist's world and works, a most satisfying journey. Memorable for very different reasons is a genuine nightmare that bleeds into two loosely-connected dreams: "Mount Fuji in Red" captures the unparalleled horror of an "end of the world" scenario, with the accidental eruption of nuclear reactors triggering Fuji's meltdown in spectacular, apocalyptic fashion. The hundreds of extras fleeing madly as all hell breaks loose makes this the most ambitious and arguably most powerful of Kurosawa's mini-episodes, capturing the helplessness and hopelessness we all experience in similar inescapable dream situations. An equally disturbing follow-up tale concerns the aftermath of man's nuclear destruction, as a weeping, one-horned "demon," in truth a wretched mutation (Chosuke Ikariya), lectures about man's folly amidst gargantuan flowers and other radiated monstrosities. The nocturnal wailing of fellow, multi-horned mutants, all in agonizing pain, is truly a vision from the pit. Fortunately, Kurosawa elects to end his primal storytelling odyssey on a positive note ("Watermill Village"), with human goodness and the refreshing simple life trumping our often grotesque and evil tendencies.

Dreams is an art-house confection by a seasoned master, to be sure; but it is also masterful and provocative filmmaking, and a brave attempt to capture the heavy, often abstract feelings conjured by our unconscious visions. With state-of-the-art special effects (George Lucas' ILM handled the Fuji sequence), exquisite cinematography and a small but passionate cast, Kurosawa's exploration of his own inner conscience speaks to us all.

The past, present, and future.

The thoughts and images of one man...for all men.

One man's dreams...for every dreamer.

Akira Kurosawa's

DREAMS

WARNER BROS. Presents
An AKIRA KUROSAWA USA Production AKIRA KUROSAWA'S DREAMS
Produced by HISAO KUROSAWA and MIKE Y. INOUE
Written and Directed by AKIRA KUROSAWA

LEFT: Mt. Fuji is about to blow in a literal nuclear nightmare.

ABOVE: Soldiers return from the dead to prey upon the guilty conscience of a reckless commander.

LEFT: Art student "I" (Akira Terao) visits a museum and inhabits the surreal landscapes of Vincent Van Gough. RIGHT: A one-horned nuclear survivor (Chosuke Ikariya) horrifies "I" with tales of post-atomic mutation and flesh-eating, demon-like humans who wail in torment.

In "The Blizzard," a lost expedition is rescued from oblivion by the appearance of a Snow Fairy (Mieko Harada). This is in the tradition of classic Asian fantasy stories.

"I" as a child disobeys parental orders and observes a woodland procession not intended for his eyes.

Internationally-acclaimed director Akira Kurosawa (here on the set of *Ran*) has been wowing film buffs for decades with classics like *Rashomon* and *The Seven Samurai*.

WHO MADE IT:

New Line Cinema (U.S.)/WingNut Films (New Zealand). Director: Peter Jackson. Producers: Peter Jackson, Michael Lynne, Mark Ordesky, Bob Weinstein, Harvey Weinstein, Robert Shaye. Writers: Fran Walsh, Philippa Boyens, Peter Jackson, from the novel by J.R.R. Tolkien. Cinematography (color): Andrew Lesnie. Music: Howard Shore. Starring Elijah Wood (Frodo Baggins), Ian McKellen (Gandalf the White), Sean Astin (Samwise Gamgee), Viggo Mortensen (Aragorn), Dominic Monaghan (Merry), Billy Boyd (Pippin), Orlando Bloom (Legolas), John Rhys-Davies (Gimli), Andy Serkis (Gollum/Smeagol), Liv Tyler (Arwen), Bernard Hill (Theoden), Miranda Otto (Eowyn), David Wenham (Faramir), John Noble (Denethor), Hugo Weaving (Elrond), Ian Holm (Bilbo Baggins), Cate Blanchett (Galadriel).

WHAT IT'S ABOUT:

As Frodo and Sam draw closer to Mt. Doom, Gollum's treachery becomes more apparent. Gandalf, meantime, defends imperiled city Midas Torith, defying its half-mad Steward, Denethor. Noble Aragorn embraces his royal heritage, calling upon a ghostly army to destroy the Uruk-Hai, while consummating his relationship with elf princess Arwen. Ultimately, the One Ring is destroyed, Sauron is foiled, and peace comes to Middle Earth at last.

WHY IT'S IMPORTANT:

Longer and even more spectacular than its predecessors, *The Return of the King* concludes Peter Jackson's astonishing *Rings* trilogy with enough thrilling battles, horrific set-pieces and poetic interludes for any ten movies. So sure is the director's hand at this stage, so powerful and satisfying were the first two acts that he earns the luxury of finishing off his spectacle at a pace and tempo of his choosing, running time be damned. With scenes such as the Battle of Minas Torith, or Shelob's venomous attack, or even the "origin" of Gollum, Jackson wows viewers with compelling characterizations and jaw-dropping action sequences, arguably the most impressive ever staged for a motion picture. New to the saga is John Noble's turn as bitter, mostly crazed monarch Denethor. As with many supporting players, he has an opportunity to express grief with Shakespearian eloquence as only a formally-trained actor of his stature can, becoming a sort of scowling yin to Bernard Hill's clear-thinking yang. Gollum also comes into his own as a nefarious villain, after Sam's description, using trickery to separate the Hobbits and steal the long-coveted Ring for himself. Of course, the movie's title refers to ranger-turned-monarch Aragorn (Viggo Mortensen), who must take the sacred blade re-forged by Elrond and use it to claim his destiny as Middle earth's new human ruler. This involves not only persuading an unpredictable phantom army to join in the fight against Sauron's minions, but spearheading a direct confrontation with the Dark Lord's forces to divert their powerful enemy from Frodo's actions at Mt. Doom. Loyal to the end, a frazzled, emotionally-pummeled Sam proves himself not only an invaluable friend but a more than competent warrior in his face-offs with giant spider Shelob and the Urak-Hai who have taken the comatose Frodo prisoner. Still, this has always been young Mr. Baggins' story, and the final stages of his taxing journey clarify the self-sacrificing Hobbit's noble intent ("This is my burden, Sam!"). A good life will go on in Middle Earth and in the Shire because of what he and his Fellowship companions have accomplished. The rule of Man will soon dominate this war-ravaged world, with a wise leader and his loving new wife at the helm, as magical races and noble supernatural entities fade into legend. When Gandalf the White and Frodo bid farewell to beloved friends and enter their gleaming, sunlit final reward, we know the grand adventure is finally over. Save for those last few pages in Frodo's book, of course, left blank so that Sam can fill them in... which he does with the love of his wife and children, assuring Frodo Baggins the most heartfelt kind of immortality. Jackson's classical, romantic, gloriously non-ironic approach to a race far nobler than ours distinguishes *Lord of the Rings*, arguably the finest fantasy epic ever achieved on film. Many of the same characters (and actors) are set to appear in the director's new trilogy, a prequel to the *Rings* adventure derived from Tolkien's *The Hobbit*. Dazzled movie viewers

Andy Serkis is never anything less than mesmerizing as Gollum, whether in human or distorted physical form (courtesy of motion-capture techniques). Gollum's tragic Ring quest ends in the fires of Mt. Doom.

ABOVE: Frodo (Elijah Wood) takes on monster spider Shelob, who eventually corners valiant Sam (Sean Astin, LEFT) within her webbed cavern lair.

ABOVE: Sword-wielding wizard Gandalf the Grey (Ian McKellan) takes on Sauron's grotesque army, even as the determined hero Aragorn (Viggo Mortensen, RIGHT) enlists the devastating supernatural services of dead warriors seeking redemption.

A very happy and proud Peter Jackson accepts the 2003 Academy Award for his remarkable work on *Return of the King*, the only fantasy film deemed Best Picture.

WHO MADE IT:

RKO Radio Pictures (U.S.). Director: Edward Schoedsack. Producers Merian C. Cooper, John Ford. Writer: Ruth Rose, based on a story by Merian C. Cooper. Cinematography (b/w and Technicolor tint): J. Roy Hunt. Music: Roy Webb. Special Visual Effects by Willis O'Brien and Ray Harryhausen. Starring Terry Moore (Jill Young), Ben Johnson (Gregg) Robert Armstrong (Max O'Hara), Frank McHugh (Windy), Douglas Fowley (Jones), Denis Green (Crawford), Paul Guilfoyle (Smith), Nestor Paiva (Brown), Regis Toomey (John Young), James Flavin (Schultz), Lora Lee Michel (Jill Young, as a Little Girl), Primo Carnera (Strongman – uncredited), Jack Pennick (Sam the Truck Driver – uncredited).

WHAT IT'S ABOUT:

In Africa, lovely Jill Young lives a tranquil life with her pet, an enormous gorilla she's named Joe. One day, a moviemaking troupe of cowboy performers invades their property and is nearly wiped out by the enraged ape. Though skeptical at first, Jill is convinced by showman Max O'Hara to bring both herself and Mr. Joseph Young to civilization, where they can be part of an elaborate nightclub act. O'Hara gets his way and everyone prospers, but eventually the gorilla is provoked into destructive action. Instead of escaping, Joe risks his life to rescue several orphans from a burning building.

WHY IT'S IMPORTANT:

Merian C. Cooper's much-beloved giant ape movies, all written by Ruth Rose and blessed with stop-motion magic by Willis O'Brien are really in a class by themselves. Grandly adventurous in the vein of Edgar Rice Burroughs, H. Rider Haggard and ultimately the *Indiana Jones* series, these films provided much-needed escapism for the reality-beset Greatest Generation, mixing exotic fantasy with two-fisted action and spectacular, jaw-dropping special effects. After WWII, the original *Kong* creative team was asked to "do it all over again," this time with a softer, more storybook approach that seemed to accommodate some of Obie's more outrageous notions. *Mighty Joe Young* is a western/jungle/monster movie with the charms of a youth-oriented romantic comedy. Guileless leads Terry Moore and Ben Johnson play like gentle variations of Ann Darrow and Jack Driscoll, while Robert Armstrong himself is back as yet another reckless P.T. Barnum-type, this time with James Cagney's best pal Frank McHugh as long-suffering sidekick. Also tossed into Cooper's ingratiating mix is a welcome touch of self-parody, although the campy excesses of *Son of Kong* have been carefully avoided.

Speaking of *Son*, kids openly bawled when little Kong's bandaged finger disappeared beneath churning waves in '33; similarly, they gasped in misty-eyed awe as a winded, wounded Mighty Joe nearly perishes rescuing tots from a burning orphanage. It's a spectacular climax, tinted Technicolor amber; with no Empire State Building to climb in this storyline, Cooper and company devised a substitute "chariot race" that more than delivers. O'Hara's astonishing, cavernous nightclub is another unforgettable creation, with dioramas filled with living African animals (take that, Museum of Natural History!), all spectacularly smashed after Joe goes on his drunken rampage.

With warmth, humor, and future fx superstar Ray Harryhausen as an asset, *Mighty Joe Young* surprised its makers in 1949 by bombing at the boxoffice, which is somewhat inexplicable, especially since *King Kong* would earn its greatest profits in a major reissue four years later. But repeated viewings on television assured the film's status as a legitimate classic, and even a tepid 1990s Disney remake

LEFT: "Beautiful Dreamer," played on a grand piano by fearless Jill (Terry Moore) is the song that soothes this savage beast, who is not especially savage when he's treated kindly. ABOVE: Jill is fast-talked by irrepressible showman Max O'Hara (Robert Armstrong), obviously a distant relative of Carl Denham. The pert and pretty Moore appeared in George Pal's charming fantasy *The Great Rupert* a few months later.

Mr. Joseph Young's nightclub career begins gloriously but ends in disaster, as baddies get the giant gorilla drunk and provoke him into violent action.

RIGHT: In a red-tinted climax, Mighty Joe pushes his enormous strength to the max as he selflessly rescues imperiled orphans from a burning building (future Grandma Walton Ellen Corby has a small part).

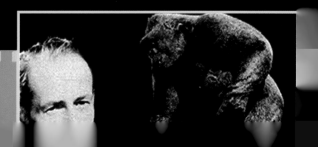

Famed stop-motion master Ray Harryhausen poses with his Mighty Joe articulated puppet. This 1949 movie classic enabled Harryhausen to work with his long-time friend and mentor, Willis (*King Kong*) O'Brien.

BEAST AND THE BEAUTY

Mr. Joseph Young of Africa, an enormous gorilla, becomes the main attraction of a super-swanky nightclub in Merian C. Cooper's 1949 follow-up to *King Kong*, the equally memorable *Mighty Joe Young*. Terry Moore (ABOVE) plays the ape's lifelong friend and reluctant showbiz partner, Jill. LEFT: Bad guys, led by *Creature from the Black Lagoon*'s Nestor Paiva, provoke normally sweet-natured Joe Young into a raging tantrum that literally brings the house down. OPPOSITE PAGE: the magnificent *Portrait of Jennie*, rendered by acclaimed artist Robert Brackman, and its inspiration, beautiful Jennifer Jones, star of the film.

WHO MADE IT:

Selznik International Pictures/Vanguard Films (U.S.). Director: William Dieterle. Producers: David O. Selznik, David Hempstead. Writers: Paul Osborn, Peter Berneis, from the novel by Robert Nathan and an adaptation by Leonardo Bercovici. Cinematography (b/w, with tints and Technicolor): Joseph August. Music: Dimitri Tiompkin. Starring Jennifer Jones (Jennie Appleton), Joseph Cotton (Eben Adams), Ethel Barrymore (Miss Spinney), Lillian Gish (Mother Mary of Mercy), Cecil Kellaway (Matthews), David Wayne (Gus O'Toole), Albert Sharpe (Moore), Henry Hull (Eke), Florence Bates (Mrs. Jekes).

WHAT IT'S ABOUT:

In Manhattan, struggling artist Eben Adams encounters a waifish young girl named Jennie Appleton, and the two become friends. Adams is inspired to paint Jennie's portrait, and becomes increasingly bewildered when she returns to him again and again, each time in a slightly older incarnation. Looking into the past, Eben learns that Jennie was a young woman who died before ever  experiencing love, and now her spirit has finally found romantic bliss. But events from years ago threaten their idyllic, surreal relationship, even as the stormy terrors of Land's End Light threaten to repeat themselves.

WHY IT'S IMPORTANT:

Fearlessly embracing the fragile and elusive qualities of ethereal love, *Portrait of Jennie* failed to connect with mainstream viewers back in '48, but has since been embraced as a legitimate fantasy classic. Star Jennifer Jones embodies Jennie Appleton, a young woman denied love in her brief lifespan. This needy, unquenchable spirit finds an equally lonely soul, painter Eben Adams (Joseph Cotton), and their relationship blossoms into nothing less than reality-challenging passion. Most significantly, it results in a magnificent portrait that captures the elusive ghost girl's sad but ultimately hopeful beauty. Director William Dieterle was clearly inspired by this melancholy tale of timeless emotional need. Using every fanciful trick in the book (including a variety of color tints and a Technicolor epilog), he shoots many of the early scenes through textured surfaces that suggest Adams' canvases. *Jennie* doesn't ignore the possibility that this comely apparition is merely a figment of the artist's restless and unhappy imagination; viewers simply put that possibility to one side as their unique romance develops, the girl older and more darkly aware of impending doom every time she appears. The climax of *Portrait of Jennie* at Land's End Light is a spectacular tour-de-force of special effects (the churning clouds are almost Spielbergian), so much so that Selznik briefly re-issued the film as *Tidal Wave*, hoping that the promise of disaster movie-style thrills might lure viewers into theaters after the fragile bliss of eternal love failed to. But even within this sequence of nature at its most terribly tangible, the elusive, impossible qualities of *Portrait*'s star-crossed union dominate. Ultimately, in the best tradition of O. Henry and Rod Serling, tangible evidence of the supernatural belies the more down-to-earth psychological explanation. Enhanced by on-location photography, a lush musical score by Tiompkin with a credited assist from Bernard Herrmann, compelling leads and some wonderful supporting performances, *Portrait of Jennie* holds up amazingly well in the hopelessly cynical 21st Century. Like romance itself, this film's gentle message of hope and the overpowering need to be cherished will never die.

nybody who could turn Lot's wife
o a pillar of salt, incinerate Sodom
Gomorrah and make it rain for
ty days and forty nights has got
be a fun guy.

A CARL REINER FILM

"Oh, God!"

A JERRY WEINTRAUB PRODUCTION
GEORGE BURNS · JOHN DENVER · "OH, GOD!"
TERI GARR
DONALD PLEASENCE · Based on the Novel by AVERY CORMAN
Screenplay by LARRY GELBART · Produced by JERRY WEINTRAUB
Directed by CARL REINER

WHO MADE IT:

Warner Bros. (U.S.). Director: Carl Reiner. Producer: Jerry Weintraub. Writer: Larry Gelbart, based on a novel by Avery Corman. Cinematography (Technicolor): Victor J. Kemper. Music: Jack Elliott. Starring John Denver (Jerry Landers), George Burns (God), Teri Garr (Bobbie Landers), Donald Pleasence (Dr. Harmon), Ralph Bellamy (Sam Raven), William Daniels (George Summers), Barnard Hughes (Judge Baker), Paul Sorvino (Reverend Willie Williams), Barry Sullivan (Bishop Reardon), Dinah Shore (Herself), Jeff Corey (Rabbi), George Furth (Briggs), David Ogden Stiers (McCarthy).

WHAT IT'S ABOUT:

A friendly, unassuming family man named Jerry Landers is contacted by God Himself, who wants His word of faith and mutual love spread throughout the world. God appears in the form of a kindly old gentleman to win Jerry's trust, and eventually the controversy caused by His proclamations leads to a major court trial, with Landers sued for slandering a pop preacher. God eventually says goodbye to Jerry, his ally and dutiful mouthpiece on Earth.

WHY IT'S IMPORTANT:

Carl Reiner's *Oh, God!* gives the Almighty a benevolent face, and such a face. Who better than kindly old codger George Burns, master of the dry one-liner, to decide our ultimate fate come Judgment Day? Mr. B is happily supplied with a plethora of choice witticisms, courtesy of Larry Gelbart's perceptive screenplay and Reiner's seasoned instincts for sharp dialogue. On the surface, these comments play like familiar Borst-belt laugh getters; but behind Burns' simple, gentle, matter-of-fact deliveries are ruminations about the universe and humanity's place in that are theologically sound and often inspiring. This is no flimsy gimmick movie, but an endearing study of why man needs God and vice-versa, prompting Him to visit our world in search of a modern-day Moses to help spread the Good Word. He finds such a person in amiable supermarket manager Jerry Landers (John Denver), a decent family man who does his best to contend with the unexpected spiritual phenomenon in his midst. Country singer Denver was never much of an actor, but he's perfect in this role, guileless and hopeful, bringing new meaning to what might be described as a profound "Father-and-son relationship." Together these two take on the media, organized religion and eventually America's justice system ("Sit down, sonny," Burns tells super-solicitor Ralph Bellamy after Landers, following God's instructions, is sued for admonishing a Jerry Falwell-like evangelist on national TV). Although entertainment is their primary goal, Reiner and Gelbert don't ignore some important theological questions along the way. "Jesus was my son," God carefully explains to doubting experts. But so is every human being on Earth, He points out, good or bad, black or white, Democrat or Republican. He even addresses humanity's escalating lack of belief in His very existence, casually citing the irony of how easy it was for the masses to accept Satanic possession as being real when they saw a little girl throwing up pea soup (*The Exorcist* was released just four years earlier, also by Warner Bros.). Nominated for a Best Screenplay Oscar, *Oh, God!* made enough money to inspire two Burns-featured sequels, neither one of them in the same quality league. When all is said and done, it's #1 that has all the laughs, fresh ideas, memorable performances, a catchy music score by Jack Elliot... and

WHO MADE IT:

Columbia Pictures (U.S.). Director: Harold Ramis. Producers: C.O. Erickson, Trevor Albert, Harold Ramis, Whitney White. Writers: Danny Rubin, Harold Ramis. Cinematography (Technicolor): John Bailey. Music: George Fenton. Starring Bill Murray (Phil), Andie MacDowell (Rita), Chris Elliott (Larry), Stephen Tobolowsky (Ned), Brian Doyle-Murray (Buster), Marita Geraghty (Nancy), Angela Paton (Mrs. Lancaster), Rick Ducommun (Gus), Rick Overton (Ralph), Robin Duke (Doris), Carol Bivins (Anchorwoman), Willie Garson (Kenny), Les Podewell (Old Man).

WHAT IT'S ABOUT:

A conceited, self-obsessed TV weather forecaster named Phil grumpily covers a popular Groundhog Day celebration – and, much to his astonishment, finds that he is reliving the same day over and over again. Caught in what might be an eternal loop, he first takes advantage of this bizarre development to satisfy his personal whims and desires, but ultimtely tries to turn himself into a better person by constructively making use what he learns from each day's repetition. Only the genuine affection of a charming co-worker eventually grounds Phil, enabling him to move pas his shortcomings and look forward to a tomorrow that will not be another Groundhog Day.

WHY IT'S IMPORTANT:

Casting an oddball personality like Bill Murray has always been an interesting challenge for Hollywood. He can be wry and Groucho-esque (*Ghostbusters*), deliriously deranged (*Caddyshack*), and even a welcome, agreeable component to a more sophisticated kind of movie (*Tootsie*). In David Rubin's original screenplay *Groundhog Day*, director Harold Ramis finds the ideal vehicle for his snarky superstar.

Like Scrooge's life-changing dream, there is a blessed simplicity to this tale's one-note premise, linked so charmingly to the real-life GD celebration in Punxsutawney, PA, which is covered throughout (with Woodstock standing in). Living the same day over and over again until "you get it right" is an irresistible notion, allowing the tale's main character every opportunity to examine the ongoing error of his ways so he can make the necessary corrections. At first used to take cheap advantages, this cosmic "edge" is eventually channeled as a force for good, with Godlike Phil able to right the daily wrongs he comes to know so well. Not surprisingly, it's nothing more than honest, selfless love (without sex, significantly) that breaks the spell and enables our finally-enlightened protagonist to move on to tomorrow.

With enough opportunity to vent his trademark irony and sarcasm, Murray shines in this showy, underplayed part, matched every step of the way by lovely co-star Andie MacDowell's soothing brand of empathy. Even the usually manic Chris Elliot is likable as Phil's put-upon cameraman, enabling Murray's self-centered obsessions to take center stage.

Smartly realized by all creative talents involved, *Groundhog Day* provides laughs, local color, and, under these most peculia circumstances, a method of self-improvement that actually works. Something to ponder the next time our alarm clock-radio goes off

YOU EVER HAD A REALLY BIG SECRET?

Tom Hanks
big
A wonderful
new comedy

TWENTIETH CENTURY FOX Presents A GRACIE FILMS Production of A PENNY MARSHALL Film TOM HANKS "BIG" ELIZABETH PERKINS ROBERT LOGGIA JOHN HEARD CO-PRODUCED BY ANNE SPIELBERG AND GARY ROSS DIRECTOR OF PHOTOGRAPHY BARRY SONNENFELD MUSIC BY HOWARD SHORE WRITTEN BY GARY ROSS & ANNE SPIELBERG PRODUCED BY ROBERT GREENHUT AND JAMES L. BROOKS DIRECTED BY PENNY MARSHALL

WHO MADE IT:

20th Century Fox/Gracie Films (U.S.). Director: Penny Marshall. Producers: James L. Brooks, Robert Greenhut. Writers: Gary Ross & Anne Spielberg. Cinematography (color): Barry Sonnenfeld. Music: Howard Shore. Starring Tom Hanks (Josh Baskin), Elizabeth Perkins (Susan), Robert Loggia (MacMillan), John Heard (Paul), Jared Rushton (Billy), David Moscow (Young Josh), Jon Lovitz (Scotty), Josh Clark (Mr. Baskin), Mercedes Ruehl (Mrs. Baskin).

WHAT IT'S ABOUT:

13 year-old Josh Baskin makes a wish that he soon wishes he hadn't: Transforming into a grown-up certainly seemed like a good idea at the time, but when it happens to him overnight, he winds up scaring the hell out of his mom (who thinks this "adult man" has kidnapped her son), and only the special rapport with best pal Billy gets the boy through a harrowing adjustment period. Unable to transform back for six weeks, Josh stumbles into a job at a toy company, and his natural instinct for what kids like to play with soon shoots him up the corporate ladder.

WHY IT'S IMPORTANT:

Big explores a fantasy that occurs to most kids sooner or later: What if I were a grown-up? Would I suddenly have unlimited power? Could I stay up all night if I wanted to, skip school, overdose on junk food? Director Penny Marshall enables everyone to take part in this wish-fulfillment adventure, offering up Tom Hanks as Josh Baskin, the boy who becomes a man, only to devolve into a (much wiser) 13 year-old again by final fade. Along the way he learns a great about the so-called adult world, although, given the family-friendly nature of this movie, Marshall and her scripters wisely pull their punches (the real adult world provides much harsher life lessons). Still, the ironic observations are solid: Tons of market research can't compete with an actual kid who loves his toys and knows what makes a good one. Josh's first girlfriend – "older woman" Susan (Elizabeth Perkins, nicely modulating a dicey role) comes to re-appreciate the simple joys she's long replaced with grim ambition, such as bouncing on a trampoline like a carefree youngster. And the preternatural importance of a loyal best friend is key to this good-natured parable, with the sing-song recognition moment that passes between Josh and 'other half' Billy (well-played by Jared Rushton) providing a crowd-pleasing highlight. Nothing, of course, matches the charm of "big" Josh and toy manufacturing boss MacMillan (Robert Loggia) dancing on those giant piano keys, making beautiful music together and cementing their unique, surrogate father-and-son relationship.

Unlike most "watch out what you wish for" fantasies, *Big* isn't about some likeable but misguided soul being set on the right moral path through cosmic intervention: little Josh happens to be a total innocent, just a normal kid smitten by a pretty girl; his only "crime" is lying to her about being at a carnival alone (she soon spots his parents), because he wants to appear like a self-sufficient grown-up. That this wish is miraculously fulfilled by a semi-demonic fortune telling machine in no way plays as judgment or punishment. It just happens, period. And, in circuitous fashion, his initial generic goal is actually accomplished: Josh finds a loving girlfriend, an "older woman" (ahem) who actually takes him over the threshold a few years prematurely.

Cute and clever, with wonderful players and a director who keeps things charmingly light without abandoning the inherent angst of its high concept, *Big* scores as a popular, gently perceptive entertainment we can all relate to.

EXCALIBUR 1981

Forged by a god.
Foretold by a wizard.
Found by a King.

EXCALIBUR

WHO MADE IT:

Orion Pictures Corporation/Warner Bros (U.S./U.K.). Director: John Boorman. Producers: John Boorman, Robert A. Eisenstein, Edgar F. Gross. Writers: Rospo Pallenberg, John Boorman, based on the book "Le Morte d'Arthur" by Thomas Malory. Cinematography (Technicolor): Alex Thomson. Original Music: Trevor Jones. Starring Nicol Williamson (Merlin), Nigel Terry (King Arthur), Helen Mirren (Morgana), Nicholas Clay (Lancelot), Cherie Lunghi (Guenevere), Paul Geoffrey (Perceval), Robert Addie (Mordred), Gabriel Byrne (Uther Pendragon), Keith Buckley (Uryens), Liam Neeson (Gawain), Patrick Stewart (Leondegrance), Katrine Boorman (Igayne), Corin Redgrave (Cornwall), Niall O'Brien (Kay).

WHAT IT'S ABOUT:

The magical sword Excalibur is passed from one generation to another. Watching events and influencing them is Merlin the Magician, who sees the eventual end of his days and the final bow of magic in the world. Young Arthur is raised by Merlin and, after drawing sword from stone and reclaiming his right as rightful heir to the throne, creates a new, gleaming kingdom of justice known as Camelot. Threats from without and within, including the ill-fated love of Sir Lancelot and Lady Guenevere, rupture the Round Table. But Excalibur and the promise of this majestic weapon survive...

WHY IT'S IMPORTANT:

Nicely recovering from the debacle that was *Exorcist II: The Heretic*, director John Boorman surprised everyone in 1981 with this splendid widescreen rendering of the popular Arthurian legends. Originally titled *Merlin*, *Excalibur* seems inspired by George Lucas' *Star Wars* epics (only fair, since Lucas mined classic fantasies of all kinds for his space saga), starting with scull-caped Nicol Williamson as a very Obi-Wan-like Merlin the Magician, that sly but benevolent manipulator of seminal events in King Arthur's life. He is supported ably by a cast boasting Helen Mirren as sexy, wicked, sympathetic Morgana, Nigel (*The Lion in Winter*) Terry as the King, Nicholas Clay as Lancelot, and a host of totally earnest Shakespearean actors in supporting roles, young Liam Nesson and Patrick Stewart among them.

Boorman blends fantasy and reality seamlessly, holding back on more tangible, conventional depictions of the fantastic (there's a great deal of talk about "the dragon's breath," but we are mercifully spared a stop-motion dinosaur breathing fire); instead, gritty bloody battles worthy of Polanski's *Macbeth* share screen time with sophisticated supernatural rituals and mysterious, hellish transmutations. Most adaptations of *King Arthur and the Knights of the Round Table* either downplay Merlin's magic or eliminate it altogether; even a grand Technicolor musical like *Camelot* doesn't fully trust this angle with skeptical modern audiences. But *Excalibur* thrives on its sumptuous other-worldly vibe. Boorman deftly uses soft focus, slow motion, post dubbing and the commanding music of Wagner to fully embrace this universe of aging wizards and vengeful blood relations, reminding us once again that while future Camelots are indeed possible, they will be forever tainted, or at least compromised, by human failing.

Best scenes: Uther's lustful transformation, Merlin's defeat, Mordred pulled out of Morgana's womb (by Morgana herself!), Arthur and his

LEFT: Young Arthur (Nigel Terry) pulls the fabled sword Excalibur from its stone, proving to loyal countrymen that he is King. ABOVE: Arthur and Guenevere (Cherie Lunghi) are married, but a torn Sir Lancelot (Nicholas Clay) will soon disrupt their wedded bliss. RIGHT: Mighty wizard Merlin (Nicol Williamson) watches over his surrogate

scion Arthur, destined to become the monarch of an imperiled kingdom.

Evil Morgana (played with a touch of sympathy by Helen Mirren) prepares her son Mordred (Robert Addie), born of King Arthur, for his blood-stained destiny.

Estranged father and son (Arthur, Mordred) united at last in a final, bloody embrace.

One of the original *Exaclibur* prop swords, on display with other rare goodies at Warner Bros. headquarters in Burbank, California.

29 THE LORD OF THE RINGS: THE TWO TOWERS 2002

WHO MADE IT:

New Line Cinema/WingNut Films (U.S./New Zealand). Director: Peter Jackson. Producers: Peter Jackson, Michael Lynne, Mark Ordesky, Robert Shayne, Bob Weinstein, Harvey Weinstein. Writers: Fran Walsh & Philippa Boyens, based on the novel by J.R.R. Tolkien. Cinematography (color): Andrew Lesnie. Music: Howard Shore. Starring: Elijah Wood (Frodo Baggins), Ian McKellen (Gandalf), Sean Astin (Samwise Gamgee), Orlando Bloom (Legolas), Christopher Lee (Saruman), Viggo Mortensen (Aragorn), Bernard Hill (Theoden), Cate Blanchett (Galadriel), Brad Dourif (Grima Wormtongue), Miranda Otto (Eowyn), Sean Bean (Boromir), Ian Holm (Bilbo Baggins), John Rhys-Davies (Gimli), Liv Tyler (Arwen), Hugo Weaving (Elrond), Dominic Monaghan (Merry), Billy Boyd (Pippin),Craig Parker (Haldir).

WHAT IT'S ABOUT:

Fellowship members Aragorn, Legolas and Gimli search for their missing comrades, even as Frodo and Sam form an uneasy alliance with the wretched, mysterious creature called Gollum. As Uruk-Hai forces attack the newly-rejuvenated King Theoden and his people, Treebeard and his fellow Ents, seeking revenge for the slaughter of their forest brethren, lay siege to Saruman's stronghold.

WHY IT'S IMPORTANT:

The Two Towers continues what filmmaker Peter Jackson started so impressively with *The Fellowship of the Ring*, confirming in the minds of viewers and critics that the brilliance of his first entry was no fluke. Picking up where *Fellowship* leaves off, *Towers* re-visits the battle between wizard Gandalf (Sir Ian McKellen) and his monster-demon opponent from the Mines of Moria, the Balrog, following these two fierce combatants into the very bowels of Hell. Meanwhile, the formidable trio of Aragorn, Legolas and Gimli (Viggo Mortensen, Orlando Bloom, John Rhys-Davies) search for their abducted Fellowship partners Merry and Pippin (Dominic Monaghan, Billy Boyd), even as a stalwart Frodo and Sam (Elijah Wood, Sean Astin) make their way to the vile land of Mordor with the dreaded One Ring in tow.

Towers lacks some of the lyrical sense-of-wonder that characterized its predecessor, as Tolkien's saga now moves into heavy war mode on several fronts. The biggest set-piece along these lines is the massive Uruk-Hai attack on Helm's Deep, where noble king Theoden (played with persuasive angst by Bernard Hill) has congregated his imperiled people. But there are other significant battles as well, all breathlessly staged and edited, including an outdoor attack on refugees, the siege of Gondor and, most impressive of all, the towering Ents' retaliation against an unwise assault on the natural world instigated by warmongering Saruman (Christopher Lee).

Which brings us to the wonderful new characters spotlighted in *Two Towers*. First and foremost is Andy Serkis as twisted Ring victim/coveter Gollum, glimpsed briefly and tantalizingly in *Fellowship*. Here he emerges as a full-fledged major character, interacting with Frodo and Sam as he guides them to Mordor. Serkis is never less than amazing, whether giddily catching a fish for breakfast or literally arguing with himself as he fathoms the true motives of his new hobbit "master." Almost as interesting is the sentient forest entity known as Treebeard, an unexpected ally who is persuaded by Merry and Pippin to join in the fight against Saruman. The scene where all of the living, walking trees of Fangorn Forest congregate to discuss their war options is a standout, as is their climactic raid on Saruman's hellish stronghold, Isengaard. Also new to the storyline is Brad Dourif as Saruman's vile ally Grima Wormtongue, who, when not indulging in evil manipulations, happens to covet possessed King Theoden's comely niece, would-be warrior Eowyn (Miranda Otto).

Thrilling, involving, and not without its own poetic interludes (Arwen's vision of deceased Aragorn's final rites certainly qualifies), *The Two Towers* is a memorable centerpiece to fantasy cinema's most consistently satisfying trilogy. Up next, one year later: *The Return of the King*, as the fate of besieged Middle Earth reaches its apocalyptic climax.

LEFT: Loyal friend, gardener and cook, Sam Gangee (Sean Astin) doesn't trust wretched Gollum (Andy Serkis), the Hobbits' new "guide" to Mt. Doom. ABOVE: A determined Frodo Baggins (Elijah Wood) uses his blade to keep violent, unpredictable Gollum in check.

The massive, bloodthirsty Uruk-Hai forces of Saruman rally for battle

Gandalf (Ian McKellen), Saruman (Christopher Lee), Grima Wormtongue (Brad Dourif).

ABOVE: Ents, the living trees of Fangorn Forest, go to war against eco-marauder Saruman, with Merry and Pippin's rescuer Treebeard (INSERT) their committed leader. Even fire can't stop this dramatic assault.

Actor Andy Serkis, wearing his motion-capture suit, makes like Gollum; eventually his movements will be computer replicated into the fully-realized screen character.

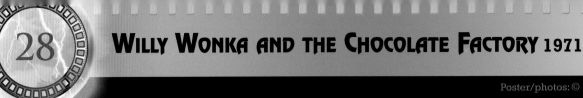
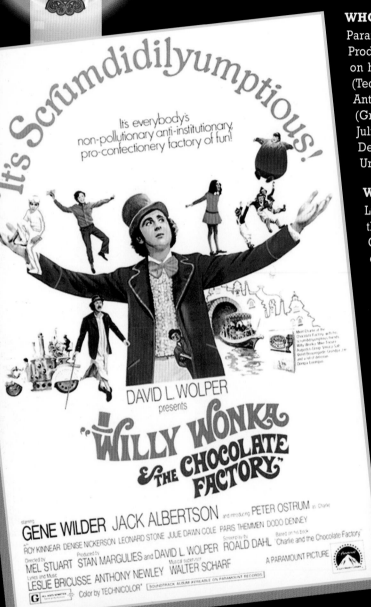

WHO MADE IT:

Paramount/David L. Wolper Productions (U.S.). Director: Mel Stuart. Producers: Stan Margulies, David L. Wolper. Writer: Roald Dahl, based on his book "Charlie and the Chocolate Factory." Cinematography (Technicolor): Arthur Ibbetson. Music, songs and lyrics: Leslie Bricusse, Anthony Newley. Starring Gene Wilder (Willy Wonka), Jack Albertson (Grandpa Joe), Peter Ostrum (Charlie Bucket), Roy Kinnear (Mr. Salt), Julie Dawn Cole (Veruca Salt), Leonard Stone (Mr. Beauregarde), Denise Nickerson (Violet Beauregarde), Nora Denny (Mrs. Teevee), Ursula Reit (Mrs. Gloop), Michael Bollner (Augustus Gloop).

WHAT IT'S ABOUT:

Little Charlie Bucket is one lucky boy; he's got the ticket to an event the entire world is talking about… a special tour of the famed Chocolate Factory, the sweetest place on Earth, by none other than owner/candy wizard Willy Wonka himself. Together with other ticket-brandishing kids and their parents, Charlie, accompanied by his beloved Grandpa Joe, is taken on a sometimes harrowing excursion into Wonka's weird wonderland, where just about everything is edible. As his fellow, far greedier ticket holders vanish, the boy eventually comes to face his unexpected destiny.

WHY IT'S IMPORTANT:

Unsuccessful when first released (even the new chocolate bar that financed the movie flopped), *Willy Wonka* managed to hook hipper critics of the day, inspired a catchy hit tune by Sammy Davis Jr., and has since been elevated to the status of legitimate, much beloved family classic. Not bad for TV documentary producer David L. Wolper, in cahoots with both Quaker Oats and trendy pop composers Anthony Newley/Leslie Bricusse. Designed as a mildly-subversive alternative to Disneyesque fluff, *Wonka*'s sweet/sour scenario is downright bizarre, no surprise given the macabre leanings of its celebrated author Roald Dahl. With only a million bucks to spend, director Mel Stuart set about creating a magical candy factory that inevitably becomes the story's multi-faceted universe of self-discovery. The lotto-like excitement of "who will find the golden ticket?" dominates *Wonka*'s dizzying first half-hour, as various kid protagonists and their keepers steal center stage, with Dickensian good boy Charlie Bucket (Peter Ostrum) in stark contrast to his hysterically bratty colleagues. Screenwriter Dahl (with invaluable help from an uncredited David Seltzer) poke mild fun at this young fellow's especially needy family and his selfless dedication to them, with optimistic Grandpa Joe (Jack Alberstson) becoming Charlie's companion on the prized factory tour. News coverage snippets are played hilariously straight as Wonka fever grips the world, a stylistic approach that mirrors what Woody Allen was parodying the very same year in *Bananas* (obviously Howard Cosell's services were too costly for the Wolper team).

But even with all the super-clever plot twists and satiric observations, it is Gene Wilder as the relentlessly charming, occasionally unhinged WW who pulls it all together. Part Wizard of Oz, part potentially dangerous bogeyman with a perverse fondness for punishing naughty tykes (who deserve far worse), Wonka plays with words incessantly, so much so that his true motive for the chocolate factory tour follows an especially nasty outburst that Wilder himself had difficulty delivering. But sweet-natured Charlie's reward is worth this difficult test, as Wonka's embrace (and a final, last-minute line provided by Seltzer) certifies the boy's new role as his chosen successor.

Not surprisingly, Tim Burton counts himself among the many fans of this fractured fairy tale, finally helming his own incarnation in 2005, with an equally appropriate Johnny Depp under the top hat. Yet somehow, this humble semi-musical from '71 is more endearing and enduring. Like young Charlie Bucket himself, it earns its stripes through sheer perseverance and a heartfelt desire to please.

Naughty little children like Veruca Salt (played with bratty perfection by Julie Dawn Cole) have much to fear in Mr. Wonka's Chocolate Factory. Only good kid Charlie Bucket passes all the tests and earns the respect and admiration of his host.

The always charming Willy Wonka (Gene Wilder) coyly welcomes all ticket-bearing guests to his self-contained universe of fantastical taste treats.

An especially scary boat ride brings out the manic qualities of WW, usually a gentle fellow.

Director Mel Stuart (who died in 2012) relaxes on the chocolate factory set with some of his delightful Oompa-Loompas.

WHO MADE IT:

Universal Pictures/Gordon Company (U.S.). Director: Phil Alden Robinson. Producers: Brian Frankish, Charles Gordon, Lawrence Gordon, Lloyd Levin. Writer: Phil Alden Robinson, based on the book "Shoeless Joe" by W.P. Kinsella. Cinematography (color): John Lindley. Music: James Horner. Starring Kevin Costner (Ray Kinsella), Amy Madigan (Annie Kinsella), Gaby Hoffman (Karin Kinsella), Ray Liotta (Shoeless Joe Jackson), James Earl Jones (Terence Mann), Burt Lancaster (Dr. Archibald 'Moonlight' Graham), Timothy Busfield (Mark), Dwier Brown (John Kinsella), Frank Whaley (Frank Graham).

WHAT IT'S ABOUT:

In Iowa, farmer Ray Kinsella hears a mysterious voice in his corn field which tells him "If you build it, he will come." This leads to Ray building a baseball field on his property, much to the concern of friends and relatives. Before long, Ray is visited by the ghosts of Shoeless Joe Jackson and seven other Chicago Black Socks players who were banned from the game after throwing the 1919 World Series. Ray ultimately seeks out a famous, reclusive author from the '60s to help him comprehend the escalating enigma in his midst. A final reconciliation with his long-deceased dad enables Ray to heal a most important personal wound, setting the stage for others to do the same.

WHY IT'S IMPORTANT:

Newly-minted superstar Kevin Costner made *Field of Dreams* right after *Bull Durham*, and many film industry observers questioned the wisdom of starring in two baseball-themed movies in a row. After these pundits saw Phil Alden Robinson's brilliant adaptation of the pseudo-autobiographical novel "Shoeless Joe," they wondered no longer. Simply stated, *Field of Dreams* provides Baby Boomers with their own *It's a Wonderful Life*, overviewing a young man's growth and personal choices in the context of small-town America. Coming of age in the '60s was a truly unprecedented social phenomenon, as resentful, perhaps unconsciously jealous offspring of the "Greatest Generation" (only a Boomer would be brash enough to create such a moniker) openly bit the hand that not only fed them, but also endured the Great Depression and rescued planet Earth from Hitler's evil just as assuredly as Flash Gordon thwarted Ming the Merciless.

And then there's baseball. What better metaphor for Americana is this most elegant and enduring of all spectator sports? And what better way for protagonist Ray Kinsella (Costner in one of his finest performances) to break the heart of his father than to reject the sport,

trashing dad's fallen hero Joe Jackson as only a peace-loving hippie can? By comparison, Capra's movie celebrates traditional values of selfless generosity and perseverance; Robinson's drama is mostly about simmering guilt. While rightfully applauding the racial and social triumphs of '60s era Boomers, *Field of Dreams* acknowledges the price decent Boomers have to pay for unrestrained selfishness in the name of progress. Calling our parents "The Greatest Generation" and movies like this one don't quite heal the wound, but at least acknowledge that the wound exists. Which is progress of sorts.

Seminal farce of romance and body-switching, enhanced by Rains...

26 **HERE COMES MR. JORDAN** 1941   94 1.37

WHO MADE IT:

Columbia Pictures (U.S.). Director: Alexander Hall. Producer: Everett Riskin. Writers: Sidney Buchman, Seton I. Miller, based on the play "Heaven Can Wait" by Harry Segall. Cinematography (b/w): Joseph Walker. Music: Friedrich Hollander. Starring Robert Montgomery (Joe Pendelton), Evelyn Keyes (Bette Logan), Claude Rains (Mr. Jordan), Rita Johnson (Julia Farnsworth), Edward Everett Horton (Messenger 7013), James Gleason (Max Corkle), John Emery (Tony Abbott), Donald MacBride (Inspector Williams), Don Costello (Lefty), Benny Rubin (Bugs).

WHAT IT'S ABOUT:

When boxer Joe Pendelton crashes in a plane accident, his spirit is prematurely snatched from his body by a well-meaning but inexperienced Heavenly Messenger. Unfortunately, Pendelton's remains are cremated, so a new body is required for an increasingly anxious Joe. The celestial Mr. Jordan pulls a few strings and arranges for him to use the one belonging to wealthy Bruce Farnsworth, who has just been murdered by his wife. In this new form, Joe tries to reform Farnsworth by employing more decent business methods, and falls deeply in love with a caring stranger. But, as Mr. Jordan warns, there are more surprises on the way... which may or may not nip this romance in the bud.

WHY IT'S IMPORTANT:

Released just a few months before the attack on Pearl Harbor, *Here Comes Mr. Jordan* was a huge hit with both audiences and critics, helping to get everyone's mind off international troubles. Unlike *A Guy Named Joe*, made at the height of the war, death doesn't resonate with the special poignancy it inevitably will, but it does provide an effective starting point for boxer hero Joe Pendelton's new life, inwardly and outwardly. Joe's arc as a character may be nowhere as pronounced as other protagonists in similar fantasies – he's pretty much the same guy in whatever body he inhabits – but his finer lights do eventually emerge when love (in the form of Evelyn Keyes) enters the already complicated mix. It all happens very swiftly, with Pendelton's fateful accident depicted within the first seven minutes (it takes almost an hour for Tracy to crash in *Guy*) and the rattled Messenger's mistake addressed almost instantly. Title character Mr. Jordan (Claude Rains) is a benevolent, eternally patient escort who calmly takes command to set things straight, personally making sure Joe is pleased with his substitute body. Played as a lovable mug by Robert Montgomery, Pendelton comes to accept Jordan as a man of his word, and so does the viewing audience. Unlike England's postwar *A Matter of Life and Death*, no one expects Joe to pay for somebody else's mistake; Heaven in the universe of *Mr. Jordan* cleans up its owned spilt milk. It's amazing how attitudes changed so quickly right after the war, victory and cynicism going hand-in-hand.

As a work of cinema, *Here Comes Mr. Jordan* hasn't aged especially well, director Alex Hall splendid with actors (important in a picture like this) but just a little stifled visually as the story methodically moves from one living room location to another. In many ways, the Warren Beatty '79 remake *Heaven Can Wait* is a better-realized movie. But *Jordan* certainly registered in its day, making a far-out cosmic displacement story personal and involving (*Back to the Future* would have the same effect on a later generation). It also happened to inspire a terrible Technicolor sequel called *Down to Earth*, showcasing Rita Hayworth. Without the ethereal Mr. Rains around to set things straight, this soggy tale of show-biz selfishness was promptly

BABE 1995

WHO MADE IT:

Universal Pictures (U.S.)/Kenny Miller Productions (Australia). Director: Chris Noonan. Producers: George Miller, Bill Miller, Doug Mitchell. Writers: George Miller, Chris Noonan, based on the novel "The Sheep Pig" by Dick King-Smith. Cinematography (color): Andrew Lesnie. Music: Nigel Westlake. Starring James Cromwell (Farmer Arthur H. Hoggett), Charistine Cavanaugh (Babe – voice), Miriam Margolyes (Fly – voice), Hugo Weaving (Rex – voice), Magda Szubanski (Mrs. Hoggett), Danny Mann (Ferdinand – voice), Miriam Flynn (Maa – voice), Brittany Byrnes (Granddaughter).

WHAT IT'S ABOUT:

Won by Farmer Hoggett at a country fair, a young piglet who calls himself Babe befriends and learns all about his animal neighbors. One of the farm sheepdogs, Fly, becomes a second mother to him, and soon Babe is as adept herding sheep as Hoggett's dutiful hounds. While all animals live in fear for their own survival, the little pig's simple friendship opens their eyes to a better way of dealing with each other. Eventually, even Hoggett himself senses something curious about Babe, and the old farmer's intuition leads to a most unusual and successful public performance that benefits all.

WHY IT'S IMPORTANT:

A charmingly offbeat contemporary fairy tale, *Babe* would have worked just fine as an animated feature in the Disney tradition. But director Chris Noonan's live-action approach has greater resonance, transforming this tale of man and pig into something unique. Although *Babe* provides the usual assortment of amusing animal characters (a neurotic duck who imitates a rooster for job security comes to mind), the film never loses sight of its simple message of tolerance. "The way things are, are the way things are," orphaned little piglet Babe is told with grim resignation. The various animal species who live on Hoggett's farm distrust one another, herd-dogs considering sheep "stupid" and vice versa. But Babe, raised by lovable mother-hound Fly after his own parents are taken away forever, is friend to one and all, bringing various animal species together in spite of their natural fears and prejudices. It's a "free to be you and me" psychology that informs this simple story, with characters realizing that anything is possible given love and faith. And this gentle altruism extends to *Babe*'s human protagonist, Farmer Hoggett (James Cromwell). In danger of losing his own precious dignity in an ever-changing world, he comes to appreciate the transcendent qualities of this little porker, the "sheep-pig" who persuades woollies to obey him by simply asking for a favor. Like the animals he loves and cares for, Hoggett defies convention and ends up winning everything – an all-important sheep-herding contest that makes him a local hero, the renewed respect of his ditsy but caring wife, and, of course, his cherished place as ongoing proprietor of the farm, more beloved parent figure to his animal charges than "boss."

Like most modern fantasy movies, *Babe* is dependent on state-of-the-art special effects, in this case a canny blend of on-set techniques and digital magic. The late Jim Henson's animatronic approach is nothing short of miraculous, easily conveying a sense of sentient life to everyday, realistically-rendered barnyard creatures. And it's all in the service of a heart-warming parable about everyone's right to dignity, no matter who our parents are or what age we've reached or how many of our feet touch the ground when we trundle forth. That's the special magic of *Babe*... a truly original ode to simple love and mutual respect.

WHO MADE IT:

RKO Radio Pictures (U.S.). Director: Joseph Losey. Producers: Dore Schary, Stephen Ames. Writers: Ben Barzman & Alfred Lewis Levitt, based on a story by Betsy Beaton. Cinematography (Technicolor): George Barnes. Music: Leigh Harline. Starring Pat O'Brien (Gramp Fry), Robert Ryan (Dr. Evans), Dean Stockwell (Peter Fry), Barbara Hale (Miss Brand), Richard Lyon (Michael), Walter Catlett (The King), Samuel S. Hinds (Dr. Knudson), Regis Toomey (Mr. Davis), David Clarke (Barber), Dwayne Hickman (Joey).

WHAT IT'S ABOUT:

A young American boy named Peter Frye, running away from home, is encouraged to explain his curious condition: he has green hair! Reluctantly, Peter tells the tale of how he was shuttled from one selfish relative to the next after his parents were killed in the London Blitz. He eventually winds up with "Gramp," a kindly ex-vaudevillean. One day, and for no apparent reason, the boy's hair turns a shocking green. Reactions from those around him range from sympathy to outright intolerance.

Eventually, Peter learns the true meaning of this bizarre miracle, and vows to represent its cause for the rest of his life.

WHY IT'S IMPORTANT:

Cut from a very different thematic cloth than most fantasy films of its era, *The Boy with Green Hair* offers a message that is both universal and timeless: war is bad for children and other living things. Soon director Joseph Losey will be forced to flee America, his leftist passions not exactly fashionable as late '40s social consciousness in Hollywood (*Gentleman's Agreement*, *Crossfire*, *Pinky*, etc.) gives way to McCarthy-era paranoia. But this genuine oddity still resonates, vindicating Losey's considerable skills as a storyteller, whatever one makes of the movie's political pamphleteering. Young war orphan protagonist Peter Fry (a remarkable Dean Stockwell) makes a fine spokesman for the evils of armed conflict, his numbed, betrayed stare symbolizing what warfare does to the innocent and unprotected. Inherent in a story about a boy's hair turning green is the study of conformity, as young Peter, understandably horrified at first, wants desperately "to be like everyone else." When he seizes upon a nobler purpose in life, perhaps instigated by his humanist guardian Gramp (Pat O'Brien, never better), the boy is attacked by vicious neighborhood children, themselves the victims of prejudice. Conformity, intolerance, fear and bigotry – Losey and his screenwriters have a field day offering up the American dream in bright Technicolor, only to shine a light on fatuous lies and the reprehensible culture of blind acceptance. In all fairness, equating "being prepared" (a strong national defense) with warmongering is a leftist reflex response, as is the total absence of perspective via some kind of counter argument (do we surrender to future Hitlers because war itself is evil?). It's a good thing worldly schoolteacher Barbara Hale doesn't have more screen time, or her struggles as a woman in a man's world might have been on Losey's laundry list of social gripes.

Still, the main point of *The Boy with Green Hair* can't be stated strongly enough, and often enough. With an enthusiastic cast, captivating flashback structure ("You won't believe me..."), a hit pop tune (Nat King Cole's "Nature Boy") and lush color photography by George Barnes that makes the most of the Boy's title condition, Joseph Losey and RKO manage to do just that.

23 EDWARD SCISSORHANDS 1990

WHO MADE IT:

20th Century Fox (U.S.). Director: Tim Burton. Producers: Tim Burton, Denise Di Novi, Richard Hashimoto. Writer: Caroline Thompson, based on a story by Thompson and Tim Burton. Cinematography (color): Stefan Czapsky. Music: Danny Elfman. Starring Johnny Depp (Edward Scissorhands), Winona Ryder (Kim), Dianne Wiest (Peg), Anthony Michael Hall (Jim), Kathy Baker (Joyce), Vincent Price (The Inventor), Alan Arkin (Bill), Robert Oliveri (Kevin), Conchata Ferrell (Helen).

WHAT IT'S ABOUT:

Created by an eccentric old inventor in a cliffside castle, an artificial young man is incomplete: his deviser died before childlike Edward's scissor-like hands could be replaced by normal ones. He is eventually discovered by kindly Avon lady Peg and introduced to suburban living, only to fall in love with Peg's comely teenage daughter. At first, the community at large accepts humble, polite and helpful Edward, but soon local citizens become frightened and turn against this bizarre stranger in their midst.

WHY IT'S IMPORTANT:

Edward Scissorhands was Tim Burton's first movie after his phenomenally-successful, fable-informed *Batman* (1989), which many felt missed the raw essence of DC's gritty Dark Knight. By contrast, *Scissorhands* fits the fanciful director's predilections like a glove over razor-sharp fingers. In its gentle depiction of a man-made entity's trials and tribulations, the well-received film not only references *Frankenstein*, but seems equally inspired by *Pinocchio*, *Adam Link* and *Astro Boy*. Johnny Depp is ideally cast as the incomplete creation of inventor Vincent Price (wonderful here, in one of his last performances), a total innocent suddenly thrust into a world of bewildering emotions. Nurtured by a caring humanist foster mom (Dianne Wiest) – only Burton would offer an Avon Lady making a call at Vincent Price's spooky castle – Edward is incorporated into her thankfully decent family with reasonable success. Fair-minded patriarch Bill (Alan Arkin) is a typically unflappable suburban dad, while little brother Kevin gets off on the cool weirdness of his houseguest's appendages. Even nosey locals are fascinated and charmed by this unexpected, super-generous haircutter in their midst, until his inherent strangeness and their own bigoted insecurities transform adulation to mindless hate. And yet, like most great fairy tales, even those set in suburban neverlands, true love trumps all inevitable conflicts. Blonde and bright-eyed Kim (Winona Ryder) is a living angel to mesmerized Edward, his ongoing inspiration not only during the course of their initial encounter, but even after many decades of separation. His decision to remain alone in his father's old castle, using those remarkable scissorhands to shred ice into Christmas snowfalls for the very community that loved/hated him, is a magical, almost Godlike role for this alienated creature. We fully understand why Kim, now an old woman reading bedtime stories to her granddaughter, still loves him, and always will.

Although it is the characters and their feelings that take center stage, *Edward Scissorhands* is also a breathtaking catalogue of technical achievements, from the remarkable scissorhands themselves (developed by Stan Winston's team), to fanciful art direction and set design: Price's mad lab embraces Willy Wonka-like absurdity, while the pastel-colored suburban universe serves as an ironic counterpoint to that scary, but benevolent, castle atop the mountain. Bridging all these diverse elements is Danny Elfman's soothingly ephemeral music score, suggesting childhood lullabies and eternal, unrequited yearning.

Best scenes: Edward discovered by Peg, the TV talk show interview, Kim's snow dance, the death of the inventor, Edward's final gift to his briefly-adopted community.

So close, so far: Edward nearly gets "real" hands from his creator (Vincent Price).

Discovered by Peg (Dianne Weist), Edward is introduced to suburban civilization, which eventually turns against him.

Kim (Winona Ryder) and Edward Scissorhands (Johnny Depp).

Director Tim Burton chats in between takes with iconic star Vincent Price.

PAN'S LABYRINTH 2006

119 | 1.85

WHO MADE IT:

Warner Bros. (Spain/U.S.). Director/Writer: Guillermo del Toro. Producers: Alvaro Augustin, Alfonso Cuaron, Belen Atienza, Elena Manrique. Cinematography (color): Guillermo Navarro. Music: Javier Navarrete. Starring Ivana Baquero (Ofelia), Sergi Lopez (Vidal), Maribel Verdu (Mercedes), Doug Jones (Fauno/Pale Man), Ariadna Gil (Carmen), Alex Angulo (Doctor), Manolo Solo (Garces), Cesar Vea (Serrano), Roger Casamajor (Pedro), Ivan Massaque (El Tarta), Lina Mira (Esposa del alcalde).

WHAT IT'S ABOUT:

Ofelia, an imaginative young girl, tries to be strong for her pregnant mother, even as she endures the harsh treatment of her new stepfather, Captain Vidal. A fascist commander trying to wipe out resistance in the hills, Vidal brings his family to this remote location, where Ofelia promptly forms a bond with local mythical creatures. A humanoid faun explains that she is a princess of legend returned for a noble and happy destiny, a dream-wish she must balance against real-life horrors.

WHY IT'S IMPORTANT:

An instant classic, Guillermo del Toro's study of fear, loneliness and the miracle of imagination uses the conventions of children's fantasy as the starting point for something far more powerful. In place of oblivious parents and standard issue pre-teen bullies, sensitive heroine Ofelia (a nice showcase for Ivana Baquero) must contend with ruthless fascists in WWII Spain, the worst of the lot being her new foster father, Captain Vidal (Sergi Lopez). Enduring an ongoing nightmare, Ofelia and her pregnant mother are taken to a remote mountain outpost where resistance activity can be monitored and smashed. The child finds solace in her fairy tales, and soon after meeting up with an attentive, vaguely intimidating humanoid faun (Doug Jones) in some nearby ruins, becomes part of a fantastic plan to "take her rightful place" as princess of a faraway kingdom. Guided by buzzing fairies, needy Ofelia follows instructions from a magical book to complete her mission, even as the horrors and atrocities of war swirl about her.

Pan's Labyrinth isn't perfect – the film's thesis of "Those who disobey orders are noble, those who do are playing into fascism" doesn't quite cover ordinarily cautious and focused Ofelia's grape-eating binge during an all-important test. But even a false step like this has a certain resonance, as it recalls the tropes of earlier myths with less complicated characters. A key question, of course, is whether these supernatural events are simply occurring in Ofelia's fevered mind. Filmmaker del Toro cleverly dances around the truth, but ultimately comes out on the side of fantasy. In a brilliant single shot, the labyrinth's dense walls open to allow a fleeing Ofelia entrance, then close again as murder-minded Vidal staggers onto the scene. This objective view confirms our belief that these miraculous events are real, which is quite important when dealing with the tragic final minutes of the story.

Technically, *Pan* is a wonder, with performer Doug Jones' emphatic mime of both "Fauno" and the monstrous Pale Man being especially memorable (Jones also played superhero Abe Sapien in del Toro's *Hellboy* movies). Still, this is pretty much little Ivana's movie, carried every step of the way on her small but steady young actor's shoulders. Not since *The Miracle of Marcelino* has childhood spirituality combined with the cosmic unknown for such a heartfelt and enriching movie experience. Sensitive as a melancholy lullaby, made by a poet at the peak of his powers, *Pan's Labyrinth* is an undeniably dark but extraordinarily rewarding place to visit.

ABOVE: Captain Vidal (Sergi Lopez) is a ruthless fascist puppet who kills without remorse and is determined to rid the Spanish hills of armed resistors. Del Toro's groundbreaking movie was rightfully praised for taking the children's fable genre into more sophisticated territory, with wartime reality's extreme pains cleverly contrasted with the comforting balm of imaginative escape. BELOW: Vidal threatens his new wife's only daughter.

Ofelia (Ivana Baquero) is drawn to mysterious old ruins with magical qualities.

LEFT, BELOW: Ofelia must past various supernatural tests in the labyrinth, including one involving the ultra-weird Pale Man (also played by Fauno performer Doug Jones) and his detachable eyes.

Imposing but warm-hearted Fauno (Doug Jones) is Ofelia's best friend during her ordeal.

Director del Toro chats with his "Fauno," Doug Jones. These two also worked together on the *Hellboy* movies, with gifted mime Jones portraying amphibious Abe Sapien.

CHILDHOOD TERRORS

Fear grips the heart and soul of a girl named Ofelia
(Ivana Baquero), who retreats from the sadism of her wicked
stepfather into an equally daunting world of fairies and
monstrous fauns. It's all part of Guillermo del Toro's unparalleled masterwork, the triple Oscar-winning *Pan's Labyrinth*.
RIGHT: Fauno (Doug Jones) comforts little Ofelia.

21 DONKEY SKIN 1970

90 1.78

WHO MADE IT:

Marianne Productions (France)/Janus Films (1975 U.S.). Director: Jacques Demy. Producer: Mag Bodard. Writer: Jacques Demy, based on the fairy tale by Charles Perrault. Cinematography (Eastmancolor): Ghislain Cloquet. Music: Michel Legrand. Starring Catherine Deneuve (The Princess), Jean Marais (The King), Jacques Perrin (The Prince), Micheline Presie (La reine rouge), Delphine Seyrig (The Fairy), Henri Cremieux (The Doctor), Sacha Pitoeff (The Minister).

WHAT IT'S ABOUT:

A distraught King resolves to fulfill his late Queen's final request... that he marry a woman as beautiful as she is. Unfortunately, only the King's comely daughter qualifies, so she must run away and disguise herself beneath smelly animal skins, a necessary ruse until she discovers true love in the form of a handsome young prince. Some help from a worldly, time-warping fairy accomplice sets things straight, and both pleased King and overjoyed Princess wind up with suitable significant others.

WHY IT'S IMPORTANT:

Lord knows why, but the French seem to have a special talent for transforming fairy tales into wonderful movies. An affectionate homage to the landmark works of Jean Cocteau (the presence of Jean Marais spells out this connection), *Donkey Skin* has an infectious charm that makes it a one-of-a-kind experience (although *The Princess Bride* gives it a run for its francs). Fresh from their international success with *The Umbrellas of Cherbourg*, director Jacques Demy, star Catherine Deneuve and composer Michel Legrand find another deliriously offbeat outlet for their considerable talents. Who but Demy would jump at the chance to film a donkey that craps jewels, an old hag who nonchalantly belches frogs and, at the heart of things, a noble king who wants to marry his own beautiful daughter? Who but Legrand would compose blissful serenades about incest and birth defects? And who but Deneuve could look absolutely ravishing even within the gross hide and hood of a skinned jackass? Yes, her lovely cheeks are stained with pitch, and everyone who sees this shunned creature considers her "ugly," but such illogic only enhances this wine-and-cheese variation of the Cinderella fable. Obviously inspired, director Demy nails exactly the right balance between earnest storytelling and unrestrained, self-aware whimsy. Nowhere is this more apparent than in the characterization of the Princess' hip, somewhat self-serving fairy godmother (Delphine Seyrig), who, like many mythological magicians (Burgess Meredith in *Clash of the Titans* among them), has eye-widening knowledge of future events and technology. Although her climactic arrival at the royal wedding via helicopter is a tad jolting, it's carefully set up by the King's volumes of poetry retrieved from times to come, and even a stray telephone perched almost unnoticeably beside her magic mirror. As for visual stylization in general,

Demy, costumer designer Gitt Magrini and cinematographer Ghislain Cloquet go Fellini and beyond, with preternatural color schemes (deep blue for the Princess' kingdom, red for the young Prince's) anticipating the works of various 21st Century fantasy filmmakers. The Princess' new dresses, requested of her father/fiancé, are unforgettable creations (nothing tops the "the color of the weather" gown – good weather, of course). And in one of the most poetic moments in any movie, the handsome young prince (Jacques Perrin) is given directions by a talking rose, sensual lips and a single eye manifesting within its pedals. Filmed in actual French chateaus that compliment these fanciful concepts, with remarkable artists doing exceptional work in all departments, Demy's ingratiating *Donkey Skin* is anything but a fool's choice.

WHO MADE IT:

Warner Bros./Paramount Pictures (U.S.). Director: David Fincher. Producers: Kathleen Kennedy, Frank Marshall, Cean Chaffin, Jim Davidson. Writers: Eric Roth, based on a story by F. Scott Fitzgerald, Roth and Robin Swicord. Cinematography (color): Claudio Miranda. Music: Alexandre Desplat. Starring Brad Pitt, Robert Towers, Peter Donald Badalamenti II, Tom Everett, Spencer Daniels, Chandler Canterbury, Charles Henry Wyson (Benjamin Button), Cate Blanchett (Adult Daisy), Julia Ormond (Adult Caroline), Tilda Swinton (Elizabeth Abbott), Jason Flemyng (Thomas Button), Taraji P. Henson (Queenie), Jared Harris (Captain Mike Clark).

WHAT IT'S ABOUT:

A soft-spoken man named Benjamin lives his life in reverse: he is born aged, and grows younger with each passing year. Abandoned as an infant, he is raised by a loving foster mother, experiences various friendships, is eventually reconciled with his guilt-ridden true father, and finds lasting love in the form of a woman named Daisy.

WHY IT'S IMPORTANT:

Although comparisons with director David Fincher's Oscar-winning triumph *Forrest Gump* are inevitable, *The Curious Case of Benjamin Button* is an accomplished work in its own right. Once again Fincher follows an offbeat protagonist through his fascinating life's journey, Benjamin Button's ups and downs unfolding against the stormy backdrop of history. This time, however, the hero is inexplicably aging in reverse, a concept conceived in thumbnail form by F. Scott Fitzgerald but fleshed-out meticulously by screenwriter Eric Roth.

At the heart of this bizarre notion is Brad Pitt's bravura performance, enhanced by astonishing CG and make-up effects. Whether portraying Benjamin as a wrinkled newbie or a handsome, aging hunk, Pitt, perfectly cast, easily conveys the feelings of a being born to gently observe, to make the most of the miracle of life in spite of fate's often extreme surprises ("You never know what's coming for ya" is an oft-repeated line that ultimately dovetails with the arrival of hurricane Katrina, part of *Button's* significant framework structure). Through it all Benjamin endures, even fathering a beautiful offspring of his own. Sharing poster space with Pitt is female co-star Cate Blanchett as Daisy, who goes through an extensive aging process of her own, evolving from self-obsessed wannabe to sensual lover to attentive pseudo-parent. Love pulls her through all of these demanding life roles, and Daisy's final moments with the infant Benjamin, dying of senility and old age as he stares weakly but knowingly at this entity he loves, seem to put the entire miraculous affair into perspective.

Ultimately, Benjamin Button's journey is everyone's journey; putting it in reverse allows a unique exploration of life unattainable in conventional stories. By savoring precious "little" moments (the comforting safety of a home after hours, when loved ones are asleep, or viewing a life-renewing dawn), director Fincher seems to catch a piece of humanity's soul, and submits it for our approval with gentlemanly grace. Thank you, sir, for a most perceptive and moving overview.

THE PRINCESS BRIDE 1987

WHO MADE IT:

20th Century Fox (U.S.). Director: Rob Reiner. Producers: Norman Lear, Andrew Scheinman, Rob Reiner. Writer: William Goldman, based on his book. Cinematography (color): Adrian Biddle. Music: Mark Knopfler. Starring Cary Elwes (Westley), Robin Wright (Buttercup), Mandy Patankin (Inigo Montoya), Chris Sarandon (Prince Humperdinck), Christopher Guest (Count Tyrone Rugen), Peter Falk (Grandfather), Fred Savage (Grandson), Wallace Shawn (Vizzini), Andre the Giant (Fezzik), Peter Cook (The Impressive Clergyman), Billy Crystal (Miracle Max), Carol Kane (Valerie).

WHAT IT'S ABOUT:

A man reads his not-exactly-thrilled grandson a bedtime story: it's a whimsical fairy tale about two star-crossed lovers, Buttercup and Westley. They are separated by fate and some dastardly characters, the evil prince Humperdinck among them. After enduring various perils, including a walk through the dreaded Fire Swamp, the lovers join forces with agenda-driven swordsman Inigo and a friendly giant to defeat Humperdinck and his minions. The villains are thwarted, Inigo's honor is reclaimed, Buttercup and Westley live happily ever after. A cool story, the grateful grandson concludes!

WHY IT'S IMPORTANT:

What is it about *The Princess Bride* that sets it apart from other good-natured fairy tale charmers? Well it isn't the pretty scenery, ladies and germs. Jewish humor has been taking the edge off regal or austere sagas since cinema's earliest days (paging Eddie Cantor), earthy responses to pompous situations and environments proving hilarious to mainstream audiences. Lovable Peter Falk reading a bedtime story to grandson Fred Savage is more than simply a serviceable framing device: it determines the tone and flavor of the fairy tale we're about to experience. Director Rob Reiner cleverly cuts away from his story-within-a-story every now and then to remind us where this specific flavoring is coming from, along with smartly charting the initially bored youngster's gradual interest in what he's hearing. Watching twinkle-eyed Falk provoke enthusiastic responses from Savage is absolutely delightful, an affectionate ploy that may be quite familiar to many parents.

As for the tale itself, it's a tongue-in-cheek romantic adventure that comes perilously close to self-parody, but never quite broadens into Mel Brooks schtick (check out *Men in Tights* to see *Princess Bride* hero Cary Elwes in complete Mad Magazine mode). Robin Wright makes for a most delicious Princess Buttercup, while Elwes is letter-perfect as the farmboy-turned-bogus pirate that she falls for in her youth. Threatening to steal the show from this comely couple (not to mention lovable Andre the Giant) is Mandy Patankin as vengeance-seeking swordsman Inigo Montoya, sworn to slay the killer of his father. Making for a handsome villain is future *Fright Night* vampire Chris Sarandon, and Billy Crystal has a Borsht-Belt field day under grotesquely heavy make-up as a helpful miracle worker. Oscar-winning screenwriter William Goldman and director Reiner are in perfect sync with this fanciful fluff, even keeping the literal fantasy elements to a welcome minimum (some oversized rats, eels, and a "fire swamp" are all we really need).

A good-hearted wink of a movie, *The Princess Bride* remains unique in its winning blend of humor, sweetness and satire. Only the animated *Shrek* movies catch a piece of this flavor (sword-wielding Puss in Boots seems to be channeling Montoya on occasion), but these confections are far broader and aimed at a wider audience. This is a movie for earnest young lovers... and grateful little kids who

ABOVE: Youngster (Fred Savage) must endure a bedtime story from doting Grandad (Peter Falk), then finds himself getting interested in the tale, which is subtly favored by the old man's dry sense

of humor. RIGHT, TOP: Unlikely bandits-turned-heroes (two out of three, anyway) Fezzik (Andre the Giant), Montoya (Mandy Patanpkin) and Vizzini (Wallace Shawn). LEFT, BELOW: Montoya is a master swordsman sworn to avenge the murder of his father. Here, he crosses blades with equally skilled Westley (Cary Elwes), who will soon become his steadfast ally.

BELOW: Young lovers Westley and Buttercup (Cary Elwes Robin Wright).

BELOW: Old lovers Valerie and Max (Carol Kane, Billy Crystal)

Director Rob Reiner has some helpful advice for horizo Cary Elwes as the torture sequence gets underway.

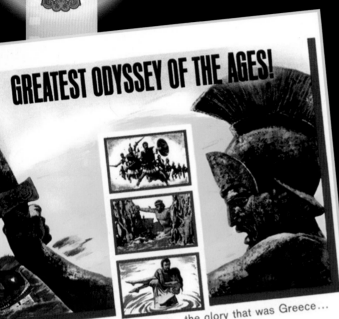

WHO MADE IT:

Columbia Pictures (U.S./U.K.). Director: Don Chaffey. Producer: Charles H. Schneer. Writers: Jan Reade, Beverley Cross. Cinematography (Eastmancolor): Wilkie Cooper. Music: Bernard Herrmann. Starring Todd Armstrong (Jason), Nancy Kovack (Medea), Gary Raymond (Acastus), Laurence Naismith (Argos), Niall MacGinnis (Zeus), Michael Gwynn (Hermes), Douglas Wilmer (Pelias), Honor Blackman (Hera), Jack Gwillim (King Aeetes), Patrick Troughton (Phineas), Nigel Green (Hercules).

WHAT IT'S ABOUT:

The rightful ruler of Thessaly, heroic Jason embarks on a fantastic quest for the Golden Fleece to avenge his slain father and reclaim his stolen kingdom. Joining him on the mighty vessel Argo are great warriors from far and wide, including the legendary Hercules, even as king of the gods Zeus and sympathetic wife Hera observe from Mount Olympus. Jason and his shipmates face a series of incredible challenges, among them the vengeful bronze giant Talos, three vicious harpies, the clashing rocks, and finally a multi-headed hydra, which protects the glimmering object of their journey. Aided by beautiful Medea, the stalwart heroes are nearly overwhelmed by six sword-wielding skeletons, unholy children of the slain hydra's teeth. But resourceful Jason manages to escape with his life… and the sacred, miraculous Golden Fleece itself.

WHY IT'S IMPORTANT:

"For some people, it's *Citizen Kane*," proclaimed Tom Hanks the night he handed Ray Harryhausen an honorary Oscar. "But for me, it's *Jason and the Argonauts*." This kind of unbridled enthusiasm pretty much says it all. At the peak of his creative powers in 1962, fx master RH decided to take a crack at one of his favorite subjects, Greek mythology. With the same self-assurance and panache that made *The 7th Voyage of Sinbad*, *The 3 Worlds of Gulliver* and *Mysterious Island* box-office sensations and critical hits, he embarked on his most ambitious movie to date, one involving three times the fx work his previous offerings required. Stop-motion pleasures aside, *Jason* is something of an oddity in that the film's leads, Todd Armstrong and Nancy Kovak (Jason and Medea) happen to be the least interesting and accomplished performers of an extraordinary ensemble. Supporting player Gary Raymond would have made a far more compelling Jason, while Olympians Honor Blackman (she appeared in *Goldfinger* the same year) and Nial (*Curse of the Demon*) MacGinnis reasonate strongly as domesticated but winsome Hera and nonchalant, endearingly pragmatic Zeus. A quick comparison with Olivier's artificial and bombastic approach to the role in *Clash of the Titans* underscores the qualitative difference between these two conceptually similar, but ultimately very different movies. Elsewhere, Douglas Wilmer underplays nicely as a dignified usurper, Jack Gwillim earns every penny of his salary as semi-hysterical King Pelias ("Kill, kill, kill them all!"), and very English Nigel Green makes a meal out of his Hercules performance, the most enjoyable since Steve Reeves put on a toga six years earlier. As one might expect from a tale built around an epic journey, there is an episodic structure to *Jason*, with expertly-crafted special effects sequences (bronze giant Talos, vindictive harpies) ultimately leading to that "tree at the end of the world" and the greatest prize of all, the Golden Fleece. Only a seven headed hydra and an army of living skeletons (former victims of the monster) stand between our Argonaut heroes and victory. Adding to these colorful proceedings is Bernard Herrmann's relentless score, and sharp-eared music historians will probably recognize his "harpy attack" cue as a direct lift from 1952's *Five Fingers*. Energetic and desperate to please, *Jason and the Argonauts* didn't match the financial success of Harryhausen's earlier films, possibly because cheaper flicks on the subject had already poisoned this particular well. But, as Tom Hanks' comments suggest, its popularity has only increased over the years. Arguably Mr. H's most impressive moment on the cinematic stage, *Jason*

ABOVE: Jason (Todd Armstrong) and his hardy shipmates. RIGHT: The Argo is saved from destruction by the sudden appearance of underwater monarch Triton. BELOW: Hera (Honor Blackman)and husband Zeus (Niall MacGinnis) listen to Jason's pleas on Mount Olympus.

Towering bronze figure Talos, restored to life by a reckless Hercules, threatens the stunned Argonauts.

LEFT, BELOW: Jason squares off against vicious harpies and a seven-headed Hydra in his quest for the legendary Golden Fleece.

Battling "Children of the Hydra's Teeth."

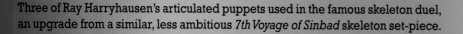

Three of Ray Harryhausen's articulated puppets used in the famous skeleton duel, an upgrade from a similar, less ambitious *7th Voyage of Sinbad* skeleton set-piece.

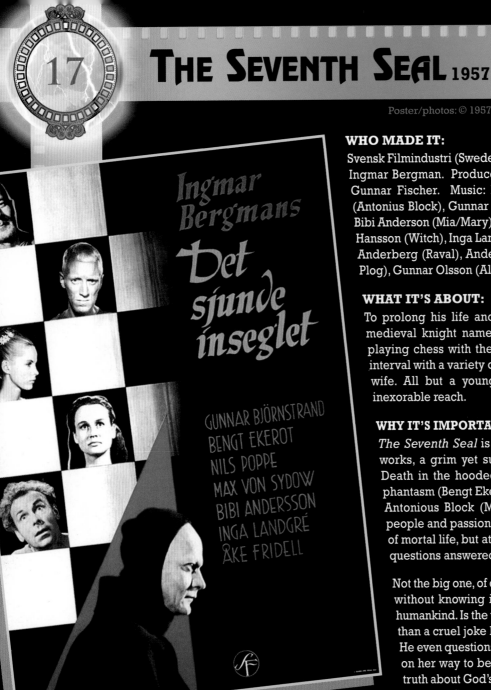

WHO MADE IT:

Svensk Filmindustri (Sweden), Janus Films (U.S.; 1958). Director/Writer: Ingmar Bergman. Producer: Allan Ekelund. Cinematography (b/w): Gunnar Fischer. Music: Erik Nordgren. Starring Max von Sydow (Antonius Block), Gunnar Bjornstrand (Jons), Nils Poppe (Jof/Joseph), Bibi Anderson (Mia/Mary), Bengt Ekerot (Death), Inga Gill (Lisa), Maud Hansson (Witch), Inga Landgre (Karin), Gunnel Lindblom (Girl), Bertil Anderberg (Raval), Anders Ek (The Monk), Ake Fridell (Blacksmith Plog), Gunnar Olsson (Albertus Pictor), Erik Strandmark (Jonas Skat).

WHAT IT'S ABOUT:

To prolong his life and find answers to meaningful questions, a medieval knight named Antonius Block keeps Death at bay by playing chess with the hooded entity. Block shares this precious interval with a variety of locals, and even re-unites with his beloved wife. All but a young couple and their child escape Death's inexorable reach.

WHY IT'S IMPORTANT:

The Seventh Seal is the most iconic of Ingmar Bergman's early works, a grim yet surprisingly hopeful parable that manifests Death in the hooded, nonjudgmental form of a chess-playing phantasm (Bengt Ekerot). The brief respite granted noble knight Antonious Block (Max von Sydow) allows him to experience people and passions that don't really alter his bleak assessment of mortal life, but at least enable him to exit with a few personal questions answered.

Not the big one, of course. Block doesn't want to leave this world without knowing if there's some caring entity watching over humankind. Is the whole maddening affair of existence no more than a cruel joke by disinterested cosmic forces, he wonders? He even questions a condemned young witch (Maud Hansson) on her way to be burned, reasoning that if anyone knows the truth about God's existence, it would logically be his opposite number, Satan. Only in one instance does Block take a significant step forward in his final ruminations, and director Bergman plays this event coyly: Impressed by the simple joyful goodness of traveling jester Jof (Nils Poppe) and his equally earthy, pregnant wife Mia (Bibi Andersson), Block distracts Death long enough so that these worthwhile innocents can slip away and escape oncoming oblivion. Whether the Lord of Finality is actually aware of his opponent's sly move and is permitting their "getaway" out of respect and pity is an open question.

As with all Bergman films, the cast of *Seventh Seal* is a potent mix of sexy young women and aging, masculine men with weather-beaten faces. Threatening to overshadow both von Sydow and Ekerot is Gunnar Bjornstrand as Block's seasoned, no-nonsense squire, an unsentimental man-at-arms with little regard for females (though he sees fit to have one around at the moment of his death). Their relationship seems to be one of unshakeable trust more than personal chemistry. When master Block gets too ponderous, his servant brings him back to earth with a dry, generally cynical observation. Eventually, it seems, we'll all be dancing with a certain tall dark stranger, facing what might be the grandest and most satisfying adventure of all. Or, as Jons might say with a resigned half-smile, merely the latest

aka Marcelino Pan e Vino

Poster/photos: © 1955 Charmartin Productions (Spain)/UMPO (U.S.)

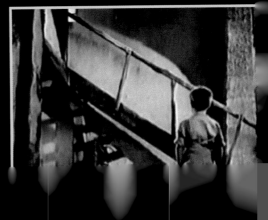

WHO MADE IT:

Chamartin Producciones (Spain), UMPO (U.S. 1956). Director: Ladislao Vajda. Producer: Vicente Sempere. Writers: Jose Maria Sanchez Silva, based on his novel; Ladislao Vajda. Cinematography (b/w): Enrique Guerner aka Heinrich Gartner. Music: Pablo Sorozabal. Starring Pablito Calvo (Marcelino), Fernando Rey (Narrator Monk), Rafael Rivelles (Father Superior), Juan Calvo (Brother Cookie), Fray Puerta (Brother Door), Jose Marco Davo (Pascual), Rafael Calvo (Don Emilio), Antonio Ferrandis (Monk), Jose Maria Ovies (Statue of Christ Voice – uncredited).

WHAT IT'S ABOUT:

A group of Franciscan monks find an abandoned infant on the doorstep of their monastery. After trying unsuccessfully to locate the child's parents, they decide to raise little Marcelino by themselves. He grows into a robust and sometimes mischievous child, adored by his foster parents but always craving the love of his unknown mother. To discipline the precocious boy, he is ordered not to climb an especially mysterious staircase leading to an equally intimidating attic. Fascinated, Marcelino investigates the upper room and is terrified by what he sees there – a towering statue of Christ on the cross. But the boy summons his courage and returns, offering this life-like figure a piece of bread. Stone fingers become flesh and dramatically accept this offering, initiating a unique relationship that will soon provide the motherless youngster with his greatest, most heartfelt wish.

WHY IT'S IMPORTANT:

One of the finest movies made, Ladislao Vajda's *The Miracle of Marcelino* is rarely seen today, and that's a shame. Combining fear of the unknown with an embrace of love and an unshakeable belief in the afterlife, Marcelino hits a unique personal note than none of Hollywood's popular religious movies can hope to achieve. There is much humor and gentle pathos as Marcelino (Pablito Calvo) grows up loving his twelve doting 'parents', but is forever saddened by the absence of his mother. Significantly, almost half of the film's running time lapses before anything remotely supernatural happens, and this careful grounding in reality makes the boy's relationship with his 'mysterious friend' from that cobwebby attic all the more evocative, and realistic. Other than a few majestic shots of Christ's nail-scarred hands breaking the bread Marcelino has brought to him, almost everything is conveyed in beautiful close-ups of Calvo reacting with joy at these miraculous events. When he first observes God descending from the wooden cross, Heinrich Gartner's camera lowers at precisely the right pace. In a later visit, Marcelino reaches directly for "us," then lowers his hands with Christ's crown of thorns that he just removed ("Did it hurt?"). This is nothing less than movie magic, crafted simply and ingeniously. Ditto the boy's fixation with the forbidden stairway that ultimately leads to the attic and his close encounter: Vajda and Gartner illuminate these ladder-like steps optically to suggest both Marcelino's obsession and the metaphysical event soon to transpire.

Based on the framework device, it's pretty obvious that Marcelino will not survive this parable. His death ("I want to see my mother"/"Then you'll have to go to sleep"/"But I'm not tired"/"Come into my arms...") provokes bittersweet joy and an avalanche of tears in the tradition of little Pud's passing in *On Borrowed Time*. Moreover, the "miracle" is not only about a living statue granting a child's ultimate wish, but about the altruistic change it causes in the local mayor (Jose Marco Davo), previously the story's resident villain. Simple love, it seems, transcends everything... selfishness, loneliness,

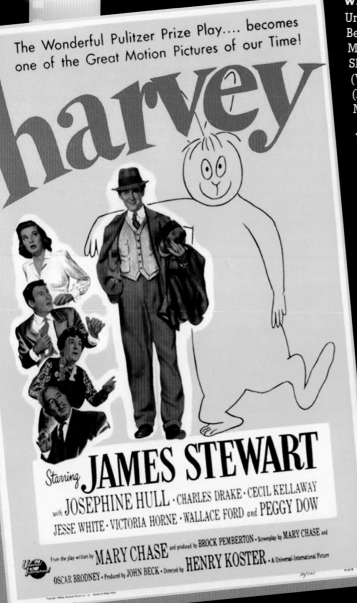

The Wonderful Pulitzer Prize Play.... becomes one of the Great Motion Pictures of our Time!

harvey

Starring JAMES STEWART

with JOSEPHINE HULL · CHARLES DRAKE · CECIL KELLAWAY
JESSE WHITE · VICTORIA HORNE · WALLACE FORD and PEGGY DOW

From the play written by MARY CHASE and produced by BROCK PEMBERTON · Screenplay by MARY CHASE and
OSCAR BRODNEY · Produced by JOHN BECK · Directed by HENRY KOSTER · A Universal-International Picture

WHO MADE IT:

Universal-International (U.S.). Director: Henry Koster. Producer: John Beck. Writers: Mary Chase and Oscar Brodney, based on the play by Mary Chase. Cinematography (b/w): William Daniels. Music: Frank Skinner. Starring James Stewart (Elwood P. Dowd), Josephine Hull (Veta Louise Simmons), Peggy Dow (Miss Kelly), Charles Drake (Dr. Sanderson), Cecil Kellaway (Dr. Chumley), Victoria Horne (Myrtle Mae Simmons), Jesse White (Wilson), William Lynn (Judge Gaffney).

WHAT IT'S ABOUT:

Elwood P. Dowd is a gentle tipper with a very special friend – an invisible, man-sized rabbit named Harvey. Also living with Elwood is his hyper-hysterical sister, Veda Louise, and his niece Myrtle Mae. Both continually frustrated women want their agreeable but embarrassing relative committed. After some mishaps at Dr Chumley's sanitarium, psychiatrist Dr. Sanderson and nurse Miss Kelly eventually catch up with Dowd at a local bar, and he casually explains how Harvey came into his life and became a most trusted ally. Even Chumley comes to believe in this entity – Harvey is in truth a "Pooka," or mischievous sprite from Celtic mythology. When Veda realizes that a new wonder drug will stop her brother from seeing the rabbit, but will also change him into a complainer, she decides she can live with Elwood – and best pal Harvey – after all.

WHY IT'S IMPORTANT:

James Stewart was never crazy about Hollywood's take on *Harvey*, believing that the Pulitzer Prize-winning material was better suited to live presentations. This is strange, because Henry Koster's adaptation deftly nails one of the most endearing and thoughtful modern parables ever written. Viewed superficially, this is a farce about a lovable drunk and the apparently real "pink elephant" that has become his bosom pal and bar-hopping companion, much to the ongoing horror of cartoonish, over-the-top relatives who want him committed. A closer and more sobering look reveals a philosophy of life that addresses concerns most of us are too busy to notice. Reality is the one thing we humans all have in common, and "winning out" over it as Elwood has is, for the most part, an admirable achievement. Writer Mary Chase provides a dizzying world of uptight professionals making wrong decisions, alienating loved ones and raising their blood pressure while doing so. Then along comes unflappable Mr. Dowd and his personable Pooka and everything settles down, truth and beauty slipping calmly into focus. Of course, there is a bittersweet side to inner tranquility. Mr. Dowd has to pay for his Pooka-induced bliss with occasional memories of what it was like to be "normal" in decades past, when he was smart rather than pleasant, when he knew the latest dance steps and women found him a desirable prospect. Harvey changed all that, enabling the human he likes best to leave reality's rat race behind and dwell in a carefree neverland based almost entirely on friendship and booze. If this is Mary Chase recipe for happiness, then it's clear she's carefully balanced the scales and concluded that Dowd is a lucky fellow indeed, some wistful nostalgia and a possibly pickled liver notwithstanding. *Harvey* is pretty much a filmed stage play, with a few locations added to open up the narrative. But director Henry Koster is careful to frame many shots of his Pooka sharing equal space with Dowd... meaning that a "hole" in the composition exists where the invisible creature is supposed to be appearing. This kind of staging is fun, and sometimes it takes a few moments to realize exactly what we're supposed to be looking at.

Clever visual touches aside, *Harvey* eschews special effects and places the emphasis where it belongs, on gentle humor and sharp characterization. Stewart is wonderful as Elwood at this stage of his life and career, and he's matched by Josephine Hull's impossible-to-replicate performance as high-strung Veta Louise. In the final analysis, this one-and-only movie version of *Harvey*, produced by Universal craftsmen at the peak of their powers, is both "smart AND pleasant." It's a combination I heartily recommend. And you may quote me.

Genial tipster Elwood P. Dowd, as portrayed by a postwar James Stewart, first on the stage, then in this well-received screen adaptation from Universal.

Stewart jokes with a bizarre attempt to visualize Harvey for this studio-issued publicity still.

Key members of the Harvey family: Miss Kelly and Dr. Sanderson (Peggy Dow, Charles Drake), Dr. Chumley (Cecil Kellaway), and Veta Louise (Josephine Hull).

BELOW: Elwood agrees that "…a painting reflects our dreams."

The Dowd home may not be as famous as Norman Bates' residence, but it's a key attraction on the Universal Studios tour (it also turns up in countless other movies and TV shows).

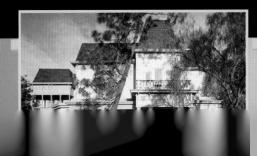

A BOY'S BEST FRIEND IS HIS POOKA

'I prefer you, too'' says Elwood P. Dowd to his best pal, a six foot-plus invisible rabbit, at the conclusion of *Harvey*. The lovable Mr. Dowd, played to perfection by James Stewart in what many critics consider his signature role appears to have "won out" over reality, at least according to author Mary Chase's pithy observations. INSERT Harvey the personable pooka by Stewart, a cartoon he's doodled countless times over the years.

WHO MADE IT:

20th Century-Fox (U.S.). Director: Joseph L. Mankiewicz. Producer: Fred Kohlmar. Writer: Philip Dunne, based on the novel by R. A. Dick. Cinematography (b/w): Charles Lang Jr. Music: Bernard Herrmann. Starring Gene Tierney (Lucy Muir), Rex Harrison (Capt. Daniel Gregg), George Sanders (Miles Fairley), Edna Best (Martha Huggins), Natalie Wood (Anna Muir as a child), Anna Lee (Mrs. Miles Fairly), Robert Coote (Mr. Coombe), Vanessa Brown (Anna Muir as an adult), Victoria Horne (Eva).

WHAT IT'S ABOUT:

An attractive young widow and her daughter move into a reputedly haunted New England cottage. Much to her surprise, Mrs. Muir is confronted by the handsome ghost of the cottage's former owner, tough but sensitive Captain Daniel Gregg. At first he tries scaring her off, but before very long Gregg comes to appreciate, and finally love, this comely stranger in his midst. Using the Captain's unvarnished life for inspiration, they write a book together, enabling the Muirs to retain Gull Cottage. Still, Lucy needs to build a new life among the living, Gregg regretfully concludes. This leads to a heartbreaking relationship with a cad, and eventually disillusioned Mrs. Muir ages into a lonely recluse. Only in death are she and her beloved sea captain reunited for all eternity.

WHY IT'S IMPORTANT:

From the first thunderous notes of Bernard Herrmann's commanding score, it's clear that *The Ghost and Mrs. Muir* has more on its mind than traditional light-hearted whimsy. Not that the film doesn't have its share of funny situations. People can hear, but not see, the salty spirit of Captain Gregg (Rex Harrison), prompting some embarrassing moments for a flustered Lucy Muir (Gene Tierney) — or Lucia, as the smitten but wise (also deceased) Captain calls her. But it's the eternal nature of human passion that seems to interest director Mankiewicz and writer Dunne, especially in the latter half of the film, where Mrs. Muir ages into a spinster rather than betray a great former romance that may or not be real. This mostly downbeat turn may have disappointed some conventionally-minded viewers of the day, but it's also what makes *Ghost and Mrs. Muir* a classic, reminding us that true love often comes at a price… even at the movies. Interestingly, Mankiewicz sets up his fanciful premise with horror movie relish, introducing Gregg into Mrs. Muir's life via a portentous thunderstorm and the darkest of interior shadows, magnified by Herrmann's ominous score. Determined to avoid genre clichés, the director avoids optical effects almost entirely, preferring conversational dramatics to fancy camera tricks and other make-believe moments. One notable exception is Daniel Gregg's farewell to his deeply-asleep Lucia, the ghost's handsome, empathic countenance slowly dissolving into nothingness even as he speaks his heartbreaking final words. Although the attractive leads take center stage, as they rightly should, a host of impressive supporting performances add to *The Ghost*'s credibility. George Sanders, just three years before he'd win an Oscar as Addison DeWitt in JLM's *All About Eve*, plays his trademark cad with customary relish. Meanwhile, little Natalie Wood is adorable as Lucy's precocious daughter Anna; although she plays no actual scenes opposite The Ghost (unlike her great exchanges with Santa Claus in *Miracle on 34th Street*), it's mentioned that she dreams about gruff but lovable father-figure Gregg, just like her beautiful mom, whose fantasies are decidedly more adult.

In the 1960s, NBC produced a TV series version of *The Ghost and Mrs. Muir*, featuring a well-cast Edward Mulhare and Hope Lange in the title roles. Although pleasant, the show lacked Mankiewicz's unique, never replicated sense of melancholy.

aka Scrooge

Poster/photos: © 1951 Renown Pictures Corporation (U.K.)/United Artists

WHO MADE IT:

Renown Pictures (U.K.)/United Artists (U.S.). Director/Producer: Brian Desmond-Hurst. Producer: Writer: Noel Langley, based on the novel by Charles Dickens. Cinematography (b/w with color tints): C. Pennington-Richards. Music: Richard Addinsell. Starring Alastair Sim (Ebenezer Scrooge), Kathleen Harrison (Mrs. Dilber), Mervyn Johns (Bob Cratchit), Hermione Baddeley (Mrs. Cratchit), Michael Hordern (Jacob Marley/Marley's Ghost), George Cole (Young Scrooge), John Charlesworth (Peter Cratchit), Francis De Wolff (Spirit of Christmas Present), Rona Anderson (Alice), Jack Warner (Mr. Jorkin), Carol Marsh (Fran Scrooge), Miles Malleson (Old Joe), Ernest Thesiger (The Undertaker), Brian Worth (Fred). Michael Dolan (Spirit of Christmas Past), Patrick MacNee (Young Marley), Peter Bull (First Businessman)

WHAT IT'S ABOUT:

The meanest miser in old London, businessman Ebenezer Scrooge receives a ghostly visit from his deceased partner, Jacob Marley, on Christmas Eve. Marley castigates Scrooge for his selfish ways and contempt for humanity, but offers a unique chance for redemption: three spirits will visit him during the course of the night, in an effort to open the reprobate's eyes and heart to a better, more charitable approach to life. The Ghost of Christmas past reveals how young Ebenezer first lost his way, becoming obsessed with financial gain; the Ghost of Christmas Present visits the poor but happy family of Bob Cratchit, Scrooge's overworked clerk, and the hopeful happiness of his cheerful nephew; the Ghost of Christmas Yet to Come forecasts a bleak fate for the old miser. Dramatically affected by these visions, Scrooge emerges from his dream with new, altruistic values.

WHY IT'S IMPORTANT:

Conceived after the first decade of popular psychoanalysis, this version of *Christmas Carol* is no Hallmark-style holiday confection, but a dark, uncompromising portrait of humanity lost… and thankfully regained. Shaking off the fuzzy charm of MGM's 1938 adaptation, Brian Desmond-Hurst zeroes in on the rich gothic atmospheric of decay and dread that a realistic portrait of Ebenezer Scrooge can't help but embrace. This subtle variation of *Dorian Gray* doesn't need a deteriorating portrait to remind us how wretched Mr. Scrooge is; it's right there in Sim's sagging face and viper eyes. In an extensive "ghost of Christmas past" sequence (shortest of the three dreams in Hollywood's take), we live through every damaging detail of a promising young life gone awry, starting with rejection at home and the tragic death of Scrooge's beloved sister Fran (Carol Marsh). Played perfectly by George Cole, who references Sim's mannerisms without mimicking them, young Scrooge and his ambitious partner Jacob Marley (Patrick MacNee in an early role) are the *Mad Men* of their day, casually engulfing competitors and increasing their power base in an indifferent world that seems to punish common decency and reward avarice. How little things seem to have changed since Dickens' day. And yet there's certainly sympathy for the devil here, even if a lifetime of sinning certifies one's fate. Marley's ghost returns decades later (once experienced, Michael Hordern's high-strung take is never forgotten), especially since his good turn for former partner Scrooge condemns him to a monstrous limbo filled with equally lost and fettered souls. Fortunately, the story's anti-hero fares somewhat better, mostly because of this generally forgotten sacrifice. It's a credit to actor Sim that he's just as convincing as a redeemed lovable eccentric as he is a shambling piker. Wisely underplaying Scrooge's most famous declarations, he is ably supported by a plethora of fine British character actors, Mervyn Johns (as Bob Cratchit), Kathleen Harrison, Miles Malleson and Ernest Thesiger among them. Best scenes: Scrooge returning home amidst expressionistic shadows and weird, bedeviling sound effects; Marley's Ghost howling at his gibbering former partner; Fran's deathbed passing; Scrooge running into close-up, only to be stopped by the methodically raised hand of Ghost of Christmas Yet to Come; funny exchange with Mrs. Dilber as she mistakes the Christmas present a rejuvenated ES has given her for a bribe

Old Jacob Marley (Michael Hordern) haunts former partner Scrooge (Alastair Sim).

The sights, sounds and experiences endured by Scrooge in this film adaptation are far more harrowing than in previous versions.

The Bergman-like Ghost of Christmas to Come stops frantic Scrooge in his tracks.

MGM's 1938 incarnation of *A Christmas Carol* (with Reginald Owen, and produced by Joseph L. Mankiewicz) is a reasonably-entertaining family movie without the spooky expressionism that characterizes Desmond-Hurst's film.

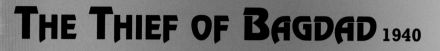

WHO MADE IT:

London Film Productions (U.K.)/United Artists (U.S.). Directors: Ludwig Berger, Michael Powell, Tim Whelan. Producers: Alexander Korda, Zoltan Korda, William Cameron Menzies. Writers: Miles Malleson, Lajos Biro. Cinematography (Technicolor): George Perinal, Osmond Borradaile. Music: Miklos Rozsa. Starring: Conrad Veidt (Jaffar), Sabu (Abu), June Duprez (Princess), John Justin (Ahmad), Rex Ingram (Djinn), Miles Malleson (Sultan), Morton Selten (The Old King), Mary Morris (Halima; Silver Maid), Bruce Winston (The Merchant).

WHAT IT'S ABOUT:

In ancient Bagdad, a young thief named Abu befriends a handsome young prince who was tricked out of his rule by a maleficent sorcerer known as Jaffar. Both boy and man manage to escape execution, swiftly embarking on a series of astonishing adventures. Complicating matters, the youthful prince is hopelessly in love with a local sultan's comely daughter – the same woman desired by evil, vengeful Jaffar. Separated from his friend, Abu uncorks a bottled genie who reveals himself as a threatening giant, and only quick thinking turns this monster into an ally. Riding a magic carpet stolen from benevolent Elders, the thief-turned-hero finally returns to Bagdad and destroys his wizard antagonist. Rightful rule is restored, the overjoyed lovers marry, and free spirit Abu narrowly escapes a fate worse than death – schoolwork!

WHY IT'S IMPORTANT:

Korda's answer to MGM's *The Wizard of Oz*, *The Thief of Bagdad* is a sumptuous Arabian fantasy built around the unique presence of star Sabu, an engaging young Indian performer who also turns up in an equally colorful adaptation of Kipling's *The Jungle Book* a few years later. Sabu as Abu is a little thief destined to become a celebrated hero, along the way helping a double-crossed prince regain his throne while matching wits with evil-eyed sorcerers and unpredictable, mountain-sized genies. With William Cameron Menzies in charge of production design (a year after his work on *Gone With the Wind*) and Miklos Rozsa delivering one of his most charming and memorable scores, including a vocal ditty for Sabu, *Thief of Bagdad* still has the power to wow youthful viewers even in the Harry Potter-centric 21st Century.

Although the romantic leads are relatively negligible (lovely June Duprez is also featured in Korda's *Four Feathers*), the film's resident villain Jaffar nearly steals the show from its youthful lead, which takes more than a little doing. Clearly up to the task is Conrad Veidt, who almost played Dracula in 1931 and will shortly achieve immortality as Nazi colonel Strassa in *Casablanca* (1942). Veidt is never less than electrifying, whether overwhelming enemies with a sustained, penetrating stare, or trying desperately to win the affections of a repulsed princess. In a standout sequence, Jaffar slays her toy-loving sultan father (Miles Malleson, who co-authored *Thief*'s screenplay) with a sexy, blue-skinned, multi-armed assassin (Mary Morris) who requires "winding up" like his other playthings. This creature's embrace is exquisitely deadly, yet fully amoral, her blank look after the killing more disturbing than a traditional villain's dark gloating. Eventually becoming an icon for the movie, Rex Ingram's brawny, pointy-eared giant of a genie, tricked into serving as both mentor and aerial transporter of resourceful Abu, enjoys some of *Thief*'s richest dialogue. Neither friend nor foe, Ingram's super-genie is something of an enigma, reveling in his new freedom as he soars into the heavens, leaving his desperate master to starve to death on a mountaintop.

Although a 1960 remake with Steve Reeves is surprisingly enjoyable, it's Korda's lavish Technicolor production, shot at the height of studio system extravagance, that rightfully steals our heart. Not even the Blue Rose of Forgetfulness can erase its lasting impact.

ABOVE: Youthful actor Sabu is the unlikely heir to silent swashbuckler Douglas Fairbanks' throne, playing the titular Thief in this grand adventure fable intended as Korda's answer to MGM's lavish *The Wizard of Oz*. RIGHT: The toy-turned-living (and flying) horse dazzles the citizens of Bagdad, who know a great special effect when they see one.

LEFT: The murderous Silver Maid (Mary Morris). RIGHT: Jaffar (Conrad Veidt) seduces Ahmad (John Justin).

RIGHT: The Princess (June Duprez) is spellbound by the magical properties of the Blue Rose, a big deal in Steve Reeves' 1960 re-working. BELOW: After saving his friends and Bagdad itself, Abu takes off on his flying carpet for more fun ("…and adventure, at last!").

ABOVE: Nominal star John Justin (Ahmad) was soon supplanted by Jon Hall in lesser Sabu adventure flicks.

Sabu sits within the full-size Genie hand prop. A giant artificial foot was also constructed (page 163), along with enormous shoulders and hair-strands for Sabu to hold on to during the flying sequences.

Movie mogul Alexander Korda of England thought big . . . in this particular case, quite literally. His mega-budgeted Arabian nights fantasy *The Thief of Bagdad* boasted among its many marvels an enormous, bald-headed genie (RIGHT, Rex Ingram), who threatens but ultimately aids little master Sabu. Lavish, special effects-filled *Thief* was Korda's Technicolor answer to MGM's *The Wizard of Oz*. Although romantic leads John Justin and June Duprez never achieved stardom (Duprez is equally exquisite in Korda's *Four Feathers*), Sabu became a Hollywood favorite during the 1940s, as did resident villain supreme Conrad Veidt.

WHO MADE IT:

Columbia Pictures (U.S.). Director/Producer: Frank Capra. Writer: Robert Riskin, based on the novel by James Hilton. Cinematography (b/w): Joseph Walker. Music: Dimitri Tiompkin. Starring Ronald Colman (Robert Conway), Jane Wyatt (Sonda), Edward Everett Horton (Lovett), John Howard (George Conway), Thomas Mitchell (Barnard), Margo (Maria), Isabel Jewell (Gloria), H.B. Warner (Chang), Sam Jaffe (High Lama).

WHAT IT'S ABOUT:

English diplomat Robert Conway helps a planeful of civilians escape death during a bloody uprising, only to find himself and his passengers abducted by the gun-wielding pilot. After an extended journey into uncharted snow-capped regions, the group crash-lands with little hope of rescue from the outside world. Miraculously, Conway and his people are escorted to a fantastic community known as Shangri-La. There, an aging wise man leader known as Father Peru, who is fearful that humanity is destroying itself, has been collecting the great artistic accomplishments of mankind to preserve them forever in this isolated paradise. Conway learns that he has been personally selected to continue Peru's noble work after the old leader's death, but Robert's restless brother George is determined to leave. An ill-advised escape with one of the locals results in a bizarre and terrifying event, proving Peru's fantastic warnings to be true. Against all odds, Conway braves the elements and manages to find his way back to Shangri-La, fulfilling his unique destiny.

WHY IT'S IMPORTANT:

Columbia's fair-haired genius after the spectacular success of *It Happened One Night*, Frank Capra had enough clout to ram his pet project, an expensive adaptation of James Hilton's *Lost Horizon*, into full production. Hollywood critics were skeptical, and not just because of the hard-to-swallow fantasy content of Hilton's utopian premise. "Nothing happens once they reach Shangri-la," naysayers groused. "This place is such a paradise, there's no conflict in the story." Unless, of course, you consider choosing between a glorious humanist dream and the harsh realities of war-torn 1937 to be a trivial mental exercise. Or how about the decision to abandon true love in favor of lonely, pointless civic duty? Then there's the primal obligation of brotherly concern to consider, along with the purely physical, ultra-daunting challenge of risking life and limb in freezing weather upon massive mountains and snowy ravines. Clearly, Capra considered these and other plot elements dramatically satisfying enough to sustain viewer interest over the long haul.

That said, there is a peculiar, possibly unintentional undercurrent of compromised morality in Hilton's fountain of youth paradise, beginning with the semi-savage abduction itself. It's a tad harsh to categorize Chang as an out-and-out liar, but he's certainly a master of half-truths and personable deception. Yes, Maria's spooky age regression suggests that he and Peru were telling the truth all along. Yet why would this apparently rational young woman rather kill herself than live another day in "paradise"? Clearly not everyone in the Valley of the New Moon is as blissfully content as Shangri-La's leaders would have us believe.

Lost Horizon was always flapdoodle, but the wish-fulfillment comfort zone provided by such a utopian dream never fails to soothe decent people looking for easy answers. Or at least a brief respite in an imaginary land without strife or conflict... a living death for some, eternal

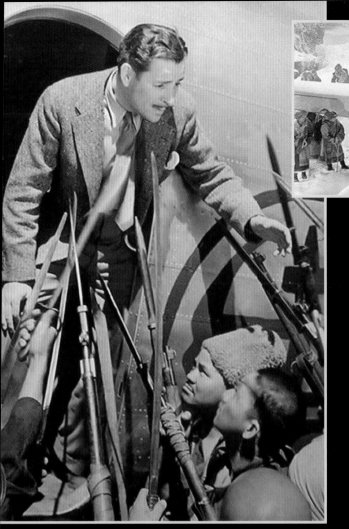

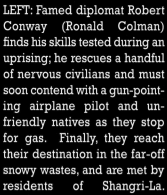

LEFT: Famed diplomat Robert Conway (Ronald Colman) finds his skills tested during an uprising; he rescues a handful of nervous civilians and must soon contend with a gun-pointing airplane pilot and unfriendly natives as they stop for gas. Finally, they reach their destination in the far-off snowy wastes, and are met by residents of Shangri-La.

BELOW: The magnificent main building of the "magical" monastery itself.
INSERT: The High Lama (Sam Jaffe) envisions a kinder, gentler world.

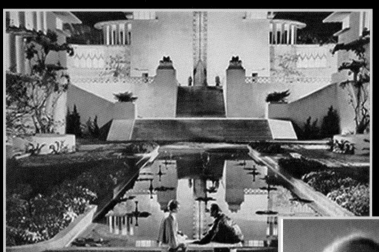

BELOW: Much of the film's dramatic conflict stems from Robert's discontented brother (the floored John Howard).

RIGHT: The love story between Conway and Shangri-La's resident "princess" Sonja (Jane Wyatt) was cut to the bone for mainstream release; it isn't even clear that she masterminded and oversaw his abduction.

In a discarded prologue, rescued Conway is stricken with amnesia; playing a Chopin composition reminds him of the fantastic extended-age miracles of Shangri-La.

165

DESIGNING A PROGRESSIVE PARADISE

In a bold touch, filmmaker Frank Capra chose to give his Shangri-La monastery a modern, quasi-futuristic look, enhancing the forward-thinking dogma of its noble inhabitants. In many ways, the temple and adjacent grounds featured in *Lost Horizon* are more than just exotic settings, but very real characters, and the contrast between glowing incandescent towers and torch-brandishing natives is startling and memorable. THIS PAGE: Shangri-La comes to life, first as a miniature (ABOVE), then a highly-detailed glass painting (RIGHT).

MIRACLE ON 34TH STREET 1947

 96 1.37

WHO MADE IT:

20th Century-Fox (U.S.). Director: George Seaton. Producer: William Pearlberg. Writer: George Seaton, based on a story by Valentine Davies. Cinematography (b/w): Lloyd Ahern, Charles Clarke. Music: Cyril Mockridge. Starring: Maureen O'Hara (Doris Walker), John Payne (Fred Gailey), Edmund Gwenn (Kris Kringle), Gene Lockhart (Judge Henry Harper), Natalie Wood (Susan Walker), Porter Hall (Granville Sawyer), William Frawley (Charles Halloran), Jerome Cowan (Dist. Atty. Thomas Mara), Philip Tonge (Julian Shellhammer), Thelma Ritter (Peter's mom).

WHAT IT'S ABOUT:

A man who calls himself Kris Kringle becomes Macy's official Santa Claus, saving the Thanksgiving Day parade from disaster and bringing joy into the lives of children everywhere. But is lovable Kris truly St. Nick, or merely a delusional old man? This is the dilemma facing department store events director Doris Walker and her serious-minded toddler daughter Susan, who befriends Kris. When the old man is placed on trial because of his allegedly unstable ways, he is defended by a worldly young lawyer who is smitten with Doris but opposed to her relentlessly realistic approach to life. Through cleverness and faith, and a little help from the U.S. postal department, he eventually proves that his client is indeed the one-and-only Santa Claus.

WHY IT'S IMPORTANT:

One look at the trailer and it's clear that 20th Century-Fox wasn't sure how to sell this whimsical holiday offering (released during the summer), although the production itself is first-rate and represents a genuine show of faith on the part of the studio. Kris Kringle's opening credits walk through Manhattan sets up the annual Thanksgiving Day parade, filmed as it happened with Hollywood performers Maureen O'Hara and Philip Tonge on location for a few brief outdoor scenes. Writer/Director George Seaton sets up two conflicts and a single theme within one small family unit: Can worldly attorney Fred Gailey (John Payne) convince once-burned divorcee Doris Walker (O'Hara) that imagination and faith are the key to personal happiness, even as Kris Kringle (Edmund Gwenn, in his signature role) tries to do the same with Doris' relentlessly reality-minded little daughter (charmer Natalie Wood)? It all hinges on the outcome of a question every kid wonders about sooner or later; Seaton and company take the eternal "Is there a Santa Claus?" controversy right into a New York City courtroom, having fun with the notion without ever fully revealing the truth about good-natured Kris. He's cleverly presented as an escapee from an old age home, allowing for a more down-to-Earth interpretation, and even the tell-tale cane left behind in Susan Walker's dream house isn't exactly proof of supernatural intervention. But in keeping with *Miracle*'s amiable theme, the viewer's conclusion says a lot about how he views the world blend his (hopefully) happy place in it. Given this movie's thesis and the utterly charming way it plays out, it's likely most observers will giddily believe that Kris Kringle a la Edmund Gwenn is indeed the genuine article. Or should be.

9 ORPHEUS 1950

WHO MADE IT:

DisCinema (France). Director/Writer: Jean Cocteau. Producer: Andre Paulve. Cinematography (b/w): Jacqueline Sadoul. Music: Georges Auric. Starring Jean Marais (Orphee), Marie Dea (Eurydice), Francois Perier (Heurtebise), Maria Casares (The Princess – Death), Juliette Greco (Aglaonice), Henri Cremieux (The Editor), Roger Bin (The Poet), Rene Worms (Judge), Edouard Dermithe (Jacques Cegeste).

WHAT IT'S ABOUT:

Popular poet Orphee, disillusioned and vaguely dissatisfied with his marriage, is taken on a bizarre journey by Death, who has assumed the form of a captivating woman known as the Princess. Orphee soon becomes obsessed with her, and also with the cryptic messages that come through the radio of the car she leaves behind. Eventually Orphee's wife

Eurydice is killed by the Princess' henchmen, and he must follow her into the Underworld. Although she still loves this mortal man, the Princess sends Orphee back to the land of he living, with his still-loving wife.

WHY IT'S IMPORTANT:

The centerpiece of a unique trilogy, Jean Cocteau's *Orpheus* is often described as a cinematic poem. Fair enough. But unlike the director's relatively graspable *La Belle et la Bette*, *Orpheus* scores as a perplexing pseudo-noir with fertile New Wave European pretentions, an exercise in symbolism and surreal special effects. Slightly miscast as the poet Orphee, preternaturally handsome and regal Jean Marais finds himself torn between worlds and two worshipful lovers, his wife Eurydice (played with coquettish warmth by Marie Dea) and Death herself, in the form of a stoic Princess (Maria Casares). As if this triangle isn't complicated enough, Cocteau ups the ante by spending a good deal of time with Princess Death's chauffeur, sad but sensitive Heurtebise (Francois Perier), charting his gentle love for Orphee's neglected wife. In a different context, one can imagine a free-wheeling romantic comedy built around these same four befuddled entities.

But that's not what Mr. Cocteau has in mind. Rather, we are treated to the textures and illogic of a living dream, clearly identified as such by the protagonist. From simple, barely noticeable touches (rear-screen backgrounds in the negative as Orphee approaches the Princess' castle, an invisible hand belonging to ghostly Heurtebise hanging up the telephone, etc.) to the showcase mirror penetrations and bleak, windy netherworlds, no one does this sort of thing better than Jean Cocteau. His trademark slow-motion reversals are in full-force here, especially effective as magical gloves envelope hands or when the Princess summons an entranced Eurydice from her deathbed. It's ironic that the best remembered sleight-of-hand in this entire movie is the stunned, post-dead heroine vanishing in an instant when Orphee accidentally catches a glimpse of her in his rear-view mirror – a simple cut-and-resume exercise that any first year film student can achieve with ease.

Not for all tastes, but mesmerizing if an indulgent escape into surreal thematics and jaw-dropping visuals are to your liking, *Orpheus* does justice to its legend while creating a significant new one in the process.

8 STAIRWAY TO HEAVEN 1946

-104- 1.37

aka A Matter of Life and Death   Poster/photos: © 1946 J. Arthur Rank/Universal Pictures

DAVID NIVEN   ROGER LIVESEY
RAYMOND MASSEY
in

A matter of
Life and
Death

IN TECHNICOLOR
KIM HUNTER
MARIUS GORING

THE FIRST BRITISH
ROYAL COMMAND
FILM

MICHAEL POWELL
EMERIC PRESSBURGER

A
PRODUCTION OF
THE ARCHERS

EAGLE-LION DISTRIBUTION

WHO MADE IT:

The Archers/Eagle-Lion Distributors Limited(U.K.)/Universal Pictures (U.S.). Directors/Producers/Writers: Michael Powell, Emeric Pressberger. Cinematography (Dye-Monochrome/Technicolor): Jack Cardiff. Music: Allan Gray. Starring David Niven (Peter Carter), Kim Hunter (June), Roger Livesey (Dr. Frank Reeves), Marius Goring (Conductor 71), Robert Coote (Bob Trubshawe), Raymond Massey (Abraham Farlan), Kathleen Bryon (An Angel), Abraham Sofaer (The Judge/The Surgeon).

WHAT IT'S ABOUT:

During WWII, pilot Peter Carter bails out of his doomed airplane, but miraculously survives. Soon he's approached by a heavenly messenger who explains that a mistake's been made, and that Peter must prepare himself for the afterlife. Carter protests, insisting that he has fallen in love with American girl June during the interim. This sets the stage for a fantastic cosmic appeal that may or my not be in the disturbed airman's mind. Dr. Reeves, a sympathetic brain specialist, assists Peter in coping with this unique delusion, but happens to die in an accident just before his patient's sanity-saving operation. The scholarly Reeves soon reappears in "Heaven" to defend Carter's right to remain on Earth as a living, and loving, human being.

WHY IT'S IMPORTANT:

A Matter of Life and Death is a witty social satire that is sometimes mistaken for a commercial farce in the American tradition of *Here Comes Mr. Jordan*. Although both films share superficial plot similarities, one is a broad character comedy, the other an oddball art house diatribe about everything from condescending U.S.O. shows to its ultimate, wryly controversial "all men are created equal, but our finer specimens should be treated better" supposition. Peter Carter (David Niven) is certainly a catch by anyone's standards, handsome, brave, romantic, even modest about his published poetry. If everything we're seeing in "Heaven" is simply his super-imaginative subconscious working overtime, Carter ultimately saves himself by incorporating Dr. Reeves into his trial for life; clearly this remarkable man deserves a second chance.

Of course, one expects something outlandish and offbeat from Powell-Pressburger's creative union. Reversing the *Wizard of Oz*-like cliché of rendering the real world in drab black-and-white, P&P experiment with subtle blue-gray dyes for their Heavenly palette and use them inventively throughout. To convey Trubshaw's return to Earth, for example, they remain on Robert Coote's grinning monochromatic close-up and gradually – almost imperceptibly – drop color in. (Infuriatingly, preparers of the recent DVD re-mastering transformed all of these subtle tones into burnished black-and-white, obliterating P&P's specific creative touches apparently without realizing it.)

As usual, charming lead David Niven acquits himself well, with sad-faced Kim Hunter fitting the bill nicely as an American "Juliet" for their star-crossed romance. They share the especially vivid spotlight with Colonel Blimp himself, Roger Livesey, Raymond Massey as a bitter Revolutionary War patriot, and, most flamboyant of all, *Red Shoes*' romantic lead Marius Goring in the "Everett Edward Horton" role of fey, flustered Conductor 71, who sets the story in motion by losing death-jumper Peter Carter in that "accursed English fog." While all aspects of art direction and visual décor are to be commended (Paradise itself is an intricate arena), special mention should be made of the film's glorious period costumes, designed to represent a plethora of different cultures from various time periods. Although Goring visits Earth enough to show off his fancy French duds, the entire main cast is invited down the stairway (and into full Tech IB) for the final scene, and their colorful costumes are, as we suspected, beyond breathtaking.

Best scenes: Peter's final moments in his burning plane, Conductor 71's flower-filled arrival on Earth, the fantastic trial itself.

ABOVE: Pilot Peter Carter (David Niven) says his last to a pretty American girl via radio, before bailing out of his burning plane sans parachute. RIGHT: Heavenly Conductor 71 (Marius Goring) clearly relishes his Technicolored time on Earth.

ABOVE: Progressive humanist Dr. Reeves (Roger Livesey, Colonel Blimp himself) pleads Carter's case before a fantastic Heavenly assembly conjured by his client's especially vivid imagination.

LEFT, BELOW: Before reaching a final verdict, the Heavenly judge and jury descend the titular (in the U.S., anyway) stairway and materialize before Carter's operation in order to question him.

Acclaimed filmmakers Powell and Pressburger often imbued their films with fantasy undertones (*The Red Shoes*, for example); but *A Matter of Life and Death* directly embraces the genre.

7 JULIET OF THE SPIRITS 1965

137 1.85

WHO MADE IT:

Rizzoli Film/Cineriz (Italy). Director: Federico Fellini. Producers: Henry Deutschmeister, Clemente Fracassi, Angelo Rizzoli (uncredited). Writers: Federico Fellini, Tullio Pinelli, Ennio Flaiano, Brunello Rondi. Cinematography (Technicolor): Gianni Di Venanzo. Music: Nino Rota. Starring: Giulietta Masina (Giulietta Boldrini), Sandra Milo (Suzy/Iris/Fanny), Mario Pisu (Giorgio), Valentina Cortesa (Valentina), Valeska Gert (Pijma), Jose De Villalonga (Giorgio's friend), Fredrich von Ledebur (Medium), Caterina Boratto (Giulietta's mother), Lou Gilbert (Grandfather), Luisa Della Noce (Adele).

WHAT IT'S ABOUT:

A married woman, who is often overshadowed by the beauty of her mother and siblings, begins to suspect that her husband of several years is unfaithful. She retreats into the world of fashionable mysticism, but wandering spirits finally suggest that she spread her wings by allowing a free-spirited neighbor to open her up sexually. Reality and fantasy interpenetrate as below-the-surface passions are indulged, infidelity is countered by effective detective work, phantom guests come calling, and the woman discovers her own unique road to emancipation.

WHY IT'S IMPORTANT:

After the critical and commercial triumphs of *La Strada* and *La Dolce Vita*, Fellini's first color endeavor failed big-time with international audiences. This is perhaps understandable, in that *Juliet of the Spirits* is a personal, aggressively elusive work, the filmmaker's most perplexing until 1970's *Satyricon* pushed his controversial predilections to the max. Although it's a self-confessed fantasy filled with mediums, astrologers and at least three party-crashing phantasms, *Spirits* spends most of its considerable running time focusing on Juliet Boldrini, played by the director's real-life spouse Giulietta Masina. This put-upon heroine must deal not only with restless spirits unleashed by her troubled psyche and some recreational occultism, but a philandering husband named Giorgio, who forgets anniversaries and seems content with frivolous, ultimately empty romantic distractions. It's perhaps inevitable that an amoral new neighbor (Sandra Milo, in one of three juicy roles), acting as surrogate for the promiscuous ghosts, becomes Juliet's "guide" to a far more exciting and uninhibited approach to life. The orgy next door provides ample temptation, and no one can blame a neglected housewife for having a little fun in her spare time.

Although Katherine Hepburn was originally mentioned for the lead (a fascinating choice), Fellini insisted on using his wife, probably because the entire project was conceived as an odd therapeutic exercise for the marriage-challenged filmmaker. He paints a thorough psychological study of his central character (some have opined that Juliet is actually Federico in drag), burdening the poor woman with a cold-fish mother (Caterina Boratto), a teenage friend who kills herself for lack of love, and a history of no sexual partners other than her husband. That Juliet starts seeing and hearing picturesque ghosts who exhort her to "open up" to other romantic experiences comes as no real surprise, given her logical dissatisfaction and Giorgio's chronic apathy.

In terms of technique, *Juliet of the Spirits* is remarkably sophisticated without being self-consciously arty, using Technicolor's unique palette to catch subtle shadings and other ethereal effects (it's interesting to compare Fellini's use of the three-strip process with Powell and Pressburger films from the '40s, such as *Red Shoes* or *Black Narcissus*). Still, this is mostly a movie about faces... Masina's, primarily. Through her sensitive features and low-key responses, we visit a world that isn't quite there, but resonates strongly. Like all great artists, Fellini shamelessly indulges his personal passions, presses friends and family into convenient service, ultimately uses the cinematic medium to better understand himself. Those who can tune into this peculiar wavelength will come away impressed, while viewers who have trouble with creative abstraction are likely to shake their heads in bewilderment.

ABOVE: Guiletta (Guiletta Masina) looks to spiritualists and fortune tellers for comfort as her marriage with Giorgio begins to disintegrate. RIGHT: Caterina Boratto as the heroine's ice cold, hard-to-please mother in a striking visual.

Guiletta's privileged background and sense of entitlement is part of what fuels her apparent fantasies. Paralleling this, Fellini family members contributed to *Juliet of the Spirits* in any number of ways, from financial to artistic.

Ghosts or fantasies? Traumatizing echoes from the past haunt Guiletta, but she's learned to live with them. Literally.

That's Federico Fellini behind the shades on the set of *Juliet of the Spirits*, his first movie in Technicolor. The film's lavish costumes cried out for a rainbow treatment.

6 THE 7TH VOYAGE OF SINBAD 1958 · 88 · 1.66 ·

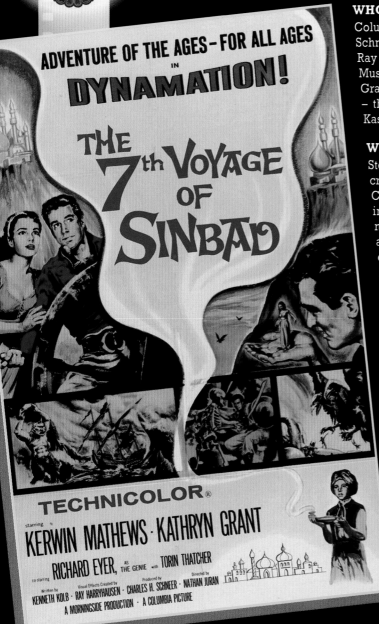

WHO MADE IT:

Columbia Pictures (U.S.). Director: Nathan Juran. Producer: Charles H. Schneer. Writer: Kenneth Kolb. Special Visual Effects (Dynamation): Ray Harryhausen. Cinematography (Technicolor): Wilke Cooper. Music: Bernard Herrmann. Starring Kerwin Mathews (Sinbad), Kathryn Grant (Princess Parisa), Torin Thatcher (Sokurah), Richard Eyer (Barani – the Genie), Alex Mango (Caliph), Danny Green (Karim), Harold Kasket (Sultan), Alfred Brown (Harufa), Nana de Herrera (Sadi).

WHAT IT'S ABOUT:

Stopping for provisions on the isle of Colossa, Sinbad and his intrepid crew rescue the magician Sokurah from the clutches of a rampaging Cyclops. The sorcerer loses his magic lamp during this skirmish and insists that they return for it, eventually forcing Sinbad's hand by miniaturizing his beloved Princess Parisa. Soon after, the rescuers are imperiled by additional Cyclops, a monstrous two-headed eagle, and an immense fire-breathing dragon controlled by the evil magician. Help from a youthful genie named Barani, who inhabits the retrieved magic lamp, enables Sinbad to finally restore the princess to her normal size and thwart Sokorah's evil schemes.

WHY IT'S IMPORTANT:

With the sci-fi creature cycle of the '50s drawing to a close, fx master Ray Harryhausen (*Beast from 20,000 Fathoms*, *Earth vs. the Flying Saucers*) took a headlong plunge into Arabian fantasy, mostly because of his own desire to see a Sinbad movie "done right." Fantastic monsters were often spoken about in previous films about the fearless sailor's exploits, but rarely visualized. This all changed in 1958 when an orange, satyr-like Cyclops stormed out of a mountain cave and into our imaginations. Simply put, *The 7th Voyage of Sinbad* was *Star Wars* for kids of its era, a groundbreaking, episodic adventure ride filled with perilous situations and astonishing bogey-beasts. And all in eye-popping Technicolor!

Reflecting the decade's sensibilities, hero Sinbad (Kerwin Mathews) is a post-WWII American male role model: handsome, athletic, straightforward and dull (Mathews would be allowed far more charm in his follow-up Harryhausen effort, *The 3 Worlds of Gulliver*). A bit livelier is Kathryn Grant as imperiled Princess Parisa, while bullet-headed sorcerer Torin Thatcher threatens to steal the scenes that tweenage antagonist Richard Eyer (previously *The Invisible Boy*) doesn't inhabit. Overall, it's a charming surrogate family unit vs. a nasty villain with all kinds of magical surprises up his sleeve, miniaturizing an unsuspecting Grant among them.

But the real stars of *Sinbad*, not surprisingly, are Harryhausen's animated monsters. The Cyclops is perhaps his most iconic creation, an ingenious, never-quite-repeated melding of mythology and weird science. Also memorable is the dinosaur-like dragon saved for Sinbad's climax, a two-headed eagle and its progeny, an exotic snake woman, and a living, dueling skeleton, precursor to the boney battlers showcased a few years later in *Jason and the Argonauts*.

Although not quite as smooth and A-level as the Harryhausen-Charles Schneer epics that followed, *Sinbad* remains an unforgettable dazzler, from RH's jaw-dropping set-pieces to the romantic, rousing music score by Bernard Herrmann. It rocked the world of fantasy-craving Baby Boomers in '58, establishing an exotic adventure formula that steadily evolved into those super-duper franchises that thrive every summer at the box-office. And it all started here, folks, on the colorful, monster-infested isle of Colossa...

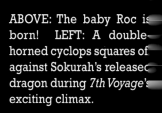

ABOVE: The baby Roc is born! LEFT: A double-horned cyclops squares of against Sokurah's released dragon during *7th Voyage's* exciting climax.

Sokurah the magician (Torin Thatcher) commands the power of a magic lamp, imperiling the lives of Princess Parisa (Kathryn Grant), Captain Sinbad (Kerwin Mathews) and his crew.

ABOVE: an alliance with the genie Barani (Richard Eyer). RIGHT: Dueling with an animated skeleton.

The illusion of Sinbad's ship at sea was achieved with a partially-built full-size set, a miniature, and some carefully-chosen stock shots from earlier Arabian nights epics.

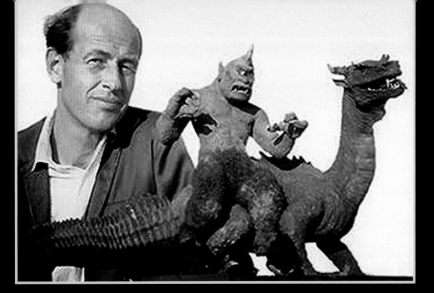

The various fabled creatures showcased in Ray Harryhausen's groundbreaking *The 7th Voyage of Sinbad* have, to their credit, a perhaps unconscious scientific flavoring as befits their atomic era origin – the Cyclops is Harryhausen's Ymir reborn, and the Dragon's a now-Technicolored Rhedosaurus, upgraded with fiery breath. ABOVE, LEFT: The master animator himself, with two of *Sinbad*'s superstars. ABOVE, RIGHT: The Cyclops armature. BELOW: Cyclops and sailor models in a posed publicity shot used in the original movie campaign. OPPOSITE PAGE: The two-headed Roc and the Dragon in all their pseudo-Darwinian glory.

MONSTERS OF SCIENCE AND SORCERY

WHO MADE IT:

Liberty Films (U.S.). Director: Frank Capra. Producer: Frank Capra. Writers: Frances Goodrich, Albert Hackett, Frank Capra, based on a story by Philip Van Doren Stern. Cinematography (b/w): Joseph Biroc, Joseph Walker. Music: Dimitri Tiompkin. Starring James Stewart (George Bailey), Donna Reed (Mary Hatch Bailey), Lionel Barrymore (Henry F. Potter), Thomas Mitchell (Uncle Billy Bailey), Henry Travers (Clarence), Beulah Bondi (Ma Bailey), Frank Faylen (Ernie Bishop), Ward Bond (Bert), Gloria Grahame (Violet Bick), H.B. Warner (Mr. Gower), Frank Albertson (Sam Wainwright), Todd Karns (Harry Bailey), Samuel S. Hinds (Peter Bailey).

WHAT IT'S ABOUT:

Novice guardian angel Clarence reviews the life of George Bailey, a decent but distraught family man who has come to the end of his rope and is contemplating suicide. Young George grows to maturity in the American hamlet of Bedford Falls, a town under the thumb of selfish, scheming Henry F. Potter. Only Bailey's Building and Loan stands between survival and bankruptcy for most of George's neighbors, and he sacrifices his own ambitions to keep this humble institution alive. When a relative loses George's money on Christmas Eve, he nearly does away with himself until Clarence steps in and shows him what life would have been like if he'd never been born. Blessed with the love of his wife Mary and a plethora of grateful friends, Bailey soon discovers that, in all the important ways, he's the richest man in town.

WHY IT'S IMPORTANT:

Unsuccessful when first released, re-discovered by film historians in the '60s, embraced with a vengeance by Baby Boomers in the late '70s and '80s to the point where it became a ubiquitous Christmas season irritant, *It's a Wonderful Life* remains a wonderful movie. Directed by Frank Capra at the peak of his considerable skills, it's the populist auteur's most personal creation, an overview of society, mortal existence and the preternatural importance of a single human life. Sentimental yet slyly subversive, the film is an ideal vehicle for everyman star Jimmy Stewart, just back from serving in WWII and himself uncertain about the future. He and Capra caught lightning in a bottle with *Mr. Smith Goes to Washington* back in 1939, and they do it all over again here… even if it takes the public a tad longer than usual to realize it.

Requiring an extended running time to chart a man's life, the guardian angel set-up is nearly forgotten when it returns to the story more than an hour in. It's actually annoying to switch from the heavy drama of George Bailey's tear-and-tumble moment in the bar to magical Clarence (Henry Travers) jumping into the river. But once the ramifications of George's non-existence begin to play out, the brilliance of this simple "what if?" concept hits home with a wallop. Yes, it's Capra's version of *A Christmas Carol*, with impeccable, wheelchair-bound Lionel Barrymore chewing the scenery as a Scrooge-inspired villain. Not to be overlooked is Donna Reed's sensitive performance as wife Mary, Thomas Mitchell as scene-stealing Uncle Billy, and the usual gang of lovable Capra character players. Still, the wonderful life in question belongs to Stewart's George Bailey, the Sam-next-door who tries to do the right thing and is stymied for his empathy and compassion. Capra nails Bailey's existential despair throughout, never more effectively than when his brother returns to Bedford Falls with a surprise wife, short-circuiting George's dreams of escape. Using a steady tracking shot to capture Stewart's tortured, deep-in-thought profile, we watch his frown gradually brighten into a warm smile, as he greets Harry's new bride and swallows this latest disappointment. It's a bittersweet feeling of helplessness, an emotion easily transmitted to most viewers. Still, *Life*'s buoyant optimism inevitably reverses all setbacks: hero George emerges from his personal purgatory to find renewal with beloved family and friends

George Bailey grows to maturity in Bedford Falls, U.S.A.

Anxious to see the world and live life to the fullest, George (James Stewart) winds up becoming a small-town family man instead. He is loved by his wife (Donna Reed), family and neighbors who help him through a life-threatening crisis one particular Christmas Eve.

A desperate George Bailey asks opposite number Mr. Potter (Lionel Barrymore) for financial help. Barrymore was scheduled to play Scrooge in 1938 when his disability prevented it.

Three key supporting players share the spotlight with Stewart: Bert the cop (TOP, Ward Bond), Uncle Billy (Thomas Mitchell), and Clarence the Angel (Henry Travers).

It's snowing in Bedford Falls, thanks to several wind machines and a beautifully-dressed Main Street set. Check out the number of studio spotlights mounted above.

Indiana Jones—the new hero from the creators of JAWS and STAR WARS.

RAIDERS of the LOST ARK

PARAMOUNT PICTURES Presents A LUCASFILM LTD. Production
A STEVEN SPIELBERG Film

Starring HARRISON FORD · JOHN RHYS-DAVIES · DENHOLM ELLIOTT
KAREN ALLEN · PAUL FREEMAN · RONALD LACEY · JOHN RHYS-DAVIES Screenplay by LAWRENCE KASDAN · ORIGINAL SOUNDTRACK ON COLUMBIA RECORDS & TAPE
and HOWARD KAZANJIAN Screenplay by LAWRENCE KASDAN Story by GEORGE LUCAS and PHILIP KAUFMAN
A PARAMOUNT PICTURE
Music by JOHN WILLIAMS Executive Producers GEORGE LUCAS and HOWARD KAZANJIAN
Produced by FRANK MARSHALL Directed by STEVEN SPIELBERG Filmed in Panavision® DOLBY STEREO®

PG PARENTAL GUIDANCE SUGGESTED
SOME MATERIAL MAY NOT BE SUITABLE FOR CHILDREN

"RAIDERS OF THE LOST ARK"

WHO MADE IT:

Paramount Pictures/Lucasfilm (U.S.). Director: Steven Spielberg. Producer: Howard Kazanjian, George Lucas, Frank Marshall, Robert Watts. Writer: Lawrence Kasden, based on a story by George Lucas and Philip Kaufman. Cinematography (Color): Douglas Slocombe. Music: John Williams. Starring Harrison Ford (Indiana Jones), Karen Allen (Marion Ravenwood), Paul Freeman (Dr. Rene Belloq), Ronald Lacey (Major Arnold Toht), John Rhys-Davies (Sallah), Denholm Elliot (Dr. Marcus Brody), Alfred Molina (Satipo), Wolf Kahler (Colonel Dietrich).

WHAT IT'S ABOUT:

Indiana Jones, adventurer, scientist and relic hunter, is approached by the government during WWII to find the fabled Lost Ark of the Covenant, a source of incredible supernatural power. Also on the trail is an unscrupulous rival scientist named Belloq, who is allied with Hitler's nefarious minions. Although the Ark is indeed found by Jones, he and feisty girlfriend Marion Ravenwood survive one jaw-dropping peril after another as both factions take turns stealing and re-stealing the precious golden chest. When it is finally opened, mystical forces emerge from within and wipe out Belloq and his Nazi partners. Spared due to their tightly-shut eyes, Indy and Marion return home with the sacred object – which is labeled top secret and shut up tight within a government warehouse.

WHY IT'S IMPORTANT:

George Lucas followed his *Flash Gordon* update with this related but somewhat different serial-inspired extravaganza, complete with rapid-paced action, old-fashioned graphics (animated map lines instead of wipes), and another rousing, gung-ho John Williams anthem. Directed with laser-like precision by Steven Spielberg, who needed a mega-hit after his extremely expensive *1941* tanked, *Raiders* scores as a charmingly inventive, slightly loopy homage to two-fisted adventure yarns of yesteryear, with influences ranging from Edgar Rice Burroughs to the James Bond films. Aware that over-the-top heroics and All-American macho posturing would appear hopelessly dated and arrogant in the post-Vietnam/Watergate era, Lucas cleverly infuses his film with the same kind of good-natured, gently self-mocking humor that characterized his *Star Wars* films. In truth, the specific idea here was to establish an intimidating, rugged, broad-shouldered man's man (*Magnum P.I.* star Tom Selleck, initially), then surprise and bemuse the audience by having this hunk respond like a sissy at the sight of a harmless snake. That's the twist. We're so sold on Dr. Jones' intensity and capabilities based on his thrilling "idol" introduction, that he remains cool even when the joke's on him. Spielberg never lets this delicate balance slip, a tonal lesson Stephen (*The Mummy*) Sommers has yet to master.

Raiders' plot may be driven by fantasy elements from antiquity, but they are rarely front-and-center; it's good guy vs. bad guy slugfests, exploding buildings and breathless car chases most patrons have come to see, the ultimate theme park rollercoaster ride, but on a movie screen. Making it all work is eventual lead Harrison Ford, Han Solo with a bullwhip, endearing himself to viewers through dry one-liners (some improvised) or by taking on oversized adversaries with amusingly grim resignation. Finally, when the Ark is ceremoniously opened a la Pandora's Box at film's end, a pre-*Poltergeist* light show dramatically commences, spewing forth Heavenly hellfire and melting stunned Nazi faces. Ironically, we learn nothing about the awesome Ark of the Covenant and its fascinating powers that we didn't already know before Indy started his hair-raising quest. But a serviceable yin/yang parallel between greedy, ruthless archeologist Belloq (Paul Freeman) and jaded but good-as-gold Jones is enough to hang this rip-roaring scenario on. Three Spielberg-directed sequels followed in the wake of *Raiders*' super-success, none of them managing to replicate the magic of this initial, perfectly-balanced foray.

LEFT: The "chased by a boulder" gag has been done in other movies (most memorably in *Journey to the Center of the Earth* '59), but as part as Spielberg's breathless introduction to Indy, it sets the stage for the over-the-top adventure to come.

LEFT: A man and his bullwhip. Harrison Ford added much to the Jones character, just as he improvised some of Han Solo's best dialogue.

ABOVE: With the help of Sallah (John Rhys-Davies), Jones manages to remove the sacred ark from its ancient burial place.

The chase is on as Indy gallops to the Nazi caravan, fights his way into the lead truck cab, slams bad guys right and left, and finally makes off with the stolen Ark.

The Ark is opened... faces melt... and our heroes survive.

Original storyboard. The character of Indy was intended for broad-shouldered Tom Selleck, who couldn't make the movie because of *Magnum P.I.* commitments.

3 BEAUTY AND THE BEAST 1946

aka La Belle et la Bette

WHO MADE IT:

Discina (France/Lopert Pictures (U.S.).   Director: Jean Cocteau. Producer: Andre Paulve. Writer: Jean Cocteau, from the story by Jeanne-Marie Leprince de Beaumont. Cinematography: Henri Alekan. Music: Georges Auric. Starring Jean Marais (The Beast/The Prince/Avenant), Josette Day (Belle), Mia Parely (Felicie), Nane Germon (Adelaide), Michel Auclair (Ludovic), Marcel Andre (Belle's Father).

WHAT IT'S ABOUT:

After a merchant loses his way in the forest and antagonizes a princely Beast , the man's lovely daughter, Belle, is compelled to return to this monster's enchanted castle as punishment.   Although initially repelled, Belle comes to pity and finally love her anguished, accursed captor. Meanwhile, the maiden's arrogant suitor learns of a treasure housed within the castle pavilion and attempts to steal it. Belle fears for the life of this creature she has come to care for, as he is dying of a broken heart. An unexpected attack from the castle's defenses slays the suitor, enabling Beauty and the now-handsome, reborn Beast to live happily ever after.

WHY IT'S IMPORTANT:

Fearlessly taking on France's most venerable fairy tale, Jean Cocteau defied conventional wisdom and scored with a straightforward live-action classic that wound up re-defining its genre. This is a children's story designed specifically for movie-going adults, especially ones with a penchant for poetry and fine art. It's also a lurid melodrama worthy of the best post-war noirs, complete with doomed anti-hero, romantic triangle and attempted heist. Although justly applauded for its use of lyrical visuals (reverse motion creating some jaw-dropping effects, like the instant creation of a necklace), it is a connection to workaday reality that gives *La Belle et la Bette* an indelible edge. Sure, there are mystical castles and enchanted forests to satisfy both story and genre requirements, all to the soaring notes of Georges Auric's characteristically grand score. But it's the consequences of unpaid bills, Belle's dreary life as a servant, and her reckless suitor's self-deceiving, doomed-to-fail ambitions that ground this adaptation, enabling us to believe the patently unbelievable.

Cocteau certainly doesn't disappoint in this latter regard, fashioning an ornate but haunted black-and-white universe that seems to emanate from the Beast's pervasive melancholy. A peculiar combination of the Cowardly Lion and Universal's Wolf Man, Marais' monster wins us over instantly with his poet's love of roses, foreshadowing the total embrace of imprisoned, but prideful, Belle. Inevitably, it is she who will come to dominate their respectful-but-nonetheless-hot (sometimes literally) personal relationship. Calling Josette Day's no-nonsense take pre-feministic may be a little extreme, but this determined young woman has known hardship and cruelty her entire life and isn't about to accept a local monarch's eloquent proclamations without a stubborn opinion or two. When he gently points out that she comforts him like a pet animal, and not the transformed prince he truly is, she thoughtlessly reminds him of his lowly nonhuman status, suggesting that what's on the outside can't totally be ignored. Eventually even the Beast must admit that the object of his transcendent affection is indeed an oddball, her contrary willfulness actually enabling their unique bond to develop. And where else is this shaggy, wiggly-eared Byron going to find a babe who actually enjoys having water slurped from her cupped hands?

Much has been made of Greta Garbo's outburst upon seeing the film's title monster switching bodies with anti-hero Avenant (also played by Marais) at the moment of this scoundrel's death. "Where is my beautiful beast?" Garbo supposedly wailed. Ironically, even Belle seems to have misgivings about this last minute swap... but that's mostly to keep her princely suitor on his toes and their relationship unpredictable, as always. Exquisite, the Beast might say... and a fitting conclusion to this cherished classic.

ABOVE, LEFT: With countless magical objects and entities on display, it's the hallway's helping hands that never fail to amaze and amuse. BELOW: Beauty (Josette Day) and Beast (Jean Marais).

Hagop Arakelian's make-up design for the Beast plays like an inspired mix of Jack Pierce's the Wolf Man and a lion-like humanoid, anticipating Roy Ashton's 1961 *The Curse of the Werewolf* as well. Unlike these other cine-monsters, the Beast can speak as well as growl, and in regal French to boot.

The Beast's rebirth in the form of arrogant Avenant is handled very differently than Larry Talbot's transformations.

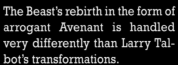

LEFT: Cocteau (with hat) on set. RIGHT: Josette Day helps co-star Marias with lunch.

WHO MADE IT:

Metro-Goldwyn-Mayer (U.S.). Director: Victor Fleming. Producer: Mervyn LeRoy Writers: Noel Langley, Florence Ryerson, Edgar Allan Woolf, from the book by Frank L. Baum. Cinematography (sepia/Technicolor): Music Harold Arlen. Starring Judy Garland (Dorothy Gale), Frank Morgan (Professor Marvel/The Wizard – Oscar Z. Diggs/Gatekeeper/Carriage Driver/Omby Amby the Palace Guard), Ray Bolger (Scarecrow/Hunk) Bert Lahr (The Cowardly Lion/Zeke), Jack Haley (The Tin Man/Hickory) Margaret Hamilton (Wicked Witch of the West/Miss Gulch), Billie Burke (Glinda), Charley Grapewin (Uncle Henry Gale), Clara Blandick (Aun Emily), Terry (Toto).

WHAT IT'S ABOUT:

A young girl from Kansas named Dorothy Gale is whisked away by a twister and deposited in a faraway fantasy land. Her only chance of returning home is to follow the Yellow Brick Road to the Emerald City for an audience with the mysterious, all-powerful Wizard of Oz Along the way, she is imperiled by the Wicked Witch of the West who will stop at nothing to obtain Dorothy's magical ruby slippers The girl is befriended by three traveling companions: an amiable scarecrow, the ax-wielding Tin Man, and a Cowardly Lion whose bark is worse than his bite. After a series of hair-raising adventures that result in the liquidation of the Wicked Witch Dorothy is returned home – only to discover that the entire exper ience in Oz was a dream, and that "there's no place like home."

WHY IT'S IMPORTANT:

There are movies, and then there's *The Wizard of Oz*, which transcended its medium by evolving into the equivalent of a national holiday for starry-eyed Baby Boomers when it was originally presented on network television during the 1960s. No that Victor Fleming's romp down the yellow brick road wasn't popular as a theatrical film in 1939; it's simply that those annual Sunday night telecasts certified its mega-classic status like a premature Christmas present right there on our fuzzy, black-and-white small screens.

Nothing less than lightning in a bottle any year it's screened, *Oz* is a broad-yet-sophisticated, in many ways unlikely project for high-brow MGM. Significantly, it busts up its own well-baked casting formula – twinkly little Shirley Temple and grouchy W.C. Fields as Professor Marvel/The Wizard– for a substitute Dorothy that makes all the difference in the world. Usually, sharp filmmakers wind up casting older actresses to play the pre-teen, pre-sexual Alices and Dorothys of these literary fables, cinema requiring a grounding in reality that the original source material can easily sidestep. With Temple in the lead, it's all about the cute little orphaned tyke and three sentimenta grown-ups who look after her. By casting slightly older and far more mature Garland, the subtext changes: now we're dealing with a young woman's coming of age trajectory, a crossover into scary adulthood where smitten friends become equal partners in the perils of day to-day survival… whether in Oz or Kansas. And what memorable friends they are! Almost like a Mad Magazine parody of anachronistic vaudevillians losing touch with reality, Dorothy's three companions sell notions that might come across as overly precious in lesser hands (see Temple's imitation *Oz* movie, *The Blue Bird*). Bert Lahr's cowardly lion in particular pushes absurdity into transcendental territory -- "Ain't it the truth?" – proving once again that earthy Jewish humor in an exotic setting will always bring the house down.

Technically, *Oz* is a showcase for all fx departments (meticulous matte paintings, that amazing first act twister), although the movie's make-up team clearly warrants special praise. In addition to the three now-iconic Road Friends, a village of Munchkins, griping, grasping trees and flying monkeys, there is the bulbous-brained Wizard himself (his alter-ego, at any rate), which predates similar sci-fi designs employed by Dick Smith and John Chambers (*Outer Limits*). The Wicked Witch's green-tinged look is also distinctive, especially since she appears to be of the same quasi-human species that serves her (the palace guards).

Lonely Kansas girl Dorothy (Judy Garland) dreams of visiting a special place over the rainbow, and, exactly one twister later, winds up in the merry old land of Oz. RIGHT: Three dancing members representing the Lollipop Guild welcome a disoriented Ms. Gale (and Toto) to Munchkinland.

LEFT: Enroute to the Emerald City. RIGHT: The Wicked Witch of the West (Margaret Hamilton) threatens all. BELOW, LEFT: After meeting the Wizard (Frank Morgan), Dorothy is sent home by Glinda (Billie Burke).

Dorothy and the Scarecrow (Ray Bolger) make a new friend on their way to Oz, the Tin Man (Jack Haley).

Buddy Ebsen, perhaps best known for his TV series *The Beverly Hillbillies* and *Barnaby Jones*, was originally cast as the Tin Man. But unexpectedly, he developed a life-threatening reaction to the metal-lic make-up being used and needed to be hospitalized.

DOROTHY'S TRAVELS

There may be no place like home, but the fantasyland of Oz is one amazing place to visit, preferably without a Wicked Witch dogging your tracks. Dorothy Gale (Judy Garland) takes in some astonishing sights and makes steadfast friends along the way. OPPOSITE PAGE: "Somewhere over the rainbow…" This beautiful publicity photo captures the endearing innocence of young Dorothy at home on her Aunt's Kansas farm, before the twister strikes. ABOVE: Gale oils up the Tin Man (Jack Haley) as an agog Scarecrow (Ray Bolger) pays close attention. RIGHT: The Wicked Witch of the West (Margaret Hamiliton) and her flying monkey accomplice revel in Dorothy's plight.

WITCHES AND WIZARDS

Dorothy is menaced and held prisoner by the foul Wicked Witch before this evil, green-skinned monarch is liquidated in her own castle. Finally, the always-resourceful Wizard himself (Frank Morgan) decides to fly stranded Miss Gale back to Kansas via a hot air balloon, although departure doesn't go exactly as planned. All images are from MGM's 1939 classic *The Wizard of Oz*, a special, highly-anticipated, once-a-year TV viewing event for Baby Boomers (even in small screen black-and-white).

1

THE LORD OF THE RINGS: THE FELLOWSHIP OF THE RING 2001 (178) 2.35

WHO MADE IT:

New Line Cinema/WingNut Films (U.S./New Zealand). Director: Peter Jackson. Producers: Peter Jackson, Michael Lynne, Mark Ordesky, Robert Shayne, Bob Weinstein, Harvey Weinstein. Writers: Fran Walsh & Philippa Boyens, based on the novel by J.R.R. Tolkien. Cinematography (color): Andrew Lesnie. Music: Howard Shore. Starring: Elijah Wood (Frodo Baggins), Ian McKellen (Gandalf), Sean Astin (Samwise Gamgee), Orlando Bloom (Legolas), Christopher Lee (Saruman), Viggo Mortensen (Aragorn), Cate Blanchett (Galadriel), Sean Bean (Boromir), Ian Holm (Bilbo Baggins), John Rhys-Davies (Gimli), Lawrence Makoare (Lurtz), Liv Tyler (Arwen), Hugo Weaving (Elrond), Dominic Monaghan (Merry), Billy Boyd (Pippin).

WHAT IT'S ABOUT:

An all-powerful Ring that threatens the ancient realm known as Middle Earth, falls into innocent hands. Sauron, the evil Dark Lord of this exotic world, intends to wipe out humanity with the help of a renegade sorcerer, who in turn creates massive monster armies. The valiant efforts of a Shire hobbit named Frodo and his steadfast friends, guided by the wizard Gandalf, eventually lead to the creation of a Fellowship dedicated to the Ring's destruction.

WHY IT'S IMPORTANT:

Defying conventional wisdom in a number of interesting ways, Peter Jackson's take on Tolkien managed to do what seasoned pros like Spielberg and Ridley Scott could not: it made movie screens safe for wizards, dragons, trolls and other fanciful entities, redefining the muscular adventure-fantasy genre for an eager new generation. With a filmmaking style that is brisk, robust, alive with sweeping camera moves and lyrical poetic passages, Jackson managed to boil down Tolkien's immense, ultra-exotic book into a mesmerizing and thoroughly captivating story. Colorful characters are played by perfectly-cast actors right down the line, from supreme conjurer Gandalf (Sir Ian McKellen, who owns the role), vigilant but still playful as he dazzles Hobbit children with a volley of fireworks), to Elijah Wood's selfless young hero Frodo, and finally to the mighty Fellowship itself, with "three musketeers" Aragorn, Legolas and Gimli (Viggo Mortensen, Orlando Bloom, John Rhys-Davies) becoming key players as the saga unfolds.

Central to the Fellowship's quest is the dreaded Ring itself, and the desperate need to destroy it in the unholy fires where it was forged. Easily taken as a metaphor for ultimate power, this object seduces one and all (even paragons like Gandalf and Aragorn are not immune to its tempting promise), and interludes in the Ring's netherworld dimension whenever Frodo places the object on his finger are remarkably eerie and portentous. Throughout this movie, director Jackson makes exactly the right creative choices, enabling grateful viewers to sit back with supreme confidence as a new battle scene or elaborate attack set-piece gets underway. Significantly, the intimate moments between characters are handled with the same textured nuances and careful attention to detail. Sean Bean, eventually the star of TV's Tolkien-inspired *Game of Thrones*, is especially sympathetic as tense, conflicted, ultimately guilt-ridden Prince Borimir. Equally interesting in his own glowering way is veteran screen villain Christopher Lee as the Judas character, imperious sorcerer Saruman.

With an inspired approach, a cast to die for and a rousing score by Howard Shore, *The Fellowship of the Ring* wowed mainstream movie viewers who couldn't give a damn about hobbits or power rings or any of the arcane flapdoodle conceived for Tolkien's books. All they knew is, this material worked gloriously, outclassing Chris Columbus' pedestrian coverage of the *Harry Potter* adventures or the chronically static staging of George Lucas' new *Star Wars* epics. Even without Gollum front-and-center in Movie #1, *Fellowship* scores as the perfect blend of fairy tale enchantment and grandiose outdoor adventure, with battle sequences that don't overstay their welcome and a sense of imaginative freshness that is thoroughly irresistible.

The beguiling One Ring tempts amiable Shire resident Bilbo Baggins (Ian Holm)...

...worrying Gandalf (Ian McKellan).

Ring-bearer Frodo (Elijah Wood) wins the respect of Elrond's Fellowship. RIGHT: Gimli (John Rhys-Davies) in action. BELOW: The darker spectral nature of Galadriel (Cate Blanchett) threatens to take control.

ABOVE: Ringwraiths pursue Arwen and an injured Frodo before they are destroyed by the elf's water-influencing magic. Female characters are given a bit more to do in Jackson's movies than in the original Tolkien books.

ABOVE: Gollum (Andy Serkis) is glimpsed swiftly and indistinctly, wetting viewer appetite.

Director Peter Jackson relaxes in the mini-dwelling of Bilbo Baggins. Several sets were built to this smaller scale, with digital fx seamlessly blending both human and Hobbit characters.

MASTER OF MIDDLE EARTH

Peter Jackson's Oscar-winning movie trilogy captured the essence of Tolkien's complex and difficult book, creating an ornate period world in the midst of upheaval. Key to this conflict is the fearsome entity known as Sauron, (RIGHT, ABOVE) a monstrous, power-craving demi-god who loses the coveted Ring (BELOW) during *Fellowship*'s opening set-piece. Some have compared the Ring's great power to atomic energy, an "ultimate weapon" that is ultimately too dangerous for any one faction to possess. ABOVE: Barad-Dur, Sauron's towering fortress in the black land of Mordor.

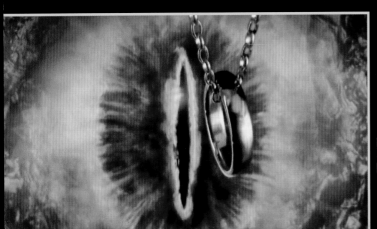

TOP: The demonic Balrog monster, complete with fiery whip, figures prominently in the exciting climax of *Fellowship*. LEFT: Gandalf the almighty wizard (Ian McKellan) senses danger while visiting his old friends in Hobbitron. ABOVE: A traitor to the sacred brotherhood, wizard Saruman (Christopher Lee) joins forces with Sauron for an all-out assault on Middle Earth. An incredible triple act for any filmmaker to follow, the original *Ring* epics are to be joined by Peter Jackson's equally ambitious adaptation of Tolkien's *The Hobbit* in 2013, with plot elements and cast members from his original visionary work figuring into the proceedings.

More so than its cousin genres (horror and sci-fi), fantasy encompasses a wide range of movie types, from alternate universe epics to drawing room comedies. The following films are all excellent, and didn't make it into the main line-up mostly because it was tougher than usual to settle on a mere 100:

BEDAZZLED (1967, 20th Century-Fox) updates the Faust parable to late '60s London with casually amoral Peter Cook bedeviling love-deprived short order cook Dudley Moore in a smart, far-ranging satire penned by the two comedy stars. Favorite bit: the record-scratching routine. Remade in the 21st Century with the Devil as a sexy woman (Elizabeth Hurly, playing against Brendon Fraser). Director: Stanley Donen. Starring Peter Cook, Dudley Moore, Eleanor Bron, Raquel Welch, Alba, Robert Russell. Color.

BEDKNOBS AND BROOMSTICKS (1971, Walt Disney Productions) is the studio's ambitious follow-up to *Mary Poppins*, with Angela Lansbury letter-perfect as an apprentice witch in WWII England whose magical abilities are ultimately put to patriotic use. Winner of a Special Effects Oscar in '71 over Jim Danforth's *When Dinosaurs Ruled the Earth*. Director: Robert Stevenson (who else?). Starring Angela Lansbury, David Tomlinson, Roddy McDowall, Sam Jaffe, John Ericson. Technicolor.

CHITTY CHITTY BANG BANG (1968, United Artists) is an elaborate super-production helmed by 007's production team, based on a popular children's novel. Dick Van Dyke is the lovable but slightly immature dad who dazzles his adoring youngsters with fantasy stories involving his miraculous, flying vehicle. Lavishly mounted in 70mm widescreen, with a few memorable songs. Director: Ken Hughes. Starring Dick Van Dyke, Sally Ann Howes, Lionel Jeffries, Gert Frobe, Anna Quayle, Benny Hill. Color.

DAMN YANKEES! (1958, Warner Bros.) is based on the popular Broadway play that re-imagines the Faust legend in a baseball setting. Stage sensation Gwen Verdon makes the most of a rare opportunity to strut her considerable stuff on screen. Great songs, and Ray Walston is unforgettable as the Devil (which probably inspired the producers of TV's *My Favorite Martian*). Directors: George Abbott, Stanley Donen. Starring Tab Hunter, Gwen Verdon, Ray Walston, Russ Brown, James Komack, Jean Stapleton. Color.

FREAKY FRIDAY (2003, Walt Disney Pictures) is a tart, family-friendly confection that employs the old body-switch premise: teenage girl and harried mom magically change places for a while, and learn more about each other's respective problems along the way. Remake of an equally good Disney flick from the '70s, which puts Barbara Harris and Jodie Foster through the same paces. Director: Mark Waters. Starring Jamie Lee Curtis, Lindsay Lohan, Mark Harmon, Harold Gould. Technicolor.

FREQUENCY (2000, New Line Cinema) takes a simple fantasy idea and extracts great pathos from it: what if you could communicate with your long-dead parent because of a freakish audio time warp? Would you – or should you – change his history and yours? Strong performances enhance a thoughtful concept, first explored in the pilot episode of ABC-TV's short-lived *Darkroom* series from the early '80s Director: Gregory Hoblit. Starring Dennis Quaid, Jim Caviezel, Shawn Doyle, Elizabeth Mitchell. Color.

HARRY POTTER AND THE DEATHLY HALLOWS: PART 2 (2011, Warner Bros.) is the ambitious, eagerly-anticipated conclusion of the mega-successful eight-part feature film series, based on J.K. Rowling's famous novels. More comic book-ey than earlier installments (is this Harry Potter or *Smallville*?), the saga nevertheless concludes with both sentiment and style. Director: David Yates. Starring Daniel Radcliffe, Emma Watson, Rupert Grint, Ralph Fiennes, John Hurt, Helena Bodham Carter. Color

HEAVEN CAN WAIT (1979, Paramount Pictures) is a worthy remake of *Here Comes Mr. Jordan*, with football replacing boxing as the spectator sport essential to hero Joe Pendelton's emotional and physical well-being. Will he find a suitable new body after his own is "claimed" prematurely? Still fresh and surprisingly funny, with baddies Grodin and Cannon stealing the show. Directors: Warren Beatty (star), Buck Henry. Starring Beatty, Julie Christie, James Mason, Charles Grodin, Dyan Cannon. Color.

HIGHLANDER (1986, 20th Century-Fox) is the first of several century-spanning action fantasies that pit eternal warriors against one another. This initial foray embraces visual style to a somewhat distracting extreme, blending pretension with legitimate hair-raising thrills. A still vital Connery is fine as always. Re-worked as a successful TV series. Director: Russell Mulcahy. Starring Christopher Lambert, Sean Connery, Roxanne Hart, Clancy Brown, Beatie Edney, Alan North. Color.

IT HAPPENS EVERY SPRING (1949, 20th Century-Fox) is the one about a college professor who accidentally creates a wood-resistant solution, so he rubs it on baseballs and winds up becoming the ultimate pitching sensation on a real team. Yet another baseball fantasy with an ingratiating cast native to this sub-genre (Paul Douglas seemed born to these confections). Directed by Lloyd Bacon. Starring Ray Milland, Jean Peters, Paul Douglas, Ed Begley, Ted de Corsia, Ray Collins, Alan Hale Jr. B/W.

JACK THE GIANT KILLER (1962, United Artists) is Edward Small's blatant imitation of *7th Voyage of Sinbad*, with Jim Danforth manipulating the stop-motion monstrosities. Despite lifting cast, director and fx style from Harryhausen's classic, Jack is far more Disney-like, embracing candy-colored, storybook sensibilities… even to the inclusion of a *Darby O'Gill*-like bottled "Imp." Directed by Nathan Juran. Starring Kerwin Mathews, Judi Meredith, Torin Thatcher, Walter Burke. Technicolor.

KING KONG (2005, Universal Pictures) is Peter Jackson's lavish re-imagining of the 1933 shocker classic, made possible by his spectacular success with the *Lord of the Rings* movies. Poetic and melancholy, spectacular but excessive, this *Kong* interprets Beauty and the Beast as the loss of personal innocence and the overdue embrace of romantic adulthood. Director: Peter Jackson. Starring Naomi Watts, Jack Black, Adrien Brody, Thomas Kretschmann, Colin Hanks, Anthony Serkis (brilliant in the title role). Color.

LADYHAWKE (1985, 20th Century-Fox/Warner Bros.) has something in common with Korda's *Thief of Bagdad* in that it offers a youthful hero (in this case a well-cast Matthew Broderick) helping fervent lovers with a most unusual problem: He takes the form of a wolf at night, while she transforms into a bird by day. Offbeat and oddly involving action romance, with a fearless pop score that only occasionally works. Director: Richard Donner. Starring Broderick, Rutger Hauer, Michelle Pfeiffer, Leo McKern. Color.

LEMONY SNICKET'S AN UNFORTUNATE SERIES OF EVENTS (2004, Paramount Pictures), based on Daniel Handler's popular books, is all about three orphaned kids who come to live with a greedy relative who is determined to steal their fortune. Weird, often disturbing, *Events* does provide Jim Carrey with an aggressively showy part worthy of his oddball talents. Director: Brad Silbering. Starring Carrey, Jude Law, Meryl Streep, Catherine O'Hara, Emily Browning, Kara and Shelby Hoffman. Color.

194

BUBBLING UNDER THE BUBBLERS: *Big Trouble in Little China, Bruce Almighty, The Enchanted Cottage, The Last Wave, The Witches of Eastwick*

MIDNIGHT IN PARIS (2011, Sony Pictures Classics) provided Woody Allen with an Oscar-winning mainstream hit, his first in some time. This study of a writer's search for inspiration explores not only the soothing balm of creativity, but the challenge it poses to our priorities when real life doesn't quite measure up. Owen Wilson is ideal as Paris' hopeless romantic, matched by Rachel McAdams and a flawless supporting cast. Director: Woody Allen. Starring Wilson, McAdams, Kurt Fuller, Mimi Kennedy. Color.

PEGGY SUE GOT MARRIED (1986, TriStar Pictures) explores the intriguing question, "If I knew then what I know now…" Like *Back to the Future*, Coppola's film uses time displacement as a device to explore the psyche of his unsettled protagonist, who is seeking a better life… and may just get one, under the fantastic circumstances. Director: Francis Ford Coppola. Starring Kathleen Turner (fearlessly playing a teenager), Nicolas Cage, Barry Miller, Catherine Hicks, Joan Allen, Jim Carrey, Kevin J. O'Connor.

QUEEN OF ATLANTIS (1932, Nero-Film AG) is one of several screen adaptations of a novel by Pierre Benoit with a most unusual premise: the ancient kingdom of Atlantis has survived, buried beneath the desert; modern-day interlopers must contend with a primitive population and a most dangerous queen, Antinea (played by Brigitte Helm of *Metropolis* fame). Director: George Wilhelm Pabst. Starring Brigitte Helm, Heinz Klingenberg, Gustav Diessl, Vladimir Sokoloiff, Tele Tchai, Florelle. B/W.

SAMSON AND DELILAH (1949, Paramount Pictures) triggered Hollywood's Bible craze in the '50s, produced with all the Technicolor opulence Cecil B. DeMille could muster. It's campy but irresistible fun, with moments that are indelible (the first-person blinding of Samson, for one) in spite of overblown Hollywood theatricality. Directed by DeMille. Starring Victor Mature, Hedy Lamarr, George Sanders, Angela Lansbury, Russ Tamblyn, Henry Wilcoxin, George Reeves. Technicolor.

SPLASH (1984, Touchstone Pictures) resurrected a genre that cinema hadn't thought about since the late '40s. Set in Manhattan, it's a warm and fuzzy romantic comedy with a difference… the leading lady happens to be a mermaid. Sometimes silly, most charming fish tail (err, tale) that made stars of newcomer Tom Hanks and director Ron Howard. Starring Tom Hanks, Daryl Hannah, Eugene Levy, John Candy, Dody Goodman, Shecky Greene. Color.

STRANGER THAN FICTION (2006, Columbia Pictures) turns the monotony of everyday living into someone else's fictional creation, a bizarre, increasingly desperate scenario for IRS agent Will Ferrell after he "overhears" talk about his upcoming demise from an inner/outer narrator. Smoothest attempt yet at the "what is real?" subgenre, helped by clever visuals and Ferrell's perceptive turn. Director: Marc Forster. Starring Ferrell, Emma Thompson, Maggie Gyllenhaal, Dustin Hoffman, William Dick. Color

THE ABSENT-MINDED PROFESSOR (1961, Buena Vista) is a delightful bit of high-flying whimsy from the Disney live-action unit in its first generation heyday. A zany but lovable small town professor, his gravity-defying creation "flubber," and an airborne antique car dodging attacks from fighter jets add up to a most original family viewing experience. Director: Robert Stevenson. Starring Fred MacMurray, Nancy Olson, Elliot Reid, Keenan Wynn, Leon Ames, Tommy Kirk, Edward Andrews. B/W.

THE BISHOP'S WIFE (1947, Samuel Goldwyn Company/RKO) provides another dashing angel in a Brooks Brothers suit, this one helping a well-intentioned bishop find the answer to his prayers. A first-rate cast brightens this holiday perennial, remade in the mid-'90s as *The Preacher's Wife*. Director: Henry Koster. Starring Cary Grant, Loretta Young, David Niven, Monte Woolley, James Gleason, Gladys Cooper, Elsa Lanchester, the Mitchell Boy Choir. B/W.

THE GREAT RUPERT (1950, Eagle-Lion Films) is a flawed but irresistible tale about a dancing squirrel, an eccentric family, and hidden fortune. George Pal's first foray into feature film producing following his Oscar-winning Puppetoons replaced the original story's mouse with a squirrel to placate Disney. Director: Irving Pichel (who would next helm *Destination Moon* for Pal). Starring Jimmy Durante, Terry Moore (right after *Mighty Joe*), Tom Drake, Frank Orth, Sara Haden, Queenie Smith, Chick Chandler. B/W.

THE MAGIC SWORD (1962, United Artists) belongs to St. George in this horror-accented, serio-comic adventure fantasy involving an evil sorcerer and seven monstrous curses. Director Bert Gordon's best movie, *Sword* benefits from a charming cast, some impressive make-ups, and a rousing music score (Richard Markowitz). Director: Bert I. Gordon. Starring Basil Rathbone, Estelle Winwood, Gary Lockwood, Ann Helm, Liam Sullivan, Danielle De Metz, Maila Nurmi (Vampira), Merritt Stone. Color.

THE PURPLE ROSE OF CAIRO (1985, Orion Pictures) is Woody Allen's indirect homage to silent classic *Sherlock Jr.* The notion of movies as a method of escape, for people on both sides of the screen, is effectively dramatized in this story about a heroic film character who leaps into harsh reality to comfort a needy, romance-starved young woman. Funny but bittersweet, as it should be. Director: Woody Allen. Starring Mia Farrow, Jeff Daniels, Danny Aiello, Irving Metzman, Stephanie Farrow. Color.

THE SECRET GARDEN (1949, MGM) is a worthwhile kid-driven fable boasting an exceptional cast, with Dean (*Boy with Green Hair*) Stockwell and Margaret (*Canterville Ghost*) O'Brien providing some nice adolescent chemistry. Black-and-white blossoms into vibrant color once they're inside the magical garden, an inoffensive, pleasing gimmick. Director: Fred M. Wilcox. Starring O'Brien, Stockwell, Herbert Marshall, Gladys Cooper, Elsa Lanchester, Brian Roper, Reginald Owen. Technicolor and B/W.

THE SECRET LIFE OF WALTER MITTY (1947, Samuel Goldwyn Company/RKO Radio Pictures) casts Danny Kaye as a chronic daydreamer who begins to suspect that enemy agents are out to get him. Never quite as buoyant as it should be (the fantasy blackouts are pretty cool), *Secret Life* at least has veteran bogeyman Boris Karloff skulking about. Director: Norman Z. McLeod. Starring Kaye, Virginia Mayo, Boris Karloff, Fay Bainter, Ann Rutherford, Thurston Hall, Gordon Jones. Technicolor.

THE TIME OF THEIR LIVES (1946, Universal Pictures) is an offbeat Abbott and Costello vehicle that smartly separates the famous duo: Lou's a Revolutionary War patriot mistaken for a traitor, Bud's the modern-day shrink haunted by his ghost. Surprisingly clever and charming, with a memorable final gag ("Odds bodkins!"). Director: Charles Barton. Starring Bud Abbott, Lou Costello, Marjorie Reynolds, Gale Sondergaard, Binnie Barnes, John Shelton, Jess Barker. B/W.

THE THIEF OF BAGHDAD (1961, Titanus/MGM) was released at the height of Italy's sword-and-sorcery imports. Boasting strong production values, charming music (Carlo Rustichelli) and the genre's unchallenged superstar, Steve Reeves, this pseudo-remake of the 1940 Korda classic has delights of its own to recommend it. Directors: Arthur Lubin, Bruno Vailati. Starring Steve Reeves, Giorgia Moll, Edy Vessel, Arturo Dominici, Daniele Vargas, Fanfulla. Eastmancolor.

WONDER MAN (1945, Samuel Goldwyn Company/RKO Radio Pictures) is one of multi-talented Danny Kaye's most watchable vehicles. His hyper-antics and some Oscar-winning special effects highlight this farce about the ghost of a guy murdered by gangsters returning to nail the culprits… with a little help from his bookworm twin. Director: H. Bruce Humberstone. Starring Danny Kaye, Virginia Mayo, Vera-Ellen, Donald Woods, S.K. Sakall, Allen Jenkins, Otto Kruger, Steve Cochran. Technicolor.

SILENT FANTASY MASTERPIECES

Fantasy and motion pictures were clearly made for each other. Special effects can bring to life gloriously unreal characters and locales with the same flamboyance of children's book illustrations, something movie-making pioneer/magician Georges Melies realized early on. His primitive but always elegant flights of fancy depicted everything from a hungry abominable snowman to mankind's first trip to the moon (a memorably painful experience for the impacted lunar surface). Among Melies' remarkable trick films are *The Alchemist's Hallucination* (1897), his own spin on *20,000 Leagues Under the Sea*, and the color-tinted *Kingdom of Fairies*, made in 1903 (LEFT). Meanwhile, German filmmakers, obsessed with this popular new art form, began to explore the intriguing possibilities of visualizing fantastic subjects. Fritz Lang's *Siegfried* (1924), based on legend, is possibly the first "super-hero" blockbuster, inspiring American action movie star Douglas Fairbanks to make *The Thief of Bagdad* a few years later (BELOW, RIGHT). Evil sorcerers and flying carpets wowed unsophisticated audiences of the day, with equally far-fetched epics like *She* (1926), *The Isle of Lost Ships* (1923-9) *The Lost World* (boasting Willis O'Brien's animated dinosaurs in '27) and *The Mysterious Island* (1929, MGM) following suit.

With robust Doug Fairbanks handling athletic fantasy, it fell to sensitive actors like Lon Chaney and Conrad Veidt to shed light on the darker, chillier side of macabre and unusual storylines. In sharp contrast, Buster Keaton's *Sherlock Jr.* (1924) is a rib-tickling masterpiece, giddily blurring the line between reality and whatever it is that exists up there on the movie screen – some compelling, irresistible parallel universe that seems to magically co-exist with our own. Also providing laughs for early sound audiences are mostly forgotten silent versions of *The Wizard of Oz* (with Oliver Hardy), *Peter Pan* (1925) and 1921's *A Connecticut Yankee in King Arthur's Court* , starring Harry Myers.

BEST FANTASY HERO: Frodo Baggins (Elijah Wood, the *Rings* Trilogy). Runner-up: Larry Daley (Ben Stiller, *Night at the Museum*).

BEST FANTASY HEROINE: Leslie Burke (Anna Sophia Robb, *Bridge to Terabithia*). Runner-up: Belle (Josette Day, *Beauty and the Beast*).

BEST FANTASY VILLAIN: Jaffar (Conrad Veidt, *The Thief of Bagdad*). Runner-up (tie): Mr. Potter (Lionel Barrymore, *It's a Wonderful Life*); Captain Vidal (Sergi Lopez, *Pan's Labyrinth*)

BEST FANTASY VILLAINESS: The Wicked Witch of the West (Margaret Hamilton, *The Wizard of Oz*). Runner-up: Morgana (Helen Mirren, *Excalibur*).

BEST ANTI-HERO: Scrooge (Alastair Sim, *A Christmas Carol*). Runner up: Eddie Kagle (Paul Muni, *Angel on My Shoulder*).

BEST PSYCHOLOGICAL DRAMA WITH FANTASY OVERTONE AND A MISLEADING TITLE: *The Curse of the Cat People*.

BEST FANTASY MOVIE THAT REALLY ISN'T A FANTASY MOVIE: *Hugo*. Runner-up: *The Shawshank Redemption*. Second Runner-up: Steven Spielberg's *Duel*.

BEST FANTASY FRAMEWORK FOR A NON-FANTASY STORY: *Wuthering Heights* (1939).

THE TOP TEN FANTASY FILMMAKERS

WALT DISNEY (1901-1966)
The legendary film producer who founded an American entertainment empire, Walter Elias "Walt" Disney is best remembered for his groundbreaking animated classics. But the master of screen fantasy was almost as remarkable in the live-action department, starting with the sci-fi adventure *20,000 Leagues Under the Sea* in '54 and including such fable-like perennials as *Darby O'Gill and the Little People*, *Mary Poppins* and *Enchanted*. Designed as family fare, Disney's offerings always represent the state-of-the-art in special visual effects and optical-animated magic.

GEORGE PAL (1908-1980)
Known in the industry as the "other" Walt Disney, George Pal established himself with Oscar-winning shorts (*Puppetoons*) and a slew of important sci-fi movies in the 1950s before moving from Paramount to MGM and embracing live-action fantasy. Pal, with that twinkle in his eye and ingratiating gentleman's smile, brought his flavorful brand of Hungarian wizardry to all screen projects. He and Disney were actually good friends, a relationship that enabled both men to adapt the works of Verne or Wells without stepping on each other's creative toes.

GEORGES MELIES (1861-1938) is the French illusionist and filmmaker whose pioneering visual techniques resulted in some of early cinema's most celebrated fantasy masterpieces. Witches, demons, imps, and plucky extraterrestrials found their way into his groundbreaking classics, such as the Jules Verne-inspired *A Trip to the Moon* (1902) and *The Impossible Journey*, made in 1904.

JEAN COCTEAU (1889-1963) transformed fantasy cinema with his unique films, although cinema is only one creative area where he excelled: Cocteau was also a poet, novelist, designer, artist and playwright. His movies are often compared to elegant fairy tales, with works like *Beauty and the Beast* and the *Orpheus* trilogy providing a showcase for his staging and visual effects set-ups.

STEVEN SPIELBERG (1945-?) became one of Hollywood's most significant director-producers in the '70s and '80s, infecting audiences with a taste for imaginative thrill rides. Although *Hook* was a misfire, *Raiders of the Lost Ark* single-handedly revived the two-fisted adventure genre, and even sci-fi trappings can't disguise 1982's *E.T.* as anything other than a children's fantasy of the highest order.

TERRY GILLIAM (1940-?) became internationally famous as the only American-born member of Britain's famed *Monty Python* comedy troupe. Kind of an anti-Disney, he soon distinguished himself as an actor, animator, screenwriter, and director of several dark and perplexing fantasy films. These include *Time Bandits*, *The Adventures of Baron Munchausen* and *Brazil*.

PETER JACKSON (1961-?) is the New Zealand fimmaker who masterminded three epic movies based on Tolkien's *The Lord of the Rings*, redefining the classical-style fantasy adventure for a new generation of viewers with sweeping CG camera moves, robust performances and striking special effects. Jackson intends to follow-up this grand achievement with a three-part adaptation of *The Hobbit*.

TIM BURTON (1958-?) is a California-born writer, artist and prodigious filmmaker who specializes in offbeat, more often than not twisted stories that celebrate the comforting magic of infantile melancholia. An eccentric stylist, his movies include *Beetlejuice*, *Edward Scissorhands*, *The Nightmare Before Christmas*, *Sleepy Hollow*, *Big Fish*, *Sweeny Todd*, and the 2012 remake of *Dark Shadows*.

ROBERT STEVENSON (1905-1966) was a distinguished film writer and director from England who wound up becoming Walt Disney's go-to filmmaker in the '60s and '70s, helming 19 successful films for the Mouse Factory. These include fantasy classics like *Mary Poppins*, *The Shaggy Dog*, *The Absent-Minded Professor*, *Darby O'Gill and the Little People* and *The Love Bug*.

GUILLERMO DEL TORO (1964-?) is a Mexican director, producer and screenwriter who specializes in macabre movies with an emotional core. The *Hellboy* pictures are fun and *Blade II* interesting, but *Pan's Labyrinth* is his incontestable masterpiece. Del Toro is currently reviving the giant monster genre with *Pacific Rim*, and has remakes of *Frankenstein* and *Beauty and the Beast* on his slate.

THE TOP TEN FANTASY FILM ACTORS

Johnny Depp	Gene Wilder
Fredric March	Robin Williams
Claude Rains	James Earl Jones
Will Smith	Liam Neeson
Jean Marius	Jim Carrey/Hugo Weaving (tie)

TOP FX CAPTURE ACTOR: Andy Serkis

THE TOP TEN FANTASY FILM COMPOSERS

Georges Auric	Jerry Goldsmith
John Williams	Howard Shore
Bernard Herrmann	Hans Zimmer
Miklos Rosza	James Horner
Danny Elfman	Alan Silvestri

INDEX

THE TOP 100 COMIC BOOK MOVIES!